DATE DUE

APR 0 1 1997	
RET'D MAR 3 1 1997	
JUN JUN 0 2 1997	

GAYLORD   PRINTED IN U.S.A.

THE POWER TO HARM

Previous books by John Cornwell

NONFICTION

COLERIDGE: POET AND REVOLUTIONARY
EARTH TO EARTH
A THIEF IN THE NIGHT
THE HIDING PLACES OF GOD
NATURE'S IMAGINATION

FICTION

THE SPOILED PRIEST
SEVEN OTHER DEMONS
STRANGE GODS

John Cornwell

THE POWER TO HARM

MIND, MEDICINE, AND MURDER ON TRIAL

VIKING

VIKING
Published by the Penguin Group
Penguin Books USA Inc., 375 Hudson Street,
New York, New York 10014, U.S.A.
Penguin Books Ltd, 27 Wrights Lane, London W8 5TZ, England
Penguin Books Australia Ltd, Ringwood, Victoria, Australia
Penguin Books Canada Ltd, 10 Alcorn Avenue,
Toronto, Ontario, Canada M4V 3B2
Penguin Books (N.Z.) Ltd, 182–190 Wairau Road,
Auckland 10, New Zealand

Penguin Books Ltd, Registered Offices:
Harmondsworth, Middlesex, England

First published in 1996 by Viking Penguin,
a division of Penguin Books USA Inc.

1 2 3 4 5 6 7 8 9 10

Photograph: The Courier-Journal

LIBRARY OF CONGRESS CATALOGING IN PUBLICATION DATA
Cornwell, John, date.
The power to harm : mind, medicine, and murder on trial / John Cornwell.
p. cm.
Includes bibliographical references and index.
ISBN 0-670-86767-5
1. Eli Lilly and Company—Trials, litigation, etc.
2. Trials (Murder)—Kentucky—Louisville.   3. Trials (Products liability)—
Kentucky—Louisville.   4. Pharmaceutical industry—Corrupt
practices—United States.   5. Wesbecker, Joseph T.   6. Fluoxetine.
I. Title.
KF224.E43C67   1996
345.73'02523'0976944—dc20
[347.30525230976944]   96-6722

This book is printed on acid-free paper.

Printed in the United States of America
Set in Times Roman · Designed by Francesca Belanger

For Crispin Rope

**Thou hast not half that power to do me harm
As I have to be hurt.**

—*Othello*, act V, scene ii

Knowledge is powerful medicine.

—Eli Lilly advertising slogan

Preface

ON SEPTEMBER 14, 1989, Joseph T. Wesbecker, a forty-seven-year-old pressman returned to Standard Gravure, his former place of work in Louisville, Kentucky, and shot twenty of his co-workers, killing eight and injuring twelve, before committing suicide in front of the pressroom supervisor's office.

It was discovered soon afterward that Wesbecker had been taking a course of the antidepressant Prozac. Thus Eli Lilly of Indianapolis, the manufacturer and distributor of the drug, became a prime target in a subsequent liability suit brought by the survivors and relatives of the dead.

Asked to write about the case for the London *Sunday Times Magazine*, I covered the court proceedings, which went to trial in Louisville on September 28, 1994, and lasted eleven weeks.

According to his psychiatrist, Wesbecker had been prescribed Prozac to alleviate depression related to workplace stress and his complaints of continuing unfair treatment by the management at Standard Gravure. Plaintiffs' counsel argued that the drug had disrupted Wesbecker's "impulse control" to a point where he was not responsible for his actions. Lilly, they insisted, had knowingly manufactured and marketed a drug that caused agitation in certain individuals, and had failed to provide appropriate package warnings in the United States.

Lilly denied negligence in their testing and marketing of Prozac. Avoiding the neurophysiological descriptions of depression the company standardly uses to promote Prozac, the defense strategy focused on Wesbecker as the product of a dysfunctional family that had suffered from hereditary mental illness in three generations. At the same time, they represented Lilly and its drug-trial procedures as irreproachable; this involved thwarting the plaintiffs' attempts to introduce testimony revealing that in 1985 Lilly had pleaded guilty in a federal court to twenty-five counts of misdemeanor in the handling of their drug Oraflex. Oraflex, an anti-inflammatory drug used in the treatment of arthritis, had killed an estimated seventy-two people in the early eighties.

It was not long before I realized that the implications of this case went far beyond the tragic incident and the subsequent postures of the litigating parties.

This was a story that embraced new brain science and profound issues of personal responsibility; competitive business practices in contracting markets and endemic workplace stress; the American mania for civil-liability suits and high-stakes contingency litigation. Crucially, it involved the gulf between authentic public-health needs and the commercial goals of the pharmaceutical industry; the public's right to know the unadorned truth about medication and the pharmaceutical industry's tendency to withhold selective information in the interest of corporate aims.

In the fall of 1994, Eli Lilly and Company, by the admission of one of its own executives, "could go down the tubes" as a result of adverse news about Prozac.

As I probed the recent history of Lilly's business, and the invention and marketing of Prozac, it became clear that the company's fortunes were inextricably linked to the fate of Prozac, which by the time of the trial was accounting for almost one-third of the company's $6.5-billion revenues.

In its determination that Prozac prevail in the market, Lilly showed a consistent pattern of conduct, marked by a tendency to manipulate information to its own ends: according to the judge, even to the extent of influencing the outcome of the Louisville trial with a secret deal.

Lilly apparently won the case by a nine-to-three jury verdict. Chief executive Randall L. Tobias immediately announced the vindication of Prozac, and the company's public-relations department cited the verdict as a token of the drug's safety in the seventy countries in which it was marketed. Lilly's stock rose, and Prozac's sales increased to make it the number-two best-selling drug in the world.

Not long after the trial ended, however, the presiding judge published a motion in his court declaring that he believed Lilly had secured its verdict with a secret payment to the plaintiffs, described by one lawyer in the know as so large that it was "mind-boggling." The judge was alleging that Lilly had paid to withhold the potentially damaging testimony about Lilly's misdemeanors in its reporting on Oraflex, evidence that in the judge's view might have affected the jury's verdict. At first, Lilly and the plaintiffs denied any arrangement, but both sides eventually acknowledged, under pressure, that there had indeed been a confidential agreement. The defendant and the plaintiffs have shown little remorse over having deprived the jury of important information relating to Lilly's Oraflex.

The plaintiffs, no longer intent on exposing the dangers of Prozac, have forged an alliance with Lilly to combat legal attempts to alter the "jury verdict" to a "settlement," or to force disclosure of any moneys paid.

The purpose of jury verdicts in civil actions is to involve members of the community in decisions about how people should behave toward each other.

This book tells the story of an individual whose community had despaired of helping him, save by offering a pharmaceutical remedy which reduced his problems and difficulties to the level of his brain chemistry.

The civil action in Louisville signally failed to discover the community's responsibility in the Wesbecker tragedy; by doing a secret deal with the plaintiffs, and effectively using the court action as a public-relations opportunity, Eli Lilly compounded that failure.

This book is written in the belief that there is much to be learned from studying the common ground that links the fate of Wesbecker and his victims to Prozac, not least the ruthless business culture inhabited by both Standard Gravure and Eli Lilly.

At the heart of this story, however, is the growing crisis over reductionist solutions to individual suffering and social disorder.

The past ten years have seen the development and marketing of new pharmaceutical products that claim to offer antidotes not only for clinical depression but for individual unhappiness and general discontent. The philosophy that underpins this notion is based on a belief that our happiness and misery, our joys and sorrows, our vices and virtues, are to be found not in the way we habitually live and work as members of families and communities, but exclusively in the state of our brain molecules. If this philosophy prevails, it follows that we shall increasingly turn from social and communitarian solutions to pharmacological ones, with inevitable and far-reaching consequences.

THE POWER
TO HARM

Joseph Wesbecker

1

THE SEVEN ROTOGRAVURE PRESSES, 150 feet long and three stories high, were housed in a windowless red-brick building adjoining the offices of the *Louisville Courier-Journal* at Broadway and Sixth. A pressman speaks of being "on the folder" at Standard Gravure, and he sees himself climbing into the belly of a thousand-ton press.

"You're driving that machine like you're driving a car. You're cramped with no space to move. You're surrounded by panels of switches, rows of flashing lights. Everything is coming at you in every direction. You screw up and there's thousands of dollars' wastage right there. The sound, the vibration, is like being inside a jet engine; you're saturated, you're breathing in a spray of solvents. You come home from being on the folder and you go on tasting and feeling and hearing that machine inside you."

Pressmen say the fumes can make them giggling "drunk" even as they operate a machine that can mangle and maim. The routine at Standard Gravure was to escort the "drunks" to the company cafeteria and pump them full of lemonade.

According to federal safety authorities, the chronic effects of the print solvents include "headache, insomnia, impaired concentration, loss of appetite, irritability, liver enlargement."

Few pressmen get out with all ten fingers. One Standard pressman lost all the digits of his left hand and the index finger and thumb of his right in a press accident; they grafted his toes onto his hands and he came back to work.

The paper rolls stand high as a man. The paper runs up from the basement through the floor and goes into the unit and then through the folder. The rotogravure press is a four-color process—yellow, red, blue, and black—and when one side is done the sheet turns over and is printed on the other side the same way. The tones are etched into the cylinders, and the depth of the etching controls the color. A darker color would have more ink; a lighter color, somewhat less. There are angle bars which turn all the papers in the proper positions to take them in. The folder grabs the paper by means of rollers and pins, then turns it forty-five degrees until it folds and cuts into a single book. By "books" a pressman means full-color magazines, catalogues, circulars.

The reel man loads the paper rolls. The ink man ensures that the inks are the right viscosity, or thickness, in order to maintain the colors. Sometimes the colors fade; sometimes they will get too bright, and the ink man will have to add solvents to control the intensity.

The folder man is the man in charge. His job is to oversee the crew, to maintain the press, to set up the job so that all the things come together in the folder at the same time, in the same place. He maintains the crew and keeps deadlines. For a pressman, the ultimate job is being a folder man.

Standard Gravure was once a premier printing plant in the Midwest and the South for newspaper supplements, advertising inserts, and free sheets. There was a time, twenty years back, when you had two folder men to a machine, two reel men, two ink men, and two flyboys checking and stacking the books. In those days, each press turned out twenty thousand books an hour. Then they automated the adjustments: brought in stacking machines, cut the personnel level to just three operators, and brought in mandatory overtime and night work. Then they started using quick-drying chemicals—toluene, xylol, and xylene—so they could speed up the machines: sixty thousand, seventy thousand books an hour, night and day, seven days a week. Most men would work three "doubles" every week: that is, three sixteen-hour shifts in a week, in addition to three eight-hour shifts on the remaining days.

"There's anger and there's stress," says a pressman. "You see the spurs are biting and you dig harder. You want to screw a man up real bad, you turn up the speed of the press, break the paper. There's always a fall guy. There's fear, there's rage. Then the bad guys get worse: there's stealing on the plant, and loan-sharking, drugs, alcohol. Workers get beaten up, get their tires slashed.

"People bring guns to work. They flash them around just so people know they're packing. Mostly they kept them in brown paper bags in their lockers. Charlie Ganote had a .375 magnum. Tommy Gosling was a gun collector. Sometimes we raffled guns. Even Jackie Miller, up in Personnel, had a .38 in her purse. Bill Ganote had a gun that fired blanks, and he would shoot it in people's faces. Wesbecker brought in guns; sometimes he had an AK-47 banana clip in his back pocket."

A pressman remembers Joe Wesbecker.

"Joe had been up on the hill—that's what we call it in Louisville when a guy gets admitted to Our Lady of Peace mental institution: up there on a hillside near Newberg Road. Somebody had written on the wall of the break room, 'Problems? Call Wesbecker—585-NUTS.' He wasn't just hurt; he wanted even. They called him 'Sexbecker' because he liked to brag about his sexual exploits down at Parents Without Partners. They called him Pillsbury Doughboy because he looked like that cook on the TV commercial—the pale face, the paunch sticking out of his T-shirt, giggling tee-hee! They called him Sweat because he was always perspiring. After he had a kind of standoff fight with Jim Mitchell in the Media 'n Mix bar, we called him Rocky—sarcastic.

"He got upset when people yelled at him and tried to, like, diagnose him. He thought they were singling him out to work the folder. They played practical jokes on him, sabotaged the reel, threw a bucket of water over him while he was taking his break by the machine.

"He said he had a hit list. He said he was going to sort things out. He said he was going to fly a remote-control plane onto the solvent-recovery plant and blow them all to smithereens. It made them laugh all the more."

"Standard Gravure," says a pressman, "was a time bomb waiting to go off."

2

THE STANDARD GRAVURE pressman who appeared in Dr. Lee Coleman's downtown office in Louisville, Kentucky, on the afternoon of Monday, September 11, 1989, had all the symptoms of severe mental stress. A paunchy, washed-out-looking fellow, five feet six inches tall, with muscular forearms and Coca-Cola-bottle-lensed glasses, Joe T. Wesbecker paced the room before the psychiatrist, waving his arms and muttering disconnectedly.

Dr. Coleman recounted later how he was struck by the patient's "labile" emotions (sudden alterations of mood), his "tangential thoughts" (a tendency to answer questions with inappropriate answers), his lack of "a fair level of control."

"I could tell fairly quickly," Coleman would recollect, "that something was changed since his previous visit, a month earlier. His affect, or mood, was quite up and down."

Dr. Coleman, aged forty-one, was a quietly spoken native of Hopkinsville, Kentucky. He had a shock of prematurely white hair, and his eyes looked deceptively sleepy. In fact, Dr. Coleman was suffering from defective eyesight. He had worked as a radiologist for fifteen years until contracting histoplasmosis, a disease spread by pigeon droppings. Dr. Coleman's vision had become so weak by 1981 that to read a printed text, he had to hold the page a few inches from his face. Following three years of retraining, Dr. Coleman started practicing psychiatry in Louisville, Kentucky, in 1984. Wesbecker had found Coleman in the Yellow Pages after being turned down for treatment by a dozen other psychiatrists.

Joe Wesbecker, as far as Coleman was concerned, was a casualty of the workplace: stress, overwork, frustration. During the very first session with Wesbecker, on July 11, 1987, Coleman had recorded that his new patient reported being depressed as a result of "job stress and employers jerking him around." In the course of the first year, Coleman had collaborated with his patient to secure long-term disability leave from Standard Gravure. Wesbecker had not been to work since September 1988.

On Coleman's desk was a yellow legal pad alongside his "office chart," notes written up after each session. Coleman's chart on Wesbecker, assembled from twenty-one twenty-minute sessions at $55 per appointment ($85 for the initial assessment) since July 8, 1987, told an average story of a stressed-out American worker in middle age. Wesbecker had been married and divorced twice, and there was a history of problems at work. Wesbecker had been employed as a journeyman pressman at the Standard Gravure printing plant for seventeen years. He was proud of his skills and industrious, but in recent years he had come to hate and fear the complicated folder. He was convinced that his foreman plotted to keep him on the machine out of spite. Years of overtime, including multiple "doubles" in a week, had left their toll. At forty-seven, Wesbecker's nerves were shot, and, as Coleman had recorded in his notes, it seemed doubtful whether he would work again.

Wesbecker lived alone ten miles out of town—near Iroquois Park, south of the city—but occasionally he dated and slept with his former second wife, Brenda, sometimes spending the night in the guest room of her father's house, seven miles away, at Blevin's Gap. There were two sons by his first marriage, now in their twenties. Kevin, the elder, suffered from scoliosis, a form of curvature of the spine. The younger, James, who had been studying economics at the University of Louisville for three years, had a history of exposing himself sexually.

Coleman would one day acknowledge that Wesbecker had volunteered nothing in detail about his place of work, or his marital relationships; nothing about his childhood, his mother, his father, his siblings, or his grandparents.

Wesbecker's current symptoms, as Coleman recorded them, were typical of the down phase of manic-depression: lack of energy, insomnia, and difficulties with memory. He had also made a note questioning whether his patient was suffering "schizoaffective disorder," indicating, according to Coleman, someone isolated, not comfortable in social settings, who might occasionally be out of touch with reality. The schizo-affective diagnosis had lurked in Wesbecker's accumulated notes from previous psychiatrists going back to 1984.

One report that had followed him to Dr. Coleman was an assessment made by a Dr. Morton Leventhal. Commenting on the observation that Wesbecker "harbors a great deal of anger," he had gone on to remark: "Currently he is attempting to contain his anger so that it doesn't jeopardize the gratification of his dependency needs by alienating support figures. To do this, he tends to turn his anger against himself." Another note, by a Dr. Vikdam Senler of Our Lady of Peace Hospital, recorded that in April 1984, Wesbecker had attempted suicide by taking a mixture of psychiatric drugs and, the next day, breathing in the fumes of his car exhaust through a water hose.

The notes on Wesbecker said little or nothing about his personal history. Dr. Coleman's chart was principally a roll call of trial-and-error drug prescriptions with observations on their effects and side effects. As Dr. Coleman later testified in court, he believed the best way to control Wesbecker's mental illness was by psychopharmacology rather than psychotherapy, chemical intervention rather than talk. Coleman believed that Wesbecker's depression was caused by imbalances in his brain chemistry.

Included in the list of drugs Wesbecker had been prescribed over the years were Valium, Percodan, Indocin, Elavil, Norpramin, Navane, Tofranil, Lithobid, Pamelor, Halcion, Desyrel, and Restoril. Just a month earlier, on August 10, 1989, Coleman had prescribed for Wesbecker, for a second time, a drug that had been strongly touted by visiting reps from Eli Lilly and Company of Indianapolis during the previous year. He had the note in front of him. "Plan: Start Prozac 20 milligrams per day."

Manufactured and marketed by Lilly, just one hundred miles north of Louisville, Prozac had been granted its license in the United States by the FDA in 1987 (the drug had not by then achieved the recognition and popularity generated by Peter Kramer's *Listening to Prozac*, published in 1993). Coleman had already prescribed it for his patient in the summer of 1988, but at that time Wesbecker felt it unsuitable and stopped taking it after two days.

Prozac was said to enhance the supply of the natural brain chemical serotonin, which tends to be at low levels in people liable to depression and aggression. Serotonin, in the view of Prozac's makers and many clinicians throughout the world, affects an individual's ability to exert control over manic or misdirected impulses, or to combat the lethargy and melancholy of depression: if you are high, it can bring you down; if you are low, it can bring you up.

Coleman had no misgivings about recommending the new medication. Prozac, technically known as fluoxetine hydrochloride, was deemed highly beneficial and safe by a large constituency of psychiatrists and general physicians. The drug tended to tackle depression swiftly. It had a low level of toxicity (an important consideration in patients prone to using their medication in suicide attempts), it required only one twenty-milligram dose daily, and it was widely thought to produce fewer side effects than other antidepressants.

Allowing for the usual delay in taking delivery of the prescription, Wesbecker was now five days into his second course of Prozac, having taken twenty-five capsules over the preceding twenty-five days. He now had fifteen left in his supply.

Witnessing the disturbed behavior of his patient that September afternoon (Coleman had never seen Wesbecker so animated in his gestures, so volatile in mood), the psychiatrist realized that something drastic had happened and assumed that Wesbecker was one of a minority of patients in whom Prozac produced marked agitation.

Coleman wrote on his yellow pad that the medication should be discontinued immediately, but as he voiced his doubts about continuing the course, Wesbecker suddenly collapsed into a chair.

According to Coleman, the following conversation took place.

"Don't take me off the Prozac. I feel it's helped me. . . ."

"Well, how has it helped you?"

"It's helped me remember this incident of sexual abuse at work."

"Remember? What was it you had forgotten, Mr. Wesbecker?"

"I forgot . . . I forgot they forced me at Standard Gravure to perform sex with one of the foremen. The foreman forced me to perform oral sex on him with my co-workers watching. That was the price to take me off the folder."

At this point, according to Coleman, Wesbecker started to sob uncontrollably. He went on weeping for a quarter of a minute. Never had Coleman seen his patient weeping in a session.

When Wesbecker finally pulled himself together, Coleman asked him, "Are you sure this really happened?"

"It happened, and I've informed the sex-crimes police. I'm filing a lawsuit."

Coleman has stated under oath that he was not sure whether he believed Wesbecker's "remembered" incident of abuse. ("I would say," he testified, "that it would be about fifty-fifty if you had to pin me down. It certainly sounded believable.") More important, Coleman believed it unlikely that Wesbecker had faked the memory.

"I'm not really sure what's going on with you," Coleman remembers saying. "I think you're a whole lot worse. I'd really like to find out what's going on and to stabilize you. Can I persuade you to go into the hospital?"

Joe Wesbecker would not be persuaded. He shook his head. "It would be better for me to go home. I don't like being around people. . . . I can go home, I've got a peaceful house; there's no one around there. I've got a big yard and I don't have to be around people."

"Are you having any thoughts about killing yourself, Mr. Wesbecker?" Coleman asked.

"No, no thoughts about killing myself."

"Then I want you to stop the Prozac, and I want you to come back next week. I'd like you to come in with somebody who could tell me how you've been getting on. Who could you bring in with you?"

"My ex-wife Brenda," said Wesbecker. "She can come in with me. But not next week; maybe in two weeks."

As Coleman noted the appointment for two weeks ahead, Wesbecker said, "If there's any problem, doctor, I'll call you; or my ex-wife will call you."

That was the last communication Dr. Coleman had with his patient.

3

ON THE MORNING of Wednesday, September 13, two days after his appointment with Dr. Coleman, Joe Wesbecker, dressed in blue jeans and white T-shirt, drove his red Chevrolet Monza over to the house of his first ex-wife, Sue, on Manslick Road, south of Louisville. Without getting out of the car, he picked up his twenty-one-year-old son, James, and took him to the University of Louisville, about three miles out of town, on Third Street. James, who wears glasses, is a younger version of his father. He was on a "home incarceration program" and had been banned from driving as a result of his compulsion to expose himself sexually in public places.

With forty-five minutes to spare by the time they reached the campus, Wesbecker drove to McDonald's on Third Street. Over breakfast, the two discussed James's decision to transfer to a master's program at North Carolina State.

"I had a letter to show him that I had got accepted at NC," James remembers. "Up till then he seemed a bit down. Then he brightened up and wanted to talk."

It seems that Wesbecker was concerned about his son's living on his own in North Carolina. He was worried that if James was alone his problems would be more difficult to manage. Wesbecker wondered if there was some way James could get a dorm apartment or have a roommate.

James did not know what his father intended doing after dropping him off. Nobody saw Wesbecker later that morning, or in the early afternoon. But at the end of classes, at three-thirty in the afternoon, Wesbecker was again at the campus, waiting to take his son home. James remembers that his father looked scruffy, his hair mussed up. "I asked him if he was all right, and he just said that he had taken a nap."

They had only been driving a few minutes on Cardinal Boulevard when a bizarre incident occurred. James says he was mentioning that he needed another manual for a class he was taking when Wesbecker brought the car to a sudden halt in the middle of the road. "It was a good job there was no traffic around. He looked real agitated. He dug into his pocket and gave me the money there and then. Then he insisted on driving straight over to the university bookstore to buy the manual."

All the way home, James remembers, his father sat in silence. "When I asked him about it, he just said something about being tired. So I let it go."

For another four hours on the afternoon of September 13, Wesbecker was alone and out of sight. But that evening, at about seven-thirty, he arrived in the Monza at Brenda's single-story house out at Blevin's Gap, southwest of Louisville. The house stands alone on a knoll surrounded by about seven acres of lawns with views along a wooded valley.

Brenda Wesbecker, aged thirty-nine, slow of voice and movement, her hair in its usual cascading dark ringlets, suggested they go out to eat. She drove Wesbecker in her white Firebird north on Dixie Highway and to Jessie's Family Restaurant.

Wesbecker was too disturbed to eat. "He was just more nervous than I'd ever seen him," remembers Brenda. "He paced more. While we were eating he got up two or three times and went to the bathroom. He didn't finish all of his meal. And I didn't either, because he just kept doing that. I finally said, 'I'll go and get a box.' "

Brenda now drove him back to her house, and they went inside. "I sat on the couch," she says, "while he paced. He walked around. He went outside and walked around a while."

Eventually he came in and said, "Can I spend the night?"

Brenda said, "Of course."

At nine-thirty, Wesbecker called his son James to wish him good night and to apologize for his jumpy behavior earlier in the day. "He seemed fine," James remembers. "He seemed like he was kind of happy again, and he was apologizing for being so short and stuff. But everything on the phone then seemed, well, back to form."

"Eventually I went to bed," Brenda says. "I slept down in the basement bedroom and left him upstairs pacing. I don't know where he slept that night. I went to bed and didn't see him till the next morning."

Testifying about Wesbecker's pacing that night, Brenda recollected the disturbance this habit had caused throughout all the years of their relationship, making it impossible for her to sleep in the same room with him.

"When he was unwell he would pace back and forth. Knock, knock, knock, knock, he would tap. Knock, knock, knock . . . all night long till you're like, I can't take no more of it. . . . You know, it was unreal."

As Brenda saw it, the pacing was connected with his medicines. "He was on so many different medicines, and I guess medicines would get in his system. Lithium was the kindest. When he was introduced to different medicines, he was sometimes nervous, sometimes he was upset."

Other times, she was convinced that his pacing was due to two decades working on the presses. "Joe was a workaholic. He would work the doubles. I would say, 'Don't work the doubles.' He'd work the doubles anyway. I'd get a telephone call at my job. 'Brenda, I'm working.' I'd say, 'Joe, you don't need to work another shift.' You know, after you work sixteen hours, how does anybody feel? You take a bath, you eat, you go to sleep for three hours.

"Have you ever walked in that plant? Rrrrrrrrrrrrrr. I'd ask him to give me earplugs when I'd meet him in there before going out to dinner. You'd come out, your ears are still going rrrrrrrrrrrrr as you drive your car home at night. I can't imagine anything like that. He worked at another printing plant before Standard Gravure—at Fawcett Printing. I can't imagine twenty years of my life listening to rrrrrrrrrrrrr. No telling what that would do to anyone's nervous system. So he would pace. In a restaurant people would stare at him and we'd just keep eating. Sometimes I would sit facing the people so they wouldn't stare at him. He would pace till he'd wear his shoes off. It might last—the longest I think I ever remember is seven hours. He couldn't sit still. It would be like telling an epileptic, 'Don't have a seizure'; it would be like telling a person in a wheelchair, 'Get up and walk.' He could not do it."

The next morning, Brenda's alarm clock woke her at seven. "I come upstairs to prepare to go to work. He already had his clothes on, because he would take Jimmy to the university. I come down the hallway—I always sleep fifteen minutes longer than my alarm clock, so I got in my normal bed and laid down for fifteen minutes, because I slept in the basement. He went in the kitchen. He come back to me. It's the last time I seen him alive. He come back to me, and we always said, 'Have a nice day.' We always said things to each other. He already had his clothes on. I'm still in my nightie shirt.

"So he leaned up against the wall in the bedroom. He looked at me and he said, 'Thanks for being a good friend.' He said, 'Thanks for always taking care of me.' He said, 'I'll call you later at work.' I said okay. So I got up and went in the hall bathroom to finish getting ready, and he turned around. That was odd. He usually said goodbye and he was gone. But that morning he turned around. He stood there and stared at me. I said, 'Joe, what's the matter?' He said, 'Nothing. I just come back to tell you goodbye again.' I said okay, I said bye, and kissed him on the cheek, and he was gone.' "

That morning, James was waiting for Wesbecker at his mother's house.

"It got to be eight-thirty, and as soon as it was just about a minute after or something, I knew something was wrong, because he's never late. And I called and called, didn't get any answer at the house on Blevin's Gap. It was raining, I thought maybe, with him, he could have had a wreck. So I called Brenda at her work and she didn't know anything about it. She said he had already left by the time that she had gotten up. And then I called my grandmother and said, 'Can you just drive me to school so I can drop my paper to turn in and then we've got to look for Dad?' Later Brenda told me on the phone that she went over to the other house they had, over there on Nottoway, and there was no car there, nothing. And so at school, that's when I started hearing on the news about what was happening. . . ."

4

ANGELA BOWMAN, an auburn-haired twenty-four-year-old print-job es-
timator, was in her second week back at Standard Gravure after two
months' maternity leave. That morning, September 14, 1989, she had
taken a four-mile detour in the rain to drop her baby son, Bradley, with a
baby-sitter. As always on Thursday, she briefly met with her husband at
a truck stop as he came off night shift: they had driven side by side so
that she could collect his paycheck through the car window and bank it
later in the day. With the financial commitments of a new family, every
banking day counted for the Bowmans.

At 8:37 A.M., Bowman was nursing a cup of coffee, standing by
Standard Gravure's reception desk with her colleague Sharon Needy, a
thirty-nine-year-old mother of three and grandmother of two. The reception area on the plant's third floor faced an elevator that carried staff directly up from the ground-floor entrance at Sixth and Armory. As the
elevator arrived once more, both women automatically turned their
heads to see who would emerge.

Joe Wesbecker was standing in the open elevator; he was dressed in
jeans and a gray bomber jacket, and he cradled a vinyl gym bag in his
arms.

"Both of us sensed that something was wrong," Bowman remembers. "He just looked so weird. His face was all scrunched up and his
eyes were squinted. . . . He looked not human." For a moment, Bowman
thought he had a stocking over his head.

As Wesbecker moved out of the elevator, he raised the gym bag by
the handles to reveal a semi-automatic assault rifle resting in the crook
of his left arm. He dropped the gym bag on the carpeted floor, raised the
weapon in his right hand, and took aim. Needy was screaming; Bowman
stood in profile to Wesbecker, paralyzed, speechless.

A hail of full-metal-jacket bullets ripped through Needy first. "Her body just flew," remembers Bowman. "She hit the wall and slid down. And as I noticed her flying, then *I* just flew. I mean it just blew me over, and I landed down behind the desk with my head by the trash can."

Moving like an automaton, Wesbecker did not break step. He walked over the bodies of the women and proceeded to the entrance of the administration hallway, where he directed a spray of bullets, after which he ran forward and fired some more; then he ran back to the reception area to retrieve his bag. The bag contained four semi-automatic pistols, a bayonet, and more than a thousand rounds of ammunition.

Bowman lay on the floor. A single bullet had passed sideways through her abdomen. Where the missile entered on her right side, it had torn a hole the size of a golf ball; where it exited, it had left a gaping wound "the size of two big fists," says Bowman.

Lifting the gym bag, Wesbecker stood staring down at the stricken women, the AK-47 poised toward Bowman's head.

"I pretended to be dead and looked through my eyelashes," she recollects. "It seemed like it was forever. And I was waiting for my head to be blown off. So I didn't open my eyes or nothing. Then I screamed: 'Please don't kill me. I have a baby.' He turned his feet—I saw his feet turn. . . . I could hear running footsteps; then I never heard a thing. It was so dead silent."

As the blood pumped out of her body, Bowman called out to her friend Sharon several times. Eventually Sharon said weakly, "Oh God, and I thought it was a joke."

"She said it," Bowman remembers, "five or six times. And I—I said 'Sharon,' and she just kept saying it until she didn't say nothing else. . . . She never spoke again."

Wesbecker was making his way through the executive suite; the clerical staff scattered, hiding under desks and in clothes closets.

Jackie Miller was a thirty-nine-year-old native of Louisville. Trained at keypunching, she had worked for various agencies for more than twenty years, including Kelly Girl and Manpower. She was divorced and lived alone on Earl Avenue. By September 1989, she had worked at Standard

Gravure for eighteen months, and was now a member of the permanent staff in Personnel.

Miller had been at her workstation checking through personnel documents since seven-thirty that morning. She started when she first heard "a sound like exploding fluorescent light bulbs"; then she heard a scream. She rose from her desk and went out into the hallway that connects the senior executives' offices to the reception area. As she turned right, she found herself at "eye level with a rifle."

She looked up at the person holding the weapon: about twenty feet away, a man she did not recognize. "I saw a man that was totally gone," she remembers, "nothing left. He looked totally dehumanized. And I knew at that time, too, that he wanted me dead."

Miller believes she "surprised him as much as he surprised me." Though she has no precise idea how long they stood staring at each other, she thinks it was "for seconds."

As she unfroze, Miller had one thought—which was to get the .38 gun she kept in her purse. Ever since she was attacked by three men in a parking lot at the Fort Knox military club, she had kept a gun handy night and day.

She turned and found herself colliding with her boss, personnel manager Paula Warman, who had come out from her inner office, beyond Miller's. Miller noticed Warman was standing "funny," leaning to one side with one shoe off. Such are the tricks time plays during a moment of terror: Miller had not realized that Warman had already taken two bullets.

As both women retreated through the door, Miller attempted to lock it behind her, but her action released rather than set the lock on the handle. Even as her hand entered her purse, perched on the paper shredder, the door was kicked in. The first bullet caught her in the chest and she doubled over her chair. Her .38 was in her hand, her finger on the trigger, when she took three more bullets—two in the stomach and one in the leg—and hit the floor.

Wesbecker moved on.

Warman, who had been shot twice from the front to the back of her abdomen, was also down. She had dragged herself across the carpet into her office and locked the door behind her. Miller was now lying on her back in the first office; when she looked down her right side, she realized her right leg was up by her head, so she had to bring the leg back down where it belonged. She remembers Warman was hollering "Jackie."

As soon as she ascertained that Miller was still alive, Warman told her to keep quiet in case the killer returned. They stopped talking. Miller kept her finger on the trigger of her weapon until she passed out.

After shooting Warman and Miller, Wesbecker, still on the third floor, proceeded down the hallway into the plant bindery. He now entered a service elevator that would take him down to the plant basement. As the doors were closing, three men approached.

Two were slightly ahead of the third. Maintenance engineers Forrest Conrad, fifty-four, and James Husband, forty-seven, were approaching a set of stairs that went up to the fifth floor, where they were due to work on a solvent-recovery unit. The third man was John Stein, a thirty-four-year-old pressman and amateur football player, who skipped ahead of the other two to catch the elevator.

The doors were almost closed; but Wesbecker opened them again, took aim, and shot Stein in the head. Even as it happened, Conrad thought: "Boy, that was a terrible trick."

Wesbecker went on firing. As Husband retreated behind Conrad, he was hit and thrown onto a row of pallets; Conrad, hit in the legs, found himself shoved up against a post, looking down at the blood spurting over his shoes.

"I looked up," remembers Conrad, "and I could see that whole elevator, and after he got done shooting he brought the gun down to his right leg, like, and held it. That's when I saw what the gun was, and I could see his whole body then. When he looked out towards us, he looked like he was in another world. He like—he looked through us. There was no eye contact or nothing. It was just like he turned the gun and shot."

As the elevator doors closed once more and Wesbecker descended to the basement, Conrad collapsed onto the floor and began to pray.

David Seidenfaden, aged forty-three, was working in the basement area with a colleague, Stanley Hatfield, under contract with an electrical-servicing company, Marine Electric. Seidenfaden and Hatfield were constructing a housing for an electric cable. Although he was not an employee of Standard Gravure, Seidenfaden knew the plant and its personnel: as a journeyman electrician, he had been involved since 1984 on various contracts there, including the installation of new folder machines.

At eight-forty-five, the two men were making couplings out of strips of aluminum to complete the cable housing. Seidenfaden was cutting with a band saw. "I was working," he remembers, "through several pieces of aluminum at a time to speed things up, so I was scrunched over a little bit to hold the weight up on them."

At this moment, Standard Gravure employee Paul Sallee came out of the grinder room, where he had been working on a lathe that trues the surface of the rubber rollers over which the paper travels. Sallee, intrigued about what Seidenfaden was doing, made some light comments on his technique of work before returning to his lathe in the grinder room.

Seidenfaden remembers: "At that point I heard a pop and I lost my wind. I didn't know what happened. I just thought something blew up. So I grabbed my chest and I had this severe pain. I couldn't breathe. And it took a while, but later I remember I looked over my shoulder and I saw Wesbecker two or three feet away. I thought to myself, 'Why are you just standing there looking like that? I'm hurt, I need help.' I didn't see the gun; I just saw his face."

Seidenfaden had been shot below his shoulder blade; the bullet had entered his back and passed through his lung and liver and diaphragm, to emerge through his chest. "There wasn't any expression on Wesbecker's face," he recalls, "and it really didn't look like he was looking at me."

Seidenfaden heard another pop and he turned to his right, away from the sound. He started staggering toward a cage where the maintenance workers kept plumbing fittings. Then he saw Hatfield, shot in the back, lying at his feet.

"I still didn't know what the pops were," says Seidenfaden, who had now dropped to the ground himself. "I thought something was blowing up. I thought it was Sallee's lathe had gone berserk and that we'd been hit by pieces of machinery."

Hatfield, despite a huge exit wound on the left side of his stomach, was also unaware that he had been shot. "It felt to me," he says, "like a practical joke or something, like somebody would come up behind you and hit you with something—it felt to me like one of these pump-up air guns."

From where he lay, Seidenfaden now saw Wesbecker approach Paul Sallee, who was bending over his lathe, wearing a pair of ear mufflers to drown the noise of the machine. Wesbecker stood in the doorway of the workshop and shot him point-blank in the back.

In the silence that followed the sudden dying of his machine, Sallee was heard to cry out, "Oh my God, help me!"

Beyond the grinder room was a tunnel that connected one section of the plant with the *Louisville Courier-Journal* building and the stairs that led up to the pressroom. Andrew Pointer, a fifty-year-old African American, had been employed at Standard Gravure as a reel man since 1967. He had worked the one-to-nine shift that morning and had just been informed that he would have to work another eight-hour shift. Weary and dejected, he was on his way to the street to move his car to a meter. As he entered the tunnel, he saw a figure coming toward him.

"I was raising my head up, and before I could raise all the way up to visualize who it was, that's when I was shot in the lower abdomen from about twenty feet distance," says Pointer.

Pointer stood in his tracks as the figure walked past him slowly "with a blank stare." That's when he recognized him as Joe Wesbecker. "He looked like he didn't have no blood in his body at all," remembers Pointer.

Leaving Pointer behind him, Wesbecker now entered the basement reel room, where paper is loaded and put over rollers on its way up to the pressroom above.

John Tingle, a forty-nine-year-old pressman who had been employed in the plant since 1966, was watching two outside contractors working on an air-conditioning system when he heard the gunshot that hit Pointer.

Mystified by the sound, Tingle began to walk slowly in the direction of the tunnel, and almost collided with Wesbecker as he came around the side of the reel machinery. He remembers that Wesbecker was holding the AK-47 across his middle with two clips taped together in his hand and a clip in the chamber. He also saw a pistol stuck in Wesbecker's waistband.

Tingle, who regarded himself as a friend of Wesbecker's, spoke first. "I said, 'What's happening, Rock.' And he just looked at me. Then he says, 'Hi, John . . . Get all the way back to the wall, stay the fuck out of my way.' I said, 'Man, what's going on?' He said, 'I said I'd be back and now I'm back! . . . I told 'em; now I'm fuckin' goin' to show 'em.' "

Tingle says that the episode seemed to him "like a cheap movie"; that he told Wesbecker as much. "I said, 'Man, it's like a cheap movie.' Wesbecker said, 'John, go all the way back to the wall and stay the fuck out of my way.' "

Tingle says he told Wesbecker, "Okay, Rock, you go for it!" Then he shouted to the contract men: "Look, get out of the way. Stay out of his way."

As Wesbecker went back around the side of the machine, Tingle joined the other two men, who had ducked down by the wall. After a few seconds, says Tingle, Wesbecker returned to look at him. "He was looking to see which way I was going. If I had been going another way it might have been different."

Tingle and his two companions now ran to a nearby restroom, where they found three other employees hiding for safety.

Now in shock, but still on his feet despite the huge wound in his abdomen, Pointer had begun to follow in the direction in which Wesbecker had gone. As he dragged himself forward, Pointer saw Wesbecker emerging from the reel room, where he had accosted Tingle.

Wesbecker was approaching a narrow set of steps "like a hunter stalking his prey," remembers Pointer. At that moment, pressman Richard Barger, who suffered from arthritic knees, was panting heavily down the steps. Pointer says that he distinctly heard Wesbecker say, "I'm sorry, Dickie," before putting five bullets into him and stepping over his body.

Pointer stood rooted to the spot for several minutes as Wesbecker disappeared from view. Eventually he heard gunfire on the floor above and thought he heard Wesbecker laughing. Inexplicably, Pointer now made his way back, slowly and painfully, to the exact spot where he had been shot, and laid himself down on the ground to wait for help.

The gunfire Pointer heard had killed two more workers in the newsroom above—Lloyd White and James Wible. But Wesbecker was still not done. Passing between the roaring machines with their harsh smells of lubricant and solvents, he headed for the snack room, or break room, where he could count on finding the majority of his former co-workers at changeover time.

Pressman Gordon Scherer, forty-eight, who had worked at Standard Gravure since 1959, had arrived at the plant that morning at eight-fifteen. He had gone to the locker room as usual and changed into his dark-blue work overalls before checking the duty list outside the fore-man's office. Then he went into the snack room, a twenty-by-twelve-foot room where there were two large tables, a dozen or so chairs, a microwave oven, a soft-drink machine, and a refrigerator in which the pressmen kept their lunch bags.

"Ordinarily there might have been up to thirty people in there at that time," says Scherer, "but for some reason or another, the traffic jams and trains and stuff, people were running late."

Scherer says he sat down and started talking to Bill Ganote about working on an old car. Also in the room were Paul Gnadinger, Kenny Fentress, Mike Campbell, Bill Hoffman, and Chuck Gorman, all veteran pressmen and former colleagues of Wesbecker's.

Eventually the men in the room began to react to the strange sounds out in the pressroom. Somebody said he thought it was a firecracker. Scherer thought it sounded like a steel plate being smacked with a lead hammer. He remembers somebody laughing and saying, "Perhaps it's Charlie come in to say good morning": Charlie Ganote (Bill Ganote's brother) had a habit of bringing firearms to work.

"A short time after those noises," continues Scherer, "I saw Wesbecker in the Plexiglas window of the door. . . . I stood up, reached out, and was going to step over to greet him when he came in. It was nothing unusual for somebody [who was] off sick or retirees to come in for a visit, and it had been a while since I'd seen Joe, and I was sort of tickled to see him. . . . Then I saw the barrel of the gun."

According to other pressmen in the room, Kenny Fentress was also smiling a greeting when Wesbecker entered the room. As Wesbecker shot him, Fentress cried out, "Oh, Joe, no!" His arms went up and he flew back against the wall. Next it was the turn of Paul Gnadinger, who crashed to the floor as the bullets hit.

"After that," says Scherer, "it moved along pretty fast. Nobody really screamed or hollered; Kenny was the only one who had said anything."

Scherer did not take a direct shot, but was hit in the right leg with shrapnel; he lay on the floor on his right side. Bill Hoffman, a fair-haired athletic-looking man, had been sitting on Scherer's right; he was shot in the leg and landed on the floor next to Scherer.

As Wesbecker sprayed the room, bullets ripped into the microwave, the drink machine, and the cooling-system pipes. The floor flooded with freezing water mingled with blood.

Mike Campbell, fifty-three, and a father of three daughters, had seen the door open and, at waist level, the barrel of the gun coming through. He says he sensed what was going to happen. "I turned away from it and I just didn't want to see it shoot me."

"At the time," Campbell remembers, "it seemed like it was in a cadence: pop-pop-pop, pop-pop-pop. I'm not sure if it was two or three or what it was. Sort of a cadence. I heard a couple of shots and I felt my body jerk and my knee burn like fire. I thought, 'God, I've been hit. That hurt.' I just bent over like I was dead. I was trying to act like I was dead so I wouldn't get shot again. But I think my leg had been up over the chair or something, but, anyway, my leg flew out when it got shot and I just leaned over the table trying to keep my eyes closed and just hoping and praying that he wouldn't come back and shoot me. And at that time I just thought, you know, 'I'm going to die and I don't know why'; you know, 'Why am I going to die in this room? I don't know why anybody would want to shoot us. I'll never see my family again.' "

The men who were still conscious were suddenly aware of a pause in the firing; Wesbecker seemed to leave the room for a few seconds. In the interval, Gorman and Gnadinger managed to drag themselves out through the back door and into the locker area.

Campbell, who was still playing dead, says, "Things got very quiet and it just ran through my mind, 'I'm going to get assassinated.' It just dawned on me, 'He's going to walk up behind me and blow me away.' "

As suddenly as Wesbecker departed, he was back in the room. Campbell says, "I heard pop-pop-pop and I felt my body jerk all over the place. And it started again, pop-pop-pop, pop-pop-pop. And at this point, I had my head down and I could hear rather than see bullets hitting furniture and it sounded like the floor and whatever ricocheting. I could hear movement of people bouncing around, like. And then the bullets stopped, the firing stopped."

Most of the men in the room had taken up to five bullets apiece. Hoffman, who had been trying to stand on a completely disjointed leg, had now taken a bullet in the chest. "He was just insane," remembers Hoffman, "he was rabid. . . . He was shooting the dead bodies . . . anywhere and anything. . . ."

Campbell had been shot in both his arms and both his legs. "I tried to get up out of the chair," says Campbell, "and my arm gave way and I fell on the floor. My arm was loose and dangling and my left leg was loose and dangling, just flopping over; I didn't have any control over it. And at this point I saw a big flap of skin hanging down off my left arm. And I could tell my legs were numb. I knew I had been shot a lot. I could feel it then, when I hit the floor."

When Wesbecker left the break room for the second time, Hoffman, despite his terrible wounds, could see him clearly through the Plexiglas. "I was sitting up now. I could see him fumbling about his waist. He had the AK-47 up to his chest and he was fumbling around. And I was worried that he was looking for another clip to put in. But he pulled out a pistol from his waistband, stuck it under his chin, and shot his face off. I saw it from the side. I saw the lurch of his body, I saw the blood spray, and I saw his body jerk, spasm; then he went down on his face."

Wesbecker's body lay in front of the foreman's office door, on which the pressmen's job assignments were posted within a glass panel.

5

As SHE LAY on the floor in the reception area bleeding from her gaping wound, Angela Bowman had one thought: to call her husband. But when she attempted to pull herself up, she could not feel her legs.

Five years later, in a packed and weeping courthouse in Louisville, Angela Bowman, permanently confined to a wheelchair, told the story of her rescue:

"I was going to get to the phone, but I couldn't feel my legs, and when I went to sit up I couldn't, so I tried getting over on my elbow and pushing up, and my arm kept sliding, and I couldn't grab the chair and pull up on it. And I looked down and there was just blood everywhere. So I grabbed the cords under the desk. I knew one of them had to be the phone cord, so I just started pulling and yanking, and then I realized there was nowhere for the phone to come back there: I was pulling to the back, and it wasn't going to fall down. And it was so quiet. I kept calling for somebody to come help us. . . .

"Then cops just started coming, and there were, like, cops guarding us, because the ambulance people came in then right away. An EMS woman started working on me, and she kept saying to the cops, 'Cover me. Cover me.' She thought they were going to come back in there and shoot us some more. And I could hear the cop's radio the whole time, all the stuff they were saying, because they were trying to flood the building with policemen. Then these SWAT guys come rushing in, leaping over my feet and going all around me. They had special vests over their uniforms. They were all carrying these big guns. They were just hollering and cussing and screaming. I suppose they did that to flush the guy out or make him make a move. They were just screaming profanities as they ran through and dispersed all through the building. Well, I just kept thinking he's coming back, and they did, too, I guess, because every-body was scared.

"I never knew anybody that had been shot before. I kept saying, 'Don't let me die. I had a baby.' And I said, 'Please don't let me die.' And they wouldn't talk to me about it. They kept telling me to calm down, not to worry about anything. Somebody went back over to Sharon, I think, once, but then nobody ever went to her no more, no policemen, nobody talked to her, and no EMS, so, I mean, I didn't ask them, but I just knew she was dead. . . .

"And so they're still working on me and my chest started to hurt and I thought I was having a heart attack, and so I told them, I said, 'I'm having a heart attack. I'm going to die of a heart attack.' And they kept telling me I just needed to calm down. And then they were trying to talk to me. I looked at this guy, and I said, 'I'm dying. I can't fight it no more. I can't fight it no more.' And I said, 'Please tell my family I loved them and I'm sorry I couldn't say goodbye.' And he looked down at me and he just picked me up in his arms and he said, 'I'm going down that elevator.' And he carried me down to the street in his arms. And when the doors opened there were cops everywhere. And he said, 'We've got to take her.'

"They put me in a car. I don't even remember if it was a police car. I just know it was a four-door car, because they kept trying to get me in the back seat and they couldn't get me in. My elbows kept hitting the doors, and they kept trying to get me in. We started off down the street. We didn't go a few feet and he slams on the brakes and he was cussing, and then he'd say, 'Excuse me, ma'am.' And he'd cuss some more, then he'd say, 'Excuse me.' They couldn't get around the roadblocks or something, he said. So then he just said to hold on and we bumped and bumped over the sidewalks. And then we started driving fast and we were at the Humana Hospital in just seconds. And I remember they jumped out and screamed, 'We've got one, we've got one.' And they put me on a stretcher and started taking me into the hospital."

At eight-thirty on the morning of September 14, patrolman Joseph A. Ball, forty-six years old and twenty-five years with the Louisville Police

Department, was walking past the Kentucky Theater on Fourth Street, when he took the call.

He, too, told his story in a crowded, tearful Louisville courtroom five years later:

"A call came that there was a man with a gun at the *Courier-Journal*. So I ran and continued listening to my radio as I ran. . . . There was an ambulance sitting there running and nothing was around it, so I said, 'Let's take an ambulance and go up and get one of them.' . . . As we were taking it up I thought to myself, 'This is not a good day to die,' but I thought that I was going to die that day. I said an Act of Contrition and a Hail Mary, and with an employee I went up in an elevator at the back of the building. . . . We had one dead here and one shot over here and another one, John Stein, that was shot over there, shot in the head. We could still hear gunshots and we thought that at any time that door was going to open up and just blow us away.

"Officer Tom Strong was there, and I took his shirt off of him and kind of wrapped it around Stein's head and tried to stop the bleeding but, you know, on head wounds you just can't stop the bleeding. It's so terrible. I can remember looking down at my hands and seeing stuff I didn't want to see. But he was still alive and I said, 'Well, let's get him out of here.' So we kind of belly-crawled out and pushed and pulled the stretcher. We got him down on the elevator, then we didn't find nobody that could drive the ambulance. . . . So we just turned everything on, and they had Broadway blocked but nobody had told us, and we bucked traffic. We were going the wrong way up Chestnut Street and we rode on sidewalks and everything. We knew this man was very seriously hurt.

"When we reached the hospital, the first thing, we pulled in, some rent-a-policeman, I believe you call them, come up and said I pulled in the wrong way. I said, 'Yeah, you better get me some doctors,' and the doctors came out and we got John inside and they went to work on him. John was also shot in the stomach, but we didn't know that. We cleaned the stretcher off and grabbed a couple more sheets and got back in the ambulance and took it back down to Standard Gravure to make sure if we had to bring somebody else back. . . .

"I went through the press area and into the break room. Everywhere I went, he had shot all the fire sprinklers, and there was so much blood that it looked like a river. It looked like a river of blood. And here you're walking through it and, you know, but [there was] something that you had to do.

"Then I saw Joe Wesbecker, a man I knew for years. I saw him lying facedown in a pool of blood. I was so mad that he wasn't man enough to face up to what he had done or get help. I wanted—I wanted to kick him and stomp him, I wanted to just do anything I could. But you know, you just—you just don't—just everything went through your head. I just figured I probably could have helped him if he would have talked to me or something like that. You know, I thought maybe I failed or something to that effect. But, God, it made me so mad that he did what he did, you know, with all this—all these poor families that he tore up, and not only the people in Standard Gravure, but the people that are involved in the police department. Some of them will never be the same again. . . . I won't never be the same again.

"And I remember, you know, after everything died down, I had on a pair of shoes—chuckle boots, they call them, they come up to your ankle—I took them off and . . . I took my socks off and my feet were completely blood-soaked. I went back to headquarters later on that evening barefooted, I would never put the stuff back on."

At 9:00 A.M. on September 14, 1989, Dr. Steve Henry, aged forty, a specialist in orthopedic surgery, was treating private patients at the Veterans Hospital, near Broadway and Third, when he received an emergency call. He rushed out of the building and drove six blocks to the Humana Hospital–University of Louisville trauma unit on Jackson Street, where the dying and the wounded were being taken.

"If there's any person coming in with gunshot wounds there's always bone splintering, and an orthopedic surgeon is called for. When I got down there, it was crazy. Nearly all the victims were in the emergency room or coming in at the time. They were all in within a space of about thirty minutes. We just started doing triage—sorting casualties into categories. When an injured person comes into Emergency, the trauma surgeon is responsible for triaging a serious injury and deciding if they need plastic surgery, orthopedic surgery, neurosurgery, or all three, or four or more.

"There were so many people coming in that we were triaging any orthopedic-type problems ourselves, because there wasn't emergency staff for each person. The first patient I saw was Mike Campbell. . . . Although he was very severely injured, he was one of the least of the wounded compared with the others.

"All his limbs had been hit. I saw him first because he had been cleared by the trauma team, which takes care of the thorax, the heart, the lungs, and the abdomen. He had gunshot wounds in all his limbs. The left knee was fractured at the kneecap, the upper part of his shinbone, the lower part of his femur, which is the thigh bone; in addition he had a shattered right elbow. . . .

"We took him to surgery around noon. We put screws and plates in the shinbone with screws and wires in the patella, or the kneecap; then we put multiple screws and multiple pins in the area right above his knee. That whole section of his knee was shattered. . . . We had him in surgery from twelve-thirty to twenty-one-thirty-five, more than nine hours. Then we felt that we had done enough surgery on him for one day, and in any case we had surgeries to do on other patients. So we decided to put off operating on his arm injury, because it was not unstable. . . . Later we put plates and screws in the arm. He received three different types of antibiotics. From noon we had him on morphine sulphate, six to eight milligrams through the muscle about every three hours, and we supplemented that with other powerful analgesics between shots."

Dr. Henry and his team worked through the night and through the following day and into the evening before taking a break. During those thirty-six hours, eight separate operations were being performed simultaneously, involving more than a hundred doctors under Dr. Frank Miller, co-director of the trauma unit. The truth of the human devastation wreaked by Joe Wesbecker and his high-velocity weapon was beginning to sink in. "It was obvious they were injured with a weapon of very high velocity," says Miller. "A slug from a .22-caliber rifle usually causes tissue damage in a narrow path through the body," he said, "but an AK-47 will cause damage to a broader area, because of the energy that's imparted through the bullet."

Kenny Fentress, who had been shot in the stomach, arm, and leg alongside Mike Campbell in the break room, underwent four separate operations and would remain on the critical list in intensive care.

John Stein, who had been shot in the head and in the abdomen as he approached the bindery elevator, was in a coma. Bill Hoffman had sustained a huge sucking wound in his chest when Wesbecker returned to shoot him a second time; the fragments had remained within his chest, causing the heart to pump out blood with nowhere to go. Angela Bowman, it was now clear, had suffered devastating injuries to her spinal cord and would almost certainly be paralyzed for life. Andrew Pointer, shot in the lower abdomen as he walked through the tunnel, underwent two operations. Also seriously injured were Paula Warman, Jackie Miller, David Seidenfaden, Stanley Hatfield, Forrest Conrad.

Those confirmed dead on arrival at the Humana were Bill Ganote and Richard Barger—shot five times each; Lloyd White—shot twice; James F. Wible, Sharon Needy, James Husband, and Paul Sallee—shot once each.

Joe Wesbecker, who died from a bullet through his brain, lay in the city morgue.

At six in the evening on September 18, four days after the shootings, and two days after the first five of the funerals, Kenneth Fentress, forty-five, would also lose his battle for life at the Humana Hospital. An ironic twist to his life and death: his own father had been shot to death seventeen years earlier in a grocery-store robbery.

6

SITUATED ALONG an eight-mile curve on the southern bank of the Ohio River, Louisville is a city of 270,0000 people that looks north across the slow-moving river to Indiana and east toward the hills they call the Floyd Knobs. Surrounded by rolling, splendidly wooded bluegrass country, Louisville lies two hundred miles east of the Mississippi and one hundred miles north of Nashville, Tennessee.

Once a year, in the first week of May, the city renews its reputation for Southern hospitality by playing host to the world on Kentucky Derby day. Out on the elegant Churchill Downs racecourse, the belles in hats and brick-faced men in bow ties gather in the grandstand to drink mint juleps and Maker's Mark bourbon, while the rest—more than 140,000 Louisvillians and visitors—disport themselves infield on whiskey and beer.

Whereas it was once a mixed and bustling street city sustained by river freight and the coal and cigarette industries (until the late 1950s, its warehouses handled a third of North America's tobacco), enthusiastic Louisvillians have been complaining for thirty years now about the dereliction of their downtown. A few Hopperesque apartment complexes survive, but the dominant architectural presence is the Providian Tower, a postmodernist erection competing for brutal dreariness with the granite cliff-face of the Humana medical-insurance headquarters.

Fourth Street, once famous for its thriving shops and restaurants, now boasts a scruffy wig emporium and a health club amid the boarded-up Greek Revival terraces. A phony motorized trolley, all mahogany and mock brass, clangs up and down its deserted length, transporting the occasional black pensioner from Broadway to the pedestrian mall on Muhammad Ali Boulevard. Known as the Galleria, this air-conditioned arcade protects an assembly of chain snack bars and tawdry knickknack shops from the extremes of Kentucky's winters and summers.

The Galleria was intended to entice the white shoppers back downtown from the cosmopolitan zest of Bardstown Road, east of the city: with its vandalized restrooms and lack of parking facilities, the Galleria has become a symbol of reinvigorated segregation. Black youths roam its walkways in droves under the keen eyes of armed security guards.

The coal and tobacco industries having vanished as in a dream, the new major employers—General Electric and Ford Motor Company—have not taken up the shortfall. Louisville, whose population has declined by eighty thousand since 1975, has more than average poverty for its size, two out of five of its African Americans living in destitution. Yet, according to the city's police department, the city ranks below the national average for crime, suffering no organized gang violence and no significant drug trafficking. In a typical year, however, some forty of its citizens are murdered, thirty-five of them by family members, friends, and co-workers. Recently Louisville's homicide chief asked a city school class for a show of hands of all students who could go home and put their hands on a gun. All but one of the twenty students present lifted their hands.

The city is divided, its West End, the largest black community in Kentucky, cut off from the white southeastern suburbs by a downtown no-man's-land and the eight-lane north-south thruways. But if there is a single institution that gives the place a semblance of cohesion, it is the *Louisville Courier-Journal*, whose sleek building—all pale limestone and curving plate glass—stands disconsolately among the parking lots and raffish bars at Broadway and Sixth. Its recent history has paralleled, and to some extent shaped, the fate of Louisville itself.

Purchased in 1916 by Judge Robert Worth Bingham with the proceeds of a $5-million legacy from his recently deceased wife (some, including his granddaughter, maintain he poisoned her for it), the *Courier-Journal* and its sister paper, the *Times*, would remain in the Bingham family until they were sold off in 1986. The Binghams did not aspire to own a chain of papers, but, accurately predicting the prospects for comics, supplements, and contract color-printing, the wily judge established in 1922 a rotogravure printing plant and called it Standard Gravure. The same year, he founded WHAS, a radio station, to complete his media empire.

Under Judge Bingham, who was United States ambassador in London during the thirties, the morning *Courier-Journal* became famous throughout the nation for courageous exposure of sleaze and the championing of civil liberties. In its heyday, despite the relatively small size of Louisville, the *Courier-Journal* was admired, and sometimes feared, as the equal of any of the nation's top ten newspapers, including *The New York Times*, *The Washington Post*, and *The Boston Globe*. During the sixties' busing campaigns, the paper's crusade in favor of desegregated schools resulted in a riot in which its windows were smashed by racist readers. Over a period of forty years the paper won eight Pulitzer prizes for investigative journalism.

After the judge's death, in 1937, his son, Barry Senior (who retired as chief executive in 1971), and then his grandson Barry Junior, continued the tradition of managing the newspaper as a public trust—a free-spending "writers' paper." And yet, "putting out a first-class paper in the forty-fifth market," Barry Bingham, Sr., would remark, "was like pulling a rabbit out of a hat." The difficulty was that the *Courier-Journal* enjoyed a small fraction of the advertising revenues of any of the top ten, and when television came those revenues were even further eroded. By the 1970s, the *Courier-Journal* was lucky to post a 2-percent profit on its annual operations, compared with *The Washington Post*'s average 12 percent.

The true cash cow of the business was Standard Gravure, whose presses started out printing wallpaper and circus posters and eventually won contracts to run off the Sunday magazines of up to twenty-five other newspapers, along with giveaways, catalogues, circulars, and preprints. It was Standard Gravure that made the shareholders' dividends look respectable, a profitability purchased with a rather different management culture from the benevolent "plantation" patriarchy exercised on the newspapers. "The process of printing was considered dirty if not actively dangerous," remembers Sallie Bingham, Barry Senior's daughter. "A general distrust of blue-collar workers seemed to unite

Standard's management and its owner, and frequent problems with strikes or threatened strikes discouraged benevolence at the top."

During the 1970s, as newsprint and energy costs soared, and circulation and advertising continued to plummet, the *Courier-Journal*, like all privately owned newspapers in the country, realized that the new computerized printing technologies were not going to restore the industry to profitability. Salvation lay in economy of scale—the irresistible concentrating of more and more newspapers into fewer hands, with all the advantages of shared overheads and massive newsprint discounts. For the Binghams, that was not an option. In consequence, Standard Gravure was squeezed all the harder to maintain overall profits; yet outside contracts were getting scarcer, since many newspapers were abandoning their expensive Sunday magazines. At the same time, the printing plant found itself falling between two technological stools: on the one hand, customers were opting for cheaper and swifter offset printing; on the other, Standard's venerable presses, despite continual additions and renovations, could not compete with the new breed of giant gravure machine that could handle, say, a Sears Catalogue running to tens of millions of copies. The pressure on Standard Gravure to perform despite these handicaps would have implications for every one of its workers—from senior management down to the most junior flyboy. "The printers," says Sallie Bingham, "were spoken of as wild men who resorted to sabotage when thwarted, and many stories were told about the vandalism that was said to increase the expenses of the operation. The blame was laid not on our inability to keep up with technological changes but on a recalcitrant union leadership."

By the late seventies, Barry Bingham, Jr., had taken the helm of the companies, his elder brother, Worth, having been decapitated by his own surfboard in a car accident at Martha's Vineyard. Barry Junior attempted to diversify into "teleconferencing" and purchased a license and franchises to sell cellular phones in Kentucky. The new enterprises failed to alleviate the problems afflicting the firm's core activity. Then the Bingham sisters and wives began to quarrel. A central issue was whether the newspaper could continue to afford its celebrated coverage and quality. The women, at least one of whom would sit through board meetings doing needlepoint, were adamant that it should, but they were not prepared to accept a reduced level of annual dividends. Hostilities between members of the Bingham family rose to such a pitch that they would communicate solely through memos.

Through the eighties, the decline continued apace. The death of downtown had ensured the eventual collapse of the circulation of the *Times*, which was essentially a street paper. At the same time, management consultants advised that it was pointless to spend money distributing the *Courier-Journal* to the rock-rib coal-mining communities of Kentucky, since those readers were unlikely to enhance the advertisers' readership profile. Tired of the family squabbles, and begrudging his younger son's control of the empire, Barry Senior, who was still chairman and ultimate controller, decided to sell.

It was as predictable as it was ironic that the *Courier-Journal*, and its stricken sister paper the *Times*, would be sold to Gannett, the fastest-growing newspaper chain in the country, and publisher of *USA Today*. No two newspaper publishers could have been more at odds in personality and vision than Gannett's CEO, Allen Neuharth, and the elitist Barry Bingham, Sr. Yet Gannett's ruthless publishing philosophy was what it took to turn the *Courier-Journal* around. As the local magazine *Louisville* commented on the purchaser and the seller: "On the one hand is the old *Courier*'s tradition of giving its readers what its owners and editors thought they needed; on the other is Gannett's eagerness to give today's *C-J* readers what they *want.*" After years of requiring a subsidiary cash cow, the *Courier-Journal became* a cash cow within the mighty Gannett chain.

At six in the morning on May 19, 1986, after jogging around Louisville's downtown in shorts and a T-shirt, Allen Neuharth, who had spent the night at the Brown Hotel, at Fourth and Broadway, panted into the *Courier-Journal* newsroom and begged a cup of coffee. For the sum of $305 million, the *Courier-Journal* had become the ninetieth paper in Neuharth's brash and profitable group.

The Gannett corporation, however, had no interest in Standard Gravure and the other businesses, which were sold off piecemeal to the highest bidders. WHAS-TV was sold for $85.7 million to the Providence Journal Co. of Rhode Island. The AM and FM radio stations went for more than $20 million to Clear Channel Communications Inc. of San Antonio. A communications enterprise called Data Courier was sold to Bell and Howell for $12 million. Finally, Standard Gravure, after its own workers had failed to achieve a buy-out, went to Michael Shea, a little-known thirty-six-year-old print broker in Atlanta, for more than $22 million. The sale of the entire Bingham media businesses garnered $448 million, making Barry Senior and his wife $100 million the richer. Each of his children received $50 million.

After the sale, Gannett's people moved quickly to close down the *Times* and rationalize editorial expenditure while beefing up the *Courier-Journal*'s circulation and advertising. "It's an economic fact," commented one newspaper reporter, not for attribution. "We don't have the bodies or resources to do what we used to do. . . . We're spread thin." Another complained, "We don't write as many stories, and we don't cover the community the way we used to."

Some journalists bemoaned the passing of the newspaper's role as a watchdog of national and international affairs; others were more concerned with the sudden decline in local public-service coverage in Louisville. All of them deplored the shrinking of what journalists call the "news hole," the parts of the newspaper that are not devoted to advertising.

Before long, media critic Bob Schulman commented that the new regime had created a "really oppressive morale problem" at the paper. "Corporate demands for vastly higher profit margins have introduced and maintained a horrendous pressure not to expand the staffs as they might want to, and did in the Bingham era. . . . The bottom-line pressure has been an enormous factor."

The pressman at Standard Gravure, who had suffered successive squeezes, job buy-outs, and a six-year pay freeze under the Binghams, initially welcomed Mike Shea. They looked forward to a new era in which profits would be plowed back into the company rather than swallowed up by the spendthrift newspaper. After the purchase, Shea addressed the gathered pressmen to assure them of expanding orders, new technology, and prosperous days ahead.

That was before the word went around that one of Shea's first acts was to take $11 million from their pension fund to pay for his purchase. Shea later insisted that the reversion of the pension money had been made clear in the original terms of the purchase. Regardless, soon the pressmen, too, began to rue the passing of the Binghams.

7

IN THE DAYS following the Standard Gravure shootings, Louisville's citizens took stock of the incident, and of the wounds that had been inflicted on the entire community. In this city, which for years had struggled to find a collective focus, hundreds of people were gravitating toward the Gothic red-brick Cathedral of the Assumption, at Fifth and Jefferson. They came just to sit and be together; they said they were showing solidarity with the victims and their families. One woman told a reporter she had come to pray for the "gunman's family, since they are suffering too and will go on suffering for the rest of their lives."

Surprised by the flow of visitors of every denomination on the morning after the incident, the Roman Catholic Archbishop Thomas Kelly announced a memorial service at his noon Mass. In an impromptu sermon before a crowded church, he said that the gathering was "us at our finest."

"Even in this most difficult and painful time," he said, "we can be together, we can have a sense of security, and even of victory."

Within twenty-four hours of the shootings, a fund was announced to help the survivors. At Standard Gravure, Mike Shea, who was thought to have been a prime target in Wesbecker's onslaught, promised to match any amount collected by the community. He also promised to pay for the victims' funerals and establish an employee-crises committee to identify and meet the needs of victims and their families. "No employer could be prepared for this tragedy," he told the *Courier-Journal*, "and there is no school to teach it to you."

Display ads announcing counseling sessions sponsored by the Humana organization were run in the *Courier-Journal*, as was a piece quoting therapists on the phenomenon of untreated shock. "Early counseling sessions in the wake of trauma are crucial in avoiding long-term psychological problems," said the paper. "Left unexplored, those frightening—and often faulty—memories can fester in one's subconscious and re-emerge months or even years later as troubling psychological problems. Eating disorders and substance abuse can be common among people exposed to such terrifying incidents, as can post-traumatic stress disorder."

In the initial bout of soul-searching, the national and local media focused on the firearms issue. The *Courier-Journal* carried a piece entitled "Sledgehammer of a Gun Can Be Bought Easily." The reporter had found a Louisville gun dealer who could inform readers that "the relationship of a low-power gun to an AK-47 is like a gnat compared to a sledgehammer. It'll go through a door, through two people, really tear up a person." Police investigating Wesbecker's house at Nottoway Circle said that they had found open on the top of the refrigerator a *Time* magazine story on assault weapons and recent murders committed with them. The article, dated February 6, 1989, was entitled "Armed in America: More Guns, More Shootings, More Massacres."

Wesbecker, it now emerged, had bought the AK-47 on May 1 from Tilford's Gun Sales, on Old Shepherdsville Road, in Louisville. The store owner, Jack Tilford, told police the AK-47 had to be ordered. It cost $349, and when Wesbecker picked it up two weeks later, he also bought eleven hundred rounds of ammunition for $139.

On Friday, the day after the shooting, there were calls for gun control on the floor of Congress; the debate would rumble on in newspapers and magazines across the nation for several days more. *Newsweek* drew a parallel between the Wesbecker incident and the January 17 massacre in a schoolyard in Stockton, California, when Patrick Purdy, wielding an AK-47, killed five Southeast Asian refugee children and wounded some thirty others. The magazine noted that eighty-eight thousand Chinese AK-47s had been imported into the United States before President Bush banned importations of semi-automatics in July 1989. "Wesbecker bought his arsenal of weapons easily and legally," said the weekly, "despite a well-documented history of mental problems."

Yet there were also the predictable responses from the pro-gun lobby. The *Chicago Tribune* quoted Jim Baker, a spokesman for the National Rifle Association: "Firearms have been around for a couple hundred years now. . . . It's the misuse of those things that I think we ought to be concerned about."

By Wednesday of the week after the shootings, the Louisville Chamber of Commerce urged that AK-47 rifles be removed from the shelves of businesses that sold them in the Louisville area. In a resolution passed by its board of directors, the chamber also called for local, state, and federal laws restricting the distribution of assault weapons. That same day, however, one of Louisville's biggest gun stores announced that orders for the AK-47 had quadrupled since the shootings.

On September 15, at the Jefferson County morgue, Wesbecker's blood and brain tissues were subjected to a battery of tests for traces of pharmaceutical products, and comparisons made with medications taken from his house at Nottoway Circle. According to Dr. Richard Greathouse, the coroner assigned to the case, the blood taken from Wesbecker's body contained two psychiatric drugs—lithium and the antidepressant Prozac, in levels normally prescribed by doctors. As recently as September 5, Wesbecker had collected a prescription for twenty capsules of Prozac, one capsule to be taken per day. The police said that they had retrieved from his house at Nottoway Circle the bottle containing the fifteen remaining Prozac capsules, indicating that he had probably taken them at least up to September 11.

By September 20, preparations were being made for an inquest on the deaths of Wesbecker's victims. In an unusual development, however, Dr. Lee Coleman, Wesbecker's psychiatrist, and a prime defendant in any liability suit, was, according to the *Courier-Journal*, thwarting the coroner, Greathouse, by refusing to release his own notes on his dead patient. Gregory J. Bubalo, attorney for Coleman, told reporters that the doctor had been asked by both city police and the coroner's office for information about Wesbecker, but had refused. "While Dr. Coleman would like to cooperate," Bubalo said, "he would decline until he is presented with a court order telling him he can talk to people about this."

It did not take Greathouse long to get his court order. Notoriously outspoken, he announced he was going call in everybody who had had anything to do with Wesbecker. "Then we'll get the whole thing laid out on the table top," he was quoted as saying.

A practicing pediatrician who was a prominent judge of national dog shows on weekends and had treated the ailments of touring rock superstars, including Mick Jagger, Greathouse told journalists from the outset that he believed Wesbecker's antidepressants had a part to play in his killing spree. His swashbuckling assurance was perhaps partly owed to the ample leeway accorded coroners in the state of Kentucky, giving them what some have described as "the biggest badge" in law enforcement. A Kentucky coroner can make arrests, carry a gun, subpoena documents, and even enter private property to search and seize.

Meanwhile, as if to plead poverty in advance of possible damages, Standard Gravure was letting it be known that they were doubtful whether the company could survive after this, their second disaster within a year. Just eleven months earlier, the plant had suffered a fire and explosion that had put three of its six presses out of action. In an interview with the *Courier-Journal* the day after the Wesbecker shootings, Vernon Rothenburger, Standard Gravure's vice-president of operations, said that the company had been dogged by bad luck ever since the days of the Binghams, when all the workers had been subjected to a six-year pay freeze.

Already raising the question of deteriorating worker relations, however, was Louisville labor lawyer Herbert L. Segal, who stated publicly that Wesbecker had come to him in mid-1988 seeking help with a complaint he had about his job. Wesbecker believed that he had been unfairly forced to do hazardous work, Segal was claiming. The lawyer said that he had met with Wesbecker's supervisors to try to resolve the complaint, yet Wesbecker remained convinced there was a plot against him at work.

But the crucial liability bombshell, possibly implicating both the plant and its security firm, Hall Security Service Inc., did not land until two weeks after the killings. Talking to journalists in the last week of September, James Lucas, a weary-looking, lantern-jawed pressman at Standard Gravure, and a longtime co-worker and friend of Wesbecker, said that Wesbecker had given him a list of people he intended to murder at Standard Gravure just three weeks before he actually did it.

Wesbecker, he said, visited him at home and, sitting in his kitchen, confided the names of people on his hit list: Michael Shea, the company owner; Don McCall, executive vice-president; Donald Cox, pressroom superintendent; Paula Warman, employee-relations manager; James Popham, pressman and onetime foreman; Sam Stizler, pressman and onetime acting foreman. "All these," Wesbecker had apparently said, "along with the rest of the office cronies."

Lucas said that he had told some of the intended victims, and had informed his co-workers and the head of his department. But, for whatever reasons, he went on, "my fears were not shared by those I told." So, while Wesbecker's scheme became common knowledge among pressroom workers and supervisors, upper management was never informed of it, according to Lucas. Lucas also revealed that Wesbecker had told him of a plan to aim a model airplane loaded with explosives at Standard Gravure's highly inflammable solvent-reclamation plant.

The coroner's inquest convened in the county courthouse in downtown Louisville before Greathouse and a six-member jury on November 22, 1989, its purpose, to reach a verdict on how the victims had met their deaths. The atmosphere was tense and tearful as relatives of the victims, and survivors well enough to attend, relived the shocking incidents of September 14. As a gruesome police videotape was played of the plant on the day of the shootings, people began to sob, and several women left the room. Various eyewitnesses gave accounts of the killings, including vivid and emotional testimony by Gordon Scherer.

But when it came to testimony about Wesbecker's job stress, the accounts sharply conflicted. Some witnesses said Wesbecker had complained that his foremen were forcing him to work on the folder. Wesbecker's son James declared he had a letter stating that his father was working the folder just before he went on medical leave in August 1988.

Mike Shea testified, however, that Wesbecker had not worked the folder since August 1986, and Scherer, who had been in charge of the team on which Wesbecker worked, backed up Shea's version, insisting that Wesbecker had worked on the paper reels, not on the folder, during his last two or three years at the plant. He added that Wesbecker had been "pretty content" with his job.

Then the fact of Wesbecker's course of Prozac was raised. Dennis Clarke, president of a group called the Citizens' Commission on Human Rights, an organization formed by the Church of Scientology, claimed that the drug was harmful. He told the court that a woman in Wisconsin had committed a murder-suicide after taking Prozac, and that many doctors had complained to the FDA about the drug's side effects.

Despite the suspicions he had voiced in September about the drug, Greathouse replied that researchers at Eli Lilly had told him that two million people had used Prozac and none had reported they had become violent. He added that Wesbecker's psychiatrists had said they prescribed the drug with good results.

Dr. Lee Coleman now gave evidence, confirming that he had tried to persuade Wesbecker to go into the hospital days before the shooting and that the patient had refused. Coleman was adamant that Wesbecker had not made even a veiled threat against Standard Gravure or anybody else during that last session. He told the court that he did not consider Wesbecker "psychotic," a condition he defined as "close-mindedly out of touch with reality." He said he believed Wesbecker probably "knew what he was doing" when he walked into the printing plant, a belief he based on the fact that Wesbecker had spared at least one co-worker, and was therefore capable of "distinguishing friend from foe."

After James Lucas had an opportunity to tell his story of Wesbecker's hit list and threats, many in the court expected that Greathouse would call Standard Gravure's middle managers to confirm whether they had heard these reports. Instead, Greathouse called the company's senior executives.

Michael Shea, Standard Gravure's owner, and Grady Throneberry, safety-and-security director, testified that they were unaware of any threatening remarks or plans by Wesbecker. Throneberry admitted, however, that the TV security camera that was supposed to scrutinize visitors at the Sixth and Armory entrance to the plant had been removed more than a year before the killings as a result of vandalism.

One of the more mysterious items to emerge during the hearings was a police statement that Wesbecker had withdrawn $70,000 from a bank account shortly before the shooting, and a further $17,000 from a trust fund. The police could not explain what had happened to the money.

Spectators and witnesses alike, moreover, were astonished at the absence of Brenda, Wesbecker's second ex-wife, who had spent the evening and night before the shootings under the same roof with him, and who was the last to see him before he set out for the plant. Questioned about her absence, Greathouse merely replied that the police had issued a subpoena but that she had not received it.

Given the complex, uneven, and in many cases conflicting testimonies, the jury verdict was extraordinarily definitive. After evidence from thirty witnesses, it took the six-member jury just one hour to rule that "excessive stress placed on Wesbecker by his employer, Standard Gravure, and possibly the effects of psychiatric drugs" were factors contributing to the shooting spree. The jury added that their statement should be "tempered with the known fact that Mr. Wesbecker was unstable." They decided, however, that Wesbecker alone was responsible for the eight deaths, thus eliminating for the time being further legal repercussions for other parties.

As he left the court, Don McCall told the *Courier-Journal*'s reporter: "I am a little disappointed, to say the least, by the jury's conclusions about stress in the workplace. Wesbecker was on long-term leave, the man was not in the workplace for well over a year."

Representatives of Eli Lilly and Company, manufacturers of Prozac, were not available for comment.

8

TWO HOURS' drive north of Louisville on Interstate 64, there takes shape on the horizon the gleaming skyline of Indianapolis, the largest land-locked city in the United States, boasting six hundred churches, twenty-three golf courses, and a million citizens. Indianapolis is also the home of Eli Lilly and Company, one of the world's largest pharmaceutical operations. Spread over ninety acres to the southeast of the city, its imposing administrative offices and research laboratories lie amid landscaped gardens and fountains.

Colonel Eli Lilly started his business out of an eighteen-by-forty-foot red-brick building on Pearl Street, Indianapolis, in 1876. A former Yankee officer in the Civil War, Lilly had an ambition to combat the quackery of patent medicines. He wanted to bring scientific discipline to the provision of medicinal substances by ensuring, for a start, that the bottle contained what the label said it did. At the same time, he was intent on appropriating for himself a slice of a growing and lucrative market.

With two employees, he procured and pounded and measured out hundreds of items with such names as Bear's Foot, Black Haw, Cramp Bark, Hardhack, Life Root, Sea Wrack, and Wormseed. When the colonel died in 1898, the total sales of his company's 2,005 medicinal products came to $322,979. Listed in the company pharmacopoeia, were Elixir of Pepsin, Bismuth, Strychnine, and a popular substance called Pil Damiana et Nux Vomica cum Phosphori, an antidote for "mental overwork, enfeebled conditions of the general system and a powerful, permanent, and determined aphrodisiac."

Among Lilly's successful milestones in the twentieth century are a patent insulin for diabetes, Liver Extract No. 343 for pernicious anemia, an early penicillin, an antiflu virus, the pregrowth weedkiller Treflan, and a revolutionary catalytic beta-blocker for heart disease. Nowadays,

Lilly employs twenty-eight thousand workers on five continents, and its gross revenues are in the region of $6.5 billion. In its laboratories in Indianapolis, more than four thousand scientists are researching pharmacological antidotes to cancer, various infections, diseases of the central nervous system, and cardiovascular and endocrine disorders.

Visitors to the facility are given a tour of Colonel Lilly's painstakingly reconstructed laboratory and shown an eight-screen film celebrating the company's history as an expanding symphony of unblemished alleviation of human disease.

The facts, however, are less exalted. Eli Lilly has suffered its fair share of the woes that afflict major pharmaceutical corporations the world over. For, if the potential rewards of commercial pharmacology have increased to gigantic proportions, so have the pressures and risks. Against the background of the U.S. government's assault on health-care spending under President Clinton, the industry has seen increased global competition, and automation at every level. The harsh economic realities have resulted in a spate of company mergers and huge staff reductions throughout the industry worldwide.

Pharmaceutical companies currently need fewer employees and more products. But the cost of developing a single new drug from early research to marketing—a period that averages ten years—has risen from $15 million in the mid-1970s to $350 million in the mid-1990s. The pressure for new products is unremitting, for it is in the nature of the industry that the most successful and profitable of patents eventually lapse or are overtaken by rival products. And despite exhaustive clinical trials, a drug might still prove defective, even dangerous, reducing investment income and revenues by many billions of dollars, engendering open-ended legal costs and compensation claims, and causing a plunge in hard-won reputation.

An eventuality that all pharmaceutical companies fear is a repeat of the Thalidomide debacle. Thalidomide, manufactured by the West German company Chemie Grünenethal, and marketed by the British company Distillers, looked promising as a hypnotic relaxant drug and was used widely in West Germany and the United Kingdom from 1958 on. It was subsequently discovered that the drug caused severe abnormalities in the offspring of women who had used it when they were twenty-nine to forty days pregnant. As a result of the Thalidomide experience, controls for new-drug approval in the United States and Europe were tightened, forcing companies to extend trial periods and make protocols more rigorous to ensure that their products were safe as well as effective. Fortunately for Distillers, which makes most of its profits from whiskey, the majority of cases were brought in West Germany and Britain, where product-liability law is less favorable to the plaintiff than in the United States. In the end, Distillers paid no more than $35 million to the Thalidomide victims, and that mainly as a result of a tenacious campaign against Distillers by the London *Sunday Times*.

Eli Lilly and Company was no stranger to product-liability litigation. During the 1950s and '60s, along with other manufacturers, the company had produced and distributed DES (diethylstilbestrol), an FDA-approved hormone-replacement substance considered beneficient in the prevention of miscarriage. In 1971, however, it was established that DES could cause vaginal cancer in the offspring of women who had ingested the drug during pregnancy. To this day, Eli Lilly, which had a major market share in DES, is involved in litigation suits brought by five hundred parties, mainly in the United States, seeking relief against the drug's manufacturers.

In 1985, Lilly found itself in another predicament when it pleaded guilty to charges brought by the United States Justice Department for failing to inform federal officials of four deaths and six illnesses in the United Kingdom after patients took Oraflex (U.K. trade name Opren).

Oraflex, an anti-inflammatory drug developed and marketed by Lilly in the 1970s, had been marketed as a remarkable scientific discovery. In 1982, the company's public-relations department issued sixty-five hundred press kits nationwide proclaiming the drug as a major medical advance in the relief of arthritis. At the same time, Lilly sent a number of scientists on tours of the country to promote the new product. Some science editors were suspicious of Lilly's claims, but the drug got extensive coverage in 150 newspapers and TV programs. Prescriptions rocketed from two thousand fo fifty-five thousand in a single week.

Between 1982 and 1985, four British patients died of liver failure after taking the drug; three others suffered kidney or liver problems, and three had jaundice. Ten of the counts against the company and its head of medical research, Dr. William Shedden, related to a failure to report these illnesses and deaths to the FDA. Fifteen further counts, which included five against Shedden, related to misbranding and mislabeling.

The FDA claimed that the drug had "possibly" been associated with forty-nine deaths in the United States and "several hundred" abroad. Yet Lilly received a fine of only $25,000. In a letter to shareholders following the conclusion of the case, Lilly's then chairman, Richard Wood, said the charges were "technical." He claimed that Lilly had agreed to plead guilty to the misdemeanors in order to avoid the time and expense of prolonged litigation, and to bring the Oraflex matter to a conclusion.

Commenting on the penalties, *The Wall Street Journal* declared that "Lilly's chief medical officer, Dr. William Shedden . . . could have been sentenced to one year in prison for each count"—a total of fifteen years, since Shedden had pleaded no contest to fifteen of the misdemeanors cited. Dr. Sidney Wolfe, director of the consumer-advocacy group Public Citizen Health Research, commented dryly that "the public will remain cynical as long as corporate criminals escape harsh punishments for crimes that would result in prison sentences for individuals."

The cost of the Oraflex debacle to Lilly was, of course, a great deal more than $25,000. As well as losing the value of more than ten years' research and development and losing revenue, Lilly would now be obliged to cope with hundreds of civil-compensation claims. In the U.K., the number of claimants would eventually rise to more than fourteen hundred. One early settlement involved a Georgia man who claimed that his eighty-one-year-old mother had died while taking the drug. The jury awarded the plaintiff $6 million; Lilly appealed, then settled the matter. Terms of that settlement were confidential, by court order, but are unlikely to have been insignificant. Ten years later, Eli Lilly's lawyers were still settling claims in the United Kingdom. By 1994, however, Lilly thought that they had put the adverse publicity surrounding the Oraflex incident well behind them.

The pharmaceutical industry had long recognized that the biggest risks for potentially defective drugs attend products that alter body chemistry. That principle would prove to be even more true of drugs designed to alter the chemistry of the brain and central nervous system. Yet, considering the potential rewards, Lilly took a calculated gamble as far back as the mid-1970s to compete in the difficult field of mind drugs, specifically those involved in treatment of depression.

Depression is probably the most common major illness seen by doctors today in Western countries (fifteen million people suffer from the disease in the United States alone). Its symptoms include feelings of intense sadness and despair, loss of mental agility, anxiety, agitation, and insomnia, plus a sense of guilt and worthlessness. Some forms of depression are characterized as "bipolar," or "manic-depressive," indicating a patient's tendency to swing periodically between excessive and unmanageable "up" phases and "down" phases.

Depression can result in loss of work, family breakup, and acute suffering. The psychologist Stuart Sutherland, who suffered a depressive illness in the 1970s, has graphically described the symptoms.

"The onset of my neurosis," he writes in his book *Breakdown*, "was marked by physical levels of anxiety that I would not have thought possible. If one is almost involved in a road accident, there is a delay of a second or two and the pit of the stomach seems to fall out and one's legs go like jelly. It was this feeling multiplied a hundredfold that seized me all hours of the day and night."

The second symptom he emphasizes is the "extreme boredom."

"I am conscious that, without being a poet, it is difficult to capture in words the quality of pain and boredom that I suffered. Indeed it is difficult to recall the bitterness of my experience, perhaps nature is merciful in making it so difficult to remember."

Such is the pain of depression that a significant proportion of sufferers contemplate taking their own lives. "The pain of severe depression is quite unimaginable to those who have not suffered it," writes the novelist William Styron in *Darkness Visible: A Memoir of Madness*, "and it kills in many instances because its anguish can no longer be borne." Up to 60 percent of depressed patients experience thoughts about suicide, and some 15 percent end up taking their lives.

Clearly, the causes of depression are numerous, and effective therapy requires a variety of strategies. Under the influence of Freud and his followers, treatment has principally been shaped by psychoanalytic theory, which understands the condition as an illness of the "psyche" or the subconscious, originating in early sexual trauma and resolved by long periods in therapy.

The main psychiatric strategy throughout the century, however, has been to equate the disease with its symptoms. Psychotropic drugs—drugs that affect mental states—have been extensively used by psychiatrists in the treatment of mental illness of every kind. Such drugs have been employed on the basis of trial and error, depending on whether they alleviate symptoms, and have been plagued by side effects such as intoxication, sedation, and addiction.

Since the 1960s, campaigning groups have argued that psychotropic drugs "imprison" the minds of patients and make them docile. More recently, feminist groups have sought to expose the deleterious effects of Valium, protesting that its production and distribution amount to a conspiracy to enslave women.

Indecisive results have been achieved with electroconvulsive therapy (ECT) since the 1940s; ECT does not benefit all patients, and there are invariably side effects, such as memory impairment. Another popular midcentury treatment was modified insulin, a drastic chemical-shock therapy that brought many patients to the brink of death. Equally controversial has been the practice, mercifully discontinued, of "quieting" patients by administering brain surgery known as prefrontal lobotomy.

The success in the early 1940s of chlorpromazine, a drug that helped patients who were suffering from illnesses like schizophrenia, prompted new optimism about the prospects of a pharmacological solution to depression. But it was not until 1957 that researchers came up with two substances that had a dramatic effect on depressive symptoms. In New York City, psychiatrist Dr. Nathan S. Kline found by chance that a compound called iproniazid, used in the treatment of tuberculosis, lifted the mood and energy of his patients. Meanwhile, in Switzerland, Dr. Roland Kuhn, at the drug firm Geigy, discovered that an antihistamine compound known as imipramine was similarly successful in relieving depressive symptoms.

In the next two decades, the quest for the ideal antidepressant was on. As a result, the market became crowded with competing compounds—including lithium, a substance found effective in the treatment of bipolar depression. And yet physicians and clinicians recognized that, in view of the wide range of side effects accompanying these drugs, no one product was ideal.

The prospects for a pharmaceutical product without side effects were vastly improved following the rapid progress of molecular biology in the 1970s and the development of noninvasive methods of imaging and measuring the activity of nerve cells. These developments led to new strategies of research that enabled scientists to discover drugs by studying the known cellular and molecular properties of the living human brain and central nervous system.

As these developments prospered, many researchers were overwhelmed by the sheer vastness and complexity of the brain and central nervous system. Pharmacologists, however, tended to take a more uncomplicated, functional view. According to the Pharmaceutical Association in its publication announcing the 1993 Discoverers Award (made that year to Prozac and its makers), "The brain is like a massive telephone exchange, all of whose numbers are interconnected through a dense spaghetti of wires (neurons that is) and among which a constant hubbub of innumerable conversations takes place."

Commercial pharmacologists concentrate on linking a condition—such as depression—to a molecular dysfunction in a "typical" cell at the point at which communication takes place—namely, the synapse, a space, or cleft, between two neurons or brain cells. Thus the root cause of depression, as envisaged by pharmacologists in the pharmaceutical industry, is an imbalance of a single chemical substance operating in assumed isolation at this crucial contact point.

Normal communication takes place, the story goes, when the transmitting neuron releases a few molecules of brain chemicals, called neurotransmitters, into the synapse. Some of these molecules cross the synapse and attach to specific receptor sites in the neighboring neuron. That moment of contact, if one works on the telephone-exchange metaphor, is the delivery of the "message." Depression is thus seen as a kind of faulty, or poorly delivered, message.

If depression is a breakdown of communication between neurons, and if that breakdown occurs as a result of an imbalance in neurotransmitter substance, then the ideal antidepressant is a substance that acts selectively on the responsible neurotransmitter or its associated receptor sites to rectify the imbalance.

In the late 1960s, three researchers at Lilly, Drs. Brian Molloy, David Wong, and Ray Fuller, were working on a theory that depression was caused by a low level of serotonin transmission in the synapses. They hypothesized that serotonin was too rapidly absorbed, or, in scientist's parlance, "reuptaken," for future reuse by the transmitting cell.

They set out to find a compound containing molecules that would lock on to the cell receptors so as to correct that "reuptake" problem: such a substance would be known as "a selective serotonin reuptake inhibitor," or an SSRI.

How was this compound to be found? In contrast to the old, serendipitous mode of substance discovery, the early 1970s saw two new research approaches in pharmacology.

One, known as rational design, investigated the properties of the neurotransmitter substances so as to produce new molecules, known as analogues, that would block or stimulate a receptor site by mimicking the real thing.

Another approach attempted to visualize the receptor sites by use of computer graphics. Receptors are usually cell-surface proteins that respond to neurotransmitters released by the nerve cell. When a receptor has been identified, the shape of the molecule that fits the active site can in theory be determined. Then researchers can attempt to devise new molecules of a similar shape to fit the binding site of the target molecule.

In 1972, using the first strategy at Lilly's laboratories in Indianapolis, Dr. Wong synthesized a compound known as fluoxetine hydrochloride and succeeded in modulating a neuron's uptake of serotonin *in vitro*—that is, in a glass, outside any human or animal body. The next step was to explore whether the compound was similarly active *in vivo,* inside a living animal. It would be another eight years before fluoxetine, eventually given the trade name Prozac, would be ready for "Phase III," the long process of clinical trials with human patients, leading to regulatory approval.

Eleven and a half years after fluoxetine had been discovered in Indianapolis, a voluminous document known as the new-drug application (NDA), including details of every patient among the thousands who had participated in the clinical trials, was submitted to the FDA. Two years later, in October 1985, an independent advisory committtee of the FDA reviewed the material and recommended that the compound be approved for the treatment of depression.

Normally a few months elapse between recommendation and formal approval. Prozac, however, did not win full approval for two more years. During the four-year gap between approval in principle and in fact, Lilly was not idle; its statisticians were also assembling clinical data in order to apply for approval of the compound's use in treating obesity, bulimia, and obsessive-compulsive disorder. At the same time, Joseph Wernicke, the clinical-trials boss at Lilly, established a crucial finding in his dose-response studies, indicating that a single twenty-milligram capsule was more effective than any other, smaller or larger combination. This meant that Prozac only needed to be given once daily in a single capsule, ensuring greater patient compliance.

Prozac was approved for marketing in Belgium and South Africa before gaining approval in the United States in 1987. During the next two years, it gained approval in some seventy countries, and by 1989 was on the market in roughly two-thirds of the world. When Lilly began marketing the drug in the United States, its eighteen hundred salesmen initially targeted psychiatrists. The appeal of the drug, they said, as they delivered their free samples and Prozac pens, was that it was as effective as the older antidepressants but had a more favorable side-effect profile.

Once experience and demand had been stimulated among the psychiatric profession, Lilly started targeting general physicians, who see and treat large numbers of depressed patients every day. Lilly's public-relations department went into full swing, sales began to accelerate, and Prozac was set to become one of the most successful drugs of the century.

9

As Mike Campbell tells it, there was no concerted rush to litigate against Eli Lilly or any other party in the immediate aftermath of the shootings. Campbell, who talks more easily and openly about this period than do the rest of the survivors, emphasizes that he was on a long and painful journey toward recovery. "I was completely absorbed with physiotherapy sessions to regain the use of my limbs. My son-in-law was a lawyer, and he would say from time to time, 'Don't talk to anybody—don't talk to company officials.' He worked for a law firm, and when he came into the hospital he used to want to kick things around—like 'Who can we sue?' And I used to say, 'I don't want to sue anybody.' " At this stage, Campbell himself favored setting up an organization called "Kentuckians Against Assault Weapons"; but that had little appeal for his injured colleagues.

The majority of the survivors, and especially the severely wounded—like Angela Bowman, who was paralyzed from the waist down, and John Stein, who had extensive neurological complications as a result of a gunshot wound to the head—were intent on piecing together their lives, physically and emotionally. The task of reassembling the pieces, as Campbell acknowledges, was going to be expensive—how expensive, no one knew—and none of them would work again.

In March 1990, Mike Shea anounced that Standard Gravure had donated $192,000 to the fund established to aid the victims of the shootings and their families. The sum matched the total collected from the community, and there would be money forthcoming from Standard Gravure's workers-insurance package, estimated at around $500,000 in total. But as the spring of 1990 approached, conversations between the widows of dead pressmen and their lawyers began to gravitate toward the possibility of a liability suit. The widows who were considering a lawsuit at this point were Joyce Fentress, Sarah Wible, and Linda Gan- ote—all represented by one lawyer, B. Hume Morris II, of Louisville. Morris was steering his clients toward filing lawsuits in pursuit of puni- tive damages against a list of defendants that included Standard Gravure, the estate of Joseph Wesbecker, Dr. Lee Coleman, Hall Secu- rity Service Inc., as well as Eli Lilly. He said he believed the other sur- vivors would not be long in joining the three widows.

Despite the multiplicity of possible defendants, Morris had Lilly in his sights as the principal target for damages, a tactic no doubt influ- enced by developments elsewhere. In February 1990, Martin Teicher, a psychiatry professor at Harvard Medical School, published an article claiming that six of his patients on Prozac had experienced strong suici- dal ideation. That article immediately became a crucial item of evidence in the hands of the Church of Scientology, whose Citizens' Commission on Human Rights (CCHR) had been criticizing Prozac since December 1989. Armed with the Teicher evidence, CCHR had gone into PR over- drive against Lilly, claiming that "up to 140,000 people in the United States had become violent on Prozac," and citing in particular the Wes- becker killing spree.

Stories were beginning to appear in newspapers across the country featuring sensational episodes experienced by patients on the drug, and the Prozac issue was being aired for the first time on national television, including "Donahue," "Geraldo," and "Home Show." According to *The Wall Street Journal*, following a February 1990 edition of "Donahue," twenty-one severely depressed patients on Prozac at Oakville-Trafalgar Memorial Hospital, near Toronto, heard Wesbecker described as "your average nice Joe turned killer by Prozac."

"The patients became distraught," said the newspaper, "some hys- terically so. Doctors and nurses had to lead them out of the hospital's day room, and it took three days to calm many of them."

One of the most vociferous spokesmen on various talk shows early in 1990 was a New York personal-injury lawyer named Leonard Finz who had emerged as lead counsel in a rash of suits citing Prozac. The system of multidistrict legislation, whereby lawyers band together under a "lead counsel" in a pending series of highly technical suits against a single defendant, has many advantages: it facilitates the acquisition, collation, and interpretation of huge volumes of relevant documents in the possession of the defendant; the selection and briefing of expert witnesses; the development and pooling of the attorneys' expertise; and the collecting of depositions. The lead counsel becomes a kind of dean of the attorneys in multidistrict litigation against a single defendant.

For its own part (with some fifty-four civil and criminal suits citing Prozac by 1990), Eli Lilly had taken steps to select a suitable trial lawyer in Kentucky, for the Wesbecker case was only one of three involving the drug in that state. The first, known as the McStoots suit, involved a Bowling Green woman who had shot a neighbor with a .22 rifle and blamed her actions on Prozac; the other involved Louisville woman Bonnie Leitch, who claimed the drug made her suicidal.

In the spring of 1990, after interviewing an unspecified number of candidates, Lilly's in-house legal team, led by the company's legal counsel, Jim Burns, chose Louisville attorney Edward H. Stopher as their potential trial lawyer for all three sets of litigation. An owlish, heavy-limbed man of forty-seven, Stopher was a member of a powerful local law firm of sixty partners called Boehl Stopher and Graves, whose offices were situated in a penthouse duplex of the Providian Tower, overlooking the Ohio River. Stopher did not specialize in the field of product liability, although he had once prepared a defense in a suit involving a glue used in mobile homes—a case that never came before a jury. Other attorneys on the team would tackle the technicalities of Prozac itself; Lilly, however, had quite a different job in mind for Stopher, one that would exploit his evident talents for thoroughness, patience, and charm, as well as his image as a solid and dependable figure in the Louisville community. The cornerstone of Lilly's defense would be the true story of Joe Wesbecker.

As the spring wore into summer, Lilly was starting to see clearly just how much might be at stake over the Wesbecker case and similar liability suits. Their fears were largely prompted by the capricious performance of Lilly stock as a result of the variable Prozac publicity. Despite the adverse stories at the beginning of 1990, *Newsweek* had published a cover story in March declaring that "nearly everyone has something nice to say about the new treatment." In consequence, Lilly's stock had risen from a low of 57$\frac{1}{4}$ earlier in the year to a high of 90$\frac{1}{8}$ in July. By July 17, however, there was a sudden drop of 4¼ points in Lilly's stock, a 5.3 percent decline in two days, after the announcement of a $150-million lawsuit accusing Prozac of prompting a New York patient to self-mutilation and attempted suicide. Then, on July 25, came the first official move in the Wesbecker case: Morris's three widows filed suits in Louisville seeking $150 million in punitive damages as well as compensatory damages against Lilly. Lilly stock plunged another 4⅛ points, to close at 79⅝. By August 13, the stock stood at 75⅞.

The problem with these ups and downs, as Lilly's people saw it, was that Prozac was clearly susceptible to media rumor. And here was the Church of Scientology spending considerable resources on whipping up a nationwide scare campaign against the drug. But if one of the suits were to go to trial, and Lilly to lose, the dormant specter of Oraflex would once again be raised. One defective drug in a decade was bad enough; two defective drugs could spell disaster.

Just before noon on September 14, 1990, the full complement of survivors and dead victims' relatives filed an expanded suit against Lilly in Louisville. There were fifteen lawyers involved, with Leonard Finz as lead counsel; several of the plaintiffs, including Mike Campbell, had come in at the last minute before the one-year statute of limitations expired. Because of her alphabetic precedence in the original list of three widows, Joyce Fentress's name would in the future be cited on behalf of all the plaintiffs.

Only one of the original injured survivors declined to join the suit: Jackie Miller, shot four times as she went to grab the gun from her purse. According to Mike Campbell, Miller had said that she did not wish to be associated with a suit that could be used in arguments for gun control.

Much as the company feared a suit's coming to trial, Ed West, Lilly's ebullient public-relations chief and a former champion salesman, was making it known from the outset that they were eager to fight the Wesbecker case in court rather than settle. "There's nothing like a victory in court to dissuade the rest," he said on more than one occasion. What heartened Lilly executives was the abundant evidence that Wesbecker had armed himself and issued his threats long before he had taken

Prozac. At the same time, his frequent hospitalizations, and his suicide attempt in 1984, established him, they believed, as somebody of unsound mind. If Lilly were forced to go to trial over Prozac, the Fentress case in Louisville seemed to them the best prospect for a resounding victory.

Lilly's principal strategy, then, was to prepare a formidable case against Wesbecker himself, arguing that he was programmed by nature and nurture throughout the course of his whole life to be a mass killer. Meanwhile Lilly's in-house counsel concentrated on preparing the arguments and evidence that would defend the drug. Ed Stopher and his team began the long process of discovery that would form one of the most detailed files ever amassed on a spree killer. "The process would carry on virtually full-time over four years," says Stopher. "We used the method of an exponential growth of witnesses—each witness suggesting others we should speak with. We interviewed members of the family, neighbors, co-workers, medical providers. We traveled as far south as Florida and as far west as Salt Lake City. We took nearly four hundred depositions under oath, and some of those depositions took from three to four days."

Lilly's expensive strategy, considering that an hour of Ed Stopher's time alone was worth $350, contained a remarkable irony: the pharmaceutical industry itself had in recent years encouraged the notion that a person is less a history than a balance of chemical levels. Indeed, this psychopharmacological view of human behavior—the notion that human identity amounts to chemical software that can be rewritten by chemical intervention—had been principally responsible for promoting the sort of litigation that led to the Fentress suit in the first place. A second irony, of course, was that Lilly and Company were preparing their massive biography not so much to defend Prozac, their drug, as to attack the very patient their drug had been designed to help.

Ed Stopher and his team were not alone, however, in exploring the life and times of Joe T. Wesbecker. The January 1990 issue of *Louisville* was filled with views and theories about Wesbecker's life and times.

"At first glance," commented the writer, "Joe Wesbecker's shooting spree at Standard Gravure last September looked like the act of a man suddenly turned mad by discontent on the job. But Wesbecker's disintegration began almost from the time he was born: a broken family, problems in school, two failed marriages, an obsession with money, manic depression."

Analyzing Joe Wesbecker had already become something of an obsession in Louisville. Strangers discussed Wesbecker's motives and state of mind in bars and on public transport, and there were frequent updates to fuel gossip as the local media aired reminiscences of Wesbecker's former friends and acquaintances.

Some argued that he was just a "crazy sonofabitch," others that he had been pushed over the edge by his medication. Another version harped on the difficulties of his childhood and youth, his scrapes with the law, and his broken marriages. But as Ed Stopher pushed forward with his research, it was increasingly clear in the accumulation of depositions that, despite his disadvantages and his manifest handicaps, Joe Wesbecker could be seen as a man who constantly had struggled to assert his humanity and decency; that he had tried hard to be a decent husband and a father, and for a number of years succeeded.

10

JOSEPH T. WESBECKER was born in Louisville on April 27, 1942, to Martha (née Montgomery) Wesbecker, who in the previous year, aged fifteen, had married a former Golden Gloves boxer with a tough torso and weak eyes named Tommy Wesbecker. Little is known about the Wesbeckers' ancestors except that they were Catholics and that Tommy's mother, Murrel, had a history of depression.

The Montgomerys and the Smiths, on Joe's mother's side, were also Catholics. The Montgomerys had been in farming for two generations in Washington State, and the Smiths came from Springfield, Kentucky. There is no evidence that either side of the family had deep roots in Louisville; but, then, neither side of the family had much sense of its history: they were working people whose main assets were their current large nuclear families and their religion.

A year after Joe Wesbecker's birth, Tommy, aged twenty-seven, fell to his death while mending the roof on the tower of St. James's Catholic Church, on Bardstown Road. According to Wesbecker's aunt Ann, his death may "not have been accidental." Another account claims he slipped while scrambling to retrieve his glasses on the steep pantiles. Relatives say that Martha showed no emotion after her husband died: she "just sat and stared."

Eventually Martha took her son to live with her own parents and her nine siblings. Leaving Joe with his grandmother Nancy Montgomery and her own brood of children, Martha went out each day to secretarial school.

When Joe was one month short of his second birthday, his thirty-eight-year-old maternal grandfather, John T. Montgomery, who had become a surrogate father, was killed in the freight yards of Louisville; his coat was caught in the wheels of a passing railroad car, and he was dragged under and cut in two.

That summer, the household moved to lodgings on South 22nd Street; his grandmother Nancy, whose youngest child, Rosie, was only five months old, was now supporting the entire family by working as a seamstress at St. Joseph's Hospital and taking in dressmaking at home. Nancy had a reputation for toughness and piety. She attended Mass daily, walking ten blocks to church in the early mornings, and said the entire fifteen mysteries of the rosary every evening.

Joe was now mostly looked after by his young uncles and aunts. A story circulated in the family that he was frequently whipped by his teenage uncle John, and that every time he was whipped he would go and kick his mother; but his uncle denies this. "I was his father figure," John Montgomery has said. "I couldn't walk without stepping on him."

When Joe was five, his mother took him to Springfield, Kentucky, to live with her maternal grandmother, Joe's great-grandmother, Cora Smith. The idea was to look after Cora, who was suffering from presenile dementia. There is a reliable family anecdote, which would gain in significance after the shootings, that in Springfield little Joe shot his mother in the leg with an air gun.

By early 1948, Martha was back in Louisville, living in an apartment on Duker Avenue. She took in her mother-in-law, Murrell Wesbecker, in order to have someone look after Joe while she was out at work. The arrangement ended after six months, when Murrell had to be taken away and put in "some kind of home." Grandma Murrell had a history of suicide attempts. Wesbecker would tell his second wife, Brenda, how at six years of age he had watched his paternal grandmother screaming as she was dragged out of the house by mental-institution attendants. He never saw her again.

Once again, mother and son returned to Nancy Montgomery's home, this time on Pope Street in Louisville. Joe's uncle John was now married and living with his wife in the basement; in addition to Martha's eight other siblings, there was an illegal-immigrant lodger from Peru who helped with the rent. At this time, Martha was working a stressful machine in the Philip Morris cigarette factory in the city. According to her brother John, she became so depressed at work that she went to a psychiatrist and eventually had ECT at Our Lady of Peace Hospital.

For three years, Joe attended the St. Francis Roman Catholic

School. He had a reputation for misbehavior and got poor grades. There were complaints about his getting into fights. He frequently played hooky, and he would throw his shoes up on the roof of the house and hide them to avoid going to school.

Aged nine, Joe moved on to the St. George School. The Montgomerys were now living in a scruffy neighborhood of frame houses, corner bars, and catalpa trees, named after an intersection—18th and Hill. Joe was always in trouble, and the head teacher, Sister Josephine, suggested he be put in an orphanage for a while. In the teeth of his grandmother's opposition, Martha agreed to send him to St. Thomas's Orphanage, on the eastern edge of Jefferson County. His grandmother and his uncle John took him there in October 1952, when he was ten years old. Every Friday, Grandmother Nancy would make the journey to and from St. Thomas's by bus and on foot, two hours each way, so that he could spend weekends at home.

By May 1953, aged eleven, Joe was back with his mother, who was now living in an apartment on West Bolling Street. The tension between mother and daughter over Joe's upbringing was deepening; Martha would say that her mother filled her with guilt feelings. While living on Bolling, Martha attempted suicide by putting rat poison in a cup of coffee; she was saved by the sudden arrival of the insurance man, who slapped it out of her hand.

The next clear impression we get of Joe is after he had turned fourteen. His friend Joe Ball, who would become a member of the Louisville Police Department, remembers him as a "cool guy," a stylish teenager who liked to act "like a protector." One night, when someone tried to pick on Ball, Wesbecker intervened and "smacked" him.

When he was sixteen, Joe bought his first car, from his uncle John, a red 1949 Ford convertible. He started hanging out at Gus's Billiards, at 18th and Gaulbert. His friend of those days, Tim Lattray, says that Joe always had money. He would drive over a hundred miles an hour on city streets, sometimes with his lights out at night, and on the wrong side of the street. Once he got into a fight with a friend in his car while driving. Lattray remembers that Joe had a "strange relationship" with his mother, that "he did not like a lot of people," and "it was real hard for him to make friends." He had a "real sad look . . . and he would kind of stare at people." Lattray also remembers that Wesbecker was "neat as a pin" and that his car was "imamaculate."

Joe entered Flaget High School as a freshman, but he soon dropped out. Next he enrolled at Parkland Junior High, only to withdraw after five days. He was spending much of his time at his grandmother's home on West Burnett. He was arrested several times for disorderly conduct and fighting. On one occasion, he spent a night in jail after siphoning gas from a truck. Friends remember that he carried a starter gun in his car. He would point it at people and shoot it to scare them.

In November 1958, Joe was brought into juvenile court, charged, along with a friend, Charlie Conn, with holding the starter gun on two fifteen-year-old girls while two other boys had sex with them. There are conflicting accounts of this incident. Conn and Wesbecker were apparently sentenced to six weeks in jail but were pardoned after a few days. As Conn remembers it, the girls' parents had Wesbecker unjustly arrested three weeks after the incident; Wesbecker had his starter pistol in the car, he said, but he did not hold it on the girls. The two boys spent several days behind bars in the Old Jailhouse on Liberty Street, alongside adult federal prisoners. Conn remembers that the other prisoners threatened to molest them sexually, and that Wesbecker talked about committing suicide by cutting an artery in his leg.

At about this time, he started traveling away from Louisville. He went to Detroit for the marriage of one of his uncles, then visited Chicago. In July 1959, aged seventeen, he drove with his aunts Rosie and Ann to Inglewood, California, to pick up his grandmother Nancy, who had been helping after the birth of his cousin.

This was the year he met Sue White, who was still attending Shawnee High School. Sue says of him, "He was witty in those days and a lot of fun to be with." They started dating, and he seemed to be quieting down a little. He had now moved in permanently with Nancy. In December 1960, when he was eighteen, Wesbecker went to work for Fawcett and Haynes Printing, starting his pressman's apprenticeship as a flyboy. He began to save money seriously and traded in the red convertible for a tame Volkswagen. The following year, he married Sue White in St. George Catholic Church in Louisville, and the reception was held at Nancy's home.

For the next twelve years or so, Wesbecker seemed to be settling down to life as a responsible young family man. In 1963, Sue gave birth to their first son, Joseph Kevin; their second son, James, was born in 1967. We hear that the couple went dancing with friends; Wesbecker enjoyed country-and-Western and was nimble on his feet. There were annual family vacations in Florida. In 1964, Sue got a job as a secretary at the *Courier-Journal*; the following year, Wesbecker received the coveted "journeyman's card" at Fawcett Printing, meaning that he could do any task expected of a pressman. Eventually he would get the pressman's Certificate of Achievement.

Co-workers from those years say he was proud of his journeyman status; he was a "serious person" and a saver. His stated ambition was for his kids to go to college. He worked all the overtime he could get, according to Lattray; sometimes he would work twelve hours a day, seven days a week. He was described as "a perfectionist." Others noticed that he could do filthy work and not get dirty. He had a "peculiarity" of washing his hands ten to fifteen times during an eight-hour shift. His nickname was Pinky because he washed his hands so much. In 1966, he and Sue bought their first home, for $10,200, a single-story three-bedroom house in a pleasant district close to Sun Valley Park, southwest of the city.

In May 1971, Wesbecker went to work at Standard Gravure after a brief period of being laid off from Fawcett. His co-workers remember him during those early days as "an industrious worker . . . just a regular guy . . . witty and easygoing." They would tease him about nursing a single beer on the rare nights he went with them to the S and H Bar, across the street from the plant.

He soon sold their first house at a profit of $7,000 and bought a larger one two miles north, on Devonshire Drive, for $25,000. After settling into the new home, he formally became a member of the parish of St. Clement's Catholic Church, and the boys were enrolled in the local Catholic school.

By the mid-1970s, however, there were signs that his punishing overtime routines were affecting his domestic life. In 1974, Wesbecker filed a suit against the previous owner of his new house, claiming water damage, and he had started quarreling with his neighbors. His attitude, remembers one, was "I'm right about everything." People would remark upon his belligerence and his aggressive strut, his muscular arms held forward. While his younger son, James, was at St. Clement's, the boy got into a fight with a schoolmate. After school, Wesbecker drove Kevin and James to the child's home and watched from the car while Kevin held the other boy down and James hit him.

After undergoing a cancer operation, his mother, Martha, moved in with the younger Wesbeckers for a time. Wesbecker's son Kevin says that Martha smoked and tended to be messy around the house; that there were frequent quarrels between his father and his grandmother. Wesbecker also quarreled with his parents-in-law, accusing them of being drunkards.

Wesbecker was working abnormally long hours, including nights. According to one foreman, he was an "overtime hog." When his son James remarked on his absence from home, Wesbecker told him he had to work extra because he did not have enough education to do other things. Sue remembers that he was "cranky and short-tempered and worn out . . . that his relationship with his sons was deteriorating."

At about this time, Wesbecker told his wife that he did not like working the folder, because it made him nervous. He said his supervisors would get on him about the way he ran the job. One foreman remembers that Wesbecker would concentrate so long on trying to solve one problem that there would be two more problems to fix, and this would make him jittery. Part of his difficulty, says another foreman, was that "Wesbecker was never able to do a good enough job to suit himself."

When James had turned ten years of age, in 1977, a woman visitor to the house saw him exposing his genitals at a window. Sue Wesbecker refused to believe that the boy had a problem until a neighbor took a photograph of him in flagrante.

The parents fought over what to do; according to Wesbecker's uncle John, Sue tended to deny the problem, while Joe insisted on getting him seen by a psychiatrist. Then Kevin's curvature of the spine seemed to get worse, and they disagreed over what to do. Wesbecker speculated that the chemicals from the Fawcett printing plant might have altered his genes and that this had affected his sons. At length, he took James to a psychiatric clinic.

After the birth of James, Sue had stopped work to stay home with them. Just as the problems with James started, she announced she was going to look for a job. Sue says Wesbecker told her calmly that, for all their sakes, her place was at home, that if she got a job he would divorce her. When she got a job as a secretary at the Life Insurance Company of America, Wesbecker was as good as his word. In June 1978 he moved out into an apartment on Rockford Lane, two miles away.

Sue blames the breakup on his working all the time, talking about nothing but money, and leaving her alone at home. At this point, Wesbecker was working "triple overtime" and making up to $50,000 a year. He told a co-worker that, to make that much, "you had to live in there." Years later, James told a social worker that the cause of the separation was his mother's parents' alcoholism, and that Sue stole money from Joe so her parents could buy liquor: "They ruined every holiday or family celebration by getting drunk and causing a scene."

Joe and Sue separated legally at the end of 1978, but by the summer of 1979 they were back together for a few months, and things seemed better—they even went dancing, something they had not done in years. During this time, Wesbecker went to evening classes and completed the GED, earning the diploma he had failed to earn as a regular student. He talked of going to Jefferson Community College to continue his education, but nothing came of it.

By the beginning of 1980, they had split up again and Wesbecker was dating other women. Co-workers say that he had all kinds of girl-friends; one remembers how he came in one day and "talked about having intercourse so much that his groin was bruised." Another co-worker remembers he was obsessed with oral sex. An acquaintance from the Fawcett days says: "Here was, I thought, a young man that the most important thing to him was his family, and come to find out he was chasing women all over town . . . complete opposite of what he was like at Fawcett." It was around this time that John Tingle nicknamed him "Sexbecker," and that, after his fight over a woman at the firm's Media 'n Mix, they called him Rocky. Having been a supportive member of St. Clement's Catholic Church for several years, he stopped going to church altogether.

Employees testified that the tensions at Standard Gravure in the early 1980s were becoming intolerable. Most pressmen were obliged to work a lot of overtime, including several sixteen-hour shifts in a row. But, according to one pressman, "if you complained, nothing happened, and you couldn't do anything bad enough to get fired." Personnel levels on the presses were halved, yet the presses were speeded up, and there were a number of job buy-outs, reducing the workforce from fourteen hundred down to six hundred. It was around this time that the Bingham family, still the owners, secured agreement to a six-year pay freeze.

The job of folder operator was becoming tougher. A co-worker remembers Joe's unhappiness in this job and the frequency with which he was assigned to it: "They evidently found out he could run a folder, and they put him up there, and they kept him up there." Pressmen say they were verbally abused by foremen—a popular expression was "shit-head." One of the foremen liked to say, "I am the lawn mower and the pressmen are the grass." Another saying among the men in charge was "I got the power of the pencil," indicating a foreman's ability to assign any job or combination of shifts that took his fancy.

Quarrels between workers were on the increase, and Wesbecker was known to be extremely touchy, "like a bundle of nerves all drawed up." The pranks and practical jokes were getting out of hand. It was possible to speed up a press so that the run would go haywire, causing hours of extra work for the team working the machine. One day, two men threw a bucket of cold water over Wesbecker from a walkway above as he sat resting between shifts.

It was during the early and mid-1980s that workers started bringing guns to work. Tommy Gosling brought in a starter pistol that everyone thought was real, and went through the plant scaring people by shooting at them, "such as when they would step into a stairwell." No one remembered anyone being disciplined for bringing a weapon or threatening with a weapon. "They had an atmosphere down there," says one pressman: "if it was considered you were half nuts you could get away with anything."

During break time, Wesbecker talked a lot about his ex-wife. Now that he had filed for divorce, he was eaten up with bitterness. He told co-workers that she was a gold digger, and would brag that he was taking her to court at least once a week. Co-worker Roger Coffey remembers that he was no longer the same person: "like he was eat up with trying to mess over his ex-wife."

Coffey said Wesbecker also talked guns. "All he wanted to tell you is the muzzle velocity of a nine-millimeter magnum or how many rounds a banana clip of an AK-47 would hold." He talked about gun magazines and *Soldier of Fortune*, and he would "tell you the force that a round would hit, how many pounds it would be if it hit you at . . . thirty or fifty feet."

At this time, he was dabbling in the stock market, buying shares in Merrill Lynch, GK Technologies, Houston Oil Minerals, Brunswick Corporation, and Humana. He was driving himself so hard at work he developed torticollis, a frozen neck and shoulder, for which he was given tranquilizers. At night he went bar-hopping. He occasionally went along to a Parents Without Partners evening, and a friend remembered how he "was looking for attention, trying to act like a clown."

It was at a Parents Without Partners Friday-night dance that he first met Brenda Beasley, who would become his second wife. Brenda had been married to a doctor and had two children in their early teens. Within a few weeks, there were tensions between Wesbecker and Brenda's ex-husband. One night, Wesbecker and Brenda were out partying and Beasley got angry because he could not locate his children. Beasley also resented Wesbecker's spending the night in Brenda's house. Wesbecker told her he thought Beasley was having him tailed by a private detective.

Wesbecker had now bought a house of his own, on Mount Holyoke Drive, a few miles north of his ex-wife and children. At first Brenda and her children moved in with Wesbecker, and James lived part of the time with them. Wesbecker's coldness toward his elder son, Kevin, dates from this period. Wesbecker wanted the boy to have surgery to correct his scoliosis and was ambitious for him educationally; but Kevin refused to finish high school and finally moved in with the parents of his girl-friend, Mary. Wesbecker believed it was Mary who had persuaded Kevin not to have surgery; he refused to communicate with the couple for several years.

On August 11, 1981, Wesbecker married Brenda in Jeffersonville, Indiana, and they went off to Gatlinburg for a three-day honeymoon. The couple appeared genuinely in love, and Wesbecker seemed at first to take considerable pride in his new family.

Things began to sour in the spring of 1982, after James, now four-teen, was repeatedly arrested for indecent exposure. On one occasion, he exposed himself seven times in public on a single day. In May 1982, Wesbecker at last brought him to live at Mount Holyoke Drive with Brenda and her two girls; her ex-husband went "through the roof." Beasley was worried about the effect of James's acting out on his fifteen-year-old daughter, Melissa.

A combination of defensiveness and anxiety over James's future prompted fresh antagonisms between Wesbecker and Sue. When Wes-becker decided to put James into Boys Haven, a Louisville boarding school for boys with emotional difficulties, Sue threatened to bring her son home. Sue claims that, after an argument about it on the telephone, Wesbecker came over and knocked her to the ground in front of the house. Wesbecker later said that Sue was using James's predicament to get back at him; he told James he was so engrossed in dealing with Sue that he was neglecting his new wife. Wesbecker told co-workers that Sue was going "berserk" and threatening to burn the house down. Both Sue and Wesbecker accused each other of making harassing phone calls; Sue denied the accusations of violent behavior. Wesbecker suc-ceeded in having Sue sentenced to a two-year probation order. Later he sued her for slander and won an out-of-court settlement.

Wesbecker was paying for an expensive course of residential psy-chiatric care for James at the Norton Hospital in Louisville; he was working seven days a week; and he was bringing a series of complicated suits against his ex-wife, while defending countersuits.

By his own admission, he was "heartbroken" over James's actions. After completing the expensive Norton course of drugs and psycho-therapy, James came back to live with his father and Brenda and her daughters, only to relapse dramatically. Within days, he had exposed himself in front of the girls next door and chased them down the street while masturbating. Dr. Beasley, Brenda's ex-husband, now attempted to alter custody arrangements for the girls by filing an affidavit saying that his ex-wife reported being fearful of James to the point of sleeping behind locked doors with her children.

James was committed to Our Lady of Peace Hospital, where he underwent a new battery of tests and assessments: he was found to have depressive neurosis with "homosexual features" and "suicidal ideation." He told his psychiatrist that he thought the root of his problem was his father's domineering attitude and the years of conflict between his parents. He claimed his first bad childhood memory was waking up to the sound of his parents' fighting.

In 1983, Wesbecker attempted to face up to his crises at work by talking with Standard Gravure's social worker, Patrick Lampton. But by November, Wesbecker decided he had no faith in the confidentiality of these sessions. He told a colleague that when he made a complaint about a foreman that foreman would be the first to hear it. He believed they were deliberately putting him on the folder, where there was enough stress to get to him.

On the last day of 1983, Wesbecker and Brenda were driving on Bardstown Road when, according to Brenda, he said "out of the clear cold blue" of her daughter Melissa, "I hate her. I ought to just kill her." Brenda explains that he was angry at his own children and at Dr. Beasley, and jealous of Melissa's relationship with her. Since James's episode with the neighbors, Melissa had moved back with her father. From that time on, Wesbecker refused to talk to her. He told Brenda, "Keep her away from me. I don't want her in the same room with me. I don't want to look at her." According to a co-worker, Wesbecker sometimes followed Beasley around Louisville and out to the airport, having convinced himself of the fantasy that the doctor was a drug smuggler. Early the following year, a Jefferson Circuit Court entered an order removing custody of Brenda's two children and granting custody to Beasley.

That spring, Brenda says, Wesbecker was "upset and tired with everything." He was tired at work, tired of his ex-wife, tired of himself, and tired of taking medicines. One evening she came home to find him running up and down the street weeping and at his wits' end. The neighbors told her he had been on the rampage for two hours, ripping up his own house inside. She called the Emergency Medical Service, but he refused to go with them.

Several days later, he took an overdose of Norpramin and had to have his stomach pumped. The day after that, Brenda woke in the night to find him attempting to breathe in carbon monoxide fumes from his car exhaust with a hose pipe. On April 16, 1984, he was committed to Our Lady of Peace Hospital and diagnosed as having "Major affective illness, depressed. Recurrent type."

The hospital's clinical psychologist, Morton Leventhal, commented that Wesbecker "perceives the world as threatening and harbors a great deal of anger at what 'they' have done to him." Leventhal described Wesbecker as a "Borderline Personality" with potential for "self-destructive behavior although not imminent." After just a week in the hospital, Wesbecker was discharged and put on the antidepressant Etrafon. The following month, Brenda moved out of the Mount Holyoke house. They did not speak to each other for another four weeks. A month later, his first wife, Sue, married Carl Chesser.

Back at Standard Gravure, Wesbecker felt no one had sympathy for his predicament. He went once more to see Lampton, the social worker, but felt he was not being listened to. He was convinced that the foremen would use the "power of the pencil" to get back at some people and reward others. Wesbecker felt he was getting "jerked around by the company" and would refer, according to his co-workers, to the management's "industrial sodomy." He begged Lampton for an easier workload, begged the foremen to listen and to stop making fun of him. Things got to the point, says one colleague, where Wesbecker "folded" under pressure. "You'd go in there and ask him if he needed help. . . . He would be running around like a headless chicken, not doing nothing, but he is looking more busy than you can imagine. . . . It was hyperfutility."

11

As ED STOPHER EMBARKED on the discovery phase of the Wesbecker case, he concentrated on those widely reported anecdotes about Wesbecker's life that indicated a vicious and vengeful nature. Wesbecker, as Stopher later insisted, came from a family that suffered mental illness. He lost two father figures early in childhood, and he lacked consistent and mature mothering. Wesbecker, in Stopher's view, was a man who from childhood believed in "getting even" at all costs, and had the habit of assigning hostile intentions to others.

Stopher believed that Wesbecker had planned his bloody revenge on Standard Gravure over several years, starting long before he had ever taken Prozac. And as for the effect of stress in the workplace, he was out of the plant on long-term disability for one whole year before his fateful return on September 14, 1989.

Meanwhile, the plaintiffs and their fifteen lawyers were making their own fitful trial preparations. In the fall of 1990, Leonard Finz was canvassing law firms around the country with a view to selecting those that were sufficiently well qualified to handle highly technical trials against a powerful and wealthy defendant.

In May 1991, Finz attended a conference of the American Trial Lawyers Association in Chicago, where he met up with Leonard Ring, a tough sixty-one-year-old attorney with a national reputation as a premier trial lawyer. Ring was being fêted for his recent success in a liability suit against Bristol-Myers Squibb involving contamination of Tylenol packages. During the conference, Ring joined Finz for breakfast along with another personal-injury lawyer, Paul Smith of Dallas, who had become a member of the Prozac litigation group representing clients in Texas. Smith, a diminutive, bespectacled forty-five-year-old with a Texan turn of phrase, had specialized throughout his career in medical negligence, personal injury, and product liability. He had his own small firm with three lawyers, and had recently won a $7.5-million suit for damages against the manufacturer of a building material that had caused an apartment-house fire. Smith had recently acquired a client whose husband had committed suicide "out of the blue" after taking Prozac, and he was now convinced that Prozac was "a dangerous substance."

The three lawyers, Finz, Ring, and Smith, agreed over breakfast that they had the expertise and the ammunition to "take Lilly down." But their enthusiasm was short-lived. As Paul Smith tells it, "After that meeting the multidistrict initiative seemed to run out of steam. Finz's strategies never seemed to get anywhere. There were a lot of cases, but they were all just fading away." Finz resigned early in 1992, at which point Smith and Ring got more active.

Smith became lead counsel for multidistrict Prozac litigation, and Ring decided to take on the Wesbecker case. Ring had working with him in Chicago a young attorney named Nancy Zettler, not long out of law school. "Although there were notionally dozens of lawyers involved in the multidistrict litigation," says Smith, "it's like the Boy Scouts or the Parent Teacher Association, there's just two or three people doing all the work. There were really just the three of us, and Lilly was not going to be helpful. At first they claimed that there were no documents in the computer. We went into a room in their headquarters in Indianapolis and there were four million pages of documents in hard copy. It was going to be a long, hard job."

In the latter part of 1992, says Smith, Nancy Zettler "started cranking this stuff up," but she was inexperienced and needed help.

Their investigations went on painfully and slowly through 1993. "I did whatever I could on a part-time basis, which wasn't enough," says Smith. "Then disaster struck. One cold morning in February 1994, a month before the Wesbecker case was to go to trial, I had a call from Nancy Zettler. She just said, 'Leonard Ring is in a coma.' He had apparently collapsed in a coffee shop, and although he wasn't exactly dead he was sure fixing to die, and died a few days later."

The trial date had been set for March 4 in Jefferson Circuit Court, Louisville, and Nancy Zettler immediately went down to Louisville to secure a postponement. Then Smith and Zettler and the plaintiffs' lawyers got into a series of circular discussions about whether they should attempt to settle, and, if not, who was to take the case.

"Judge Potter, who was to preside over the case, told Nancy she should take it herself," says Smith. "And she said, 'Well, wait a minute, Your Honor, thanks for your respect, but I'm just two years out of law school. I just don't feel I have the experience to represent twenty-seven plaintiffs in a multimillion-dollar suit.'

"And Lilly was not open to a settlement anyway; it seems that they really wanted this thing to come to trial down there in Louisville rather than risk a first case locally in Indianapolis, where they might get their butt kicked.

"The plaintiffs were asking me to take it over, and I wasn't keen. My initial feeling was that this had been billed as a dog case, and I couldn't see myself dropping everything for it. In fact, both Nancy and I thought it had problems: it was Lilly's best case of the bunch, and our worst. . . ."

As the arguments went back and forth between the various parties representing the plaintiffs, however, Smith began to see some advantage in taking on the case. He felt it would be useful even if they lost, "because Lilly would be forced to show their hand." He was impressed, moreover, with the "total innocence of these plaintiffs, who had done nothing to deserve what had happened to them."

Smith says he was especially heartened when Nancy showed him Dr. Lee Coleman's note on Wesbecker written three days before the shootings. "She said Wesbecker's psychiatrist had blamed the whole thing on Prozac—right there in his notes. Added to which, the coroner's report and verdict laid a big emphasis on Prozac, too."

Smith accepted the invitation to be the plaintiffs' trial lawyer in early March 1994, on a contingency, no-win-no-fee basis. He declines to say what the deal was, but confirms that his arrangements typically involve a fifty-fifty split of all damages awarded, with all the costs coming out of the clients' split. "This is a high-risk business," he says. "You can't be in this kind of law unless you've got several million in the bank to lose. But the rewards are very substantial if you get to win." He was estimating that his own firm's costs in the Wesbecker trial, which was scheduled to run for three and a half months, would approach a million dollars. As for damages—should the plaintiffs win—the estimates were varying between $150 million and $500 million.

Starting in the spring of 1994, Smith and Zettler traveled around the country collecting depositions from Lilly scientists involved with the development and production of Prozac—fifty-six in all, for a total of 20,822 pages with 944 accompanying exhibits. "I was spending four days a week getting on and off of planes, traveling down as far as Fort Myers and up as far as Seattle in Washington," says Smith.

At the same time, Smith was hunting for expert witnesses—specialists in psychopharmacology and psychiatry prepared to testify in court that Prozac was a potentially harmful substance. According to Smith, there were some 320 experts in psychopharmacology who could satisfy the demanding criteria for witness status in such a case in the United States, but he maintained that Lilly had managed to retain most of them already. On their side, Lilly claimed that the plaintiffs' counsel found it hard to come up with a potential witness hostile to Prozac because most experts were convinced of the drug's efficacy and safety. In any case, Stopher would later insist, they had not "retained" large numbers of expert witnesses as such; they had merely "consulted" many of them, as was their right.

Assisting Paul Smith as his chief expert witness was fifty-eight-year-old Peter Breggin, a psychiatrist based in Maryland who had been conducting a personal crusade against the excessive use of electro-convulsive therapy and drugs in psychiatric treatment, and had written a book on the subject entitled *Toxic Psychiatry*, published in 1991. Breggin, a stocky, combative man with a mop of silver hair, was well known on the TV talk-show circuit. He was no psychopharmacologist, and he would not be able to point to specific behavioral abnormalities as a result of a patient's taking Prozac; his antagonism toward the drug, and others like it, was mainly sociopolitical. Although he was not as radical as the Thomas Szasz–R. D. Laing school of antipsychiatry, he believed that there was a "medical-pharmaceutical establishment" in operation in the United States foisting drugs on millions of people in the interest of profits rather than health.

After the trial, Smith admitted to me that his relationship with Breggin "had gotten difficult" early on; that there were times when the psychiatrist "wanted to tell me how to conduct my case, and I had to tell him where to get off."

As the trial date (postponed now to mid-September) approached, both sides were happy to evade the issue of workplace tension raised at the coroner's inquest in November 1989. The coroner's jury had focused on the effect on Wesbecker of stresses at Standard Gravure, referring specifically to the pressure put on him by the foremen and bosses. During the preliminary-motions phase of the trial, Judge John Potter of the Jefferson Circuit Court had for technical reasons ruled that Standard Gravure (as represented by Shea Communications), Hall Security, and Dr. Lee Coleman had no case to answer. The first two defendants had offered the plaintiffs money that had been accepted, and Judge Potter had ruled that, under Kentucky law, a psychiatrist cannot be sued if he has given drugs in good faith. This meant that a jury could still apportion a percentage liability to Standard Gravure, Hall, and Coleman, but actual payment of potential damages was unlikely.

As far as Smith was concerned, there was no future in demonstrating that excessive pressure in the workplace had been a substantial cause of Wesbecker's actions, since there was no financial percentage in it. Smith's most profitable course of action was to tackle Lilly head-on, focusing the entire blame on Prozac.

For Lilly, on the other hand, it made qualified sense to divert attention to Standard Gravure, but Stopher and his team were conscious that some of the leading plaintiffs had been foremen and managers at the plant. As Stopher confessed to me after the trial, "We were worried that by attacking Standard Gravure we would be attacking the plaintiffs, who were sympathetic figures."

As the trial date approached, both sides were increasingly preoccupied with the story of the last four or five years of Wesbecker's life, the course of his manic-depressive illness, its diagnoses and prognoses, and the drugs he had taken. Even though both sides intended to play down the issue of workplace tensions, the discovery process was telling a chilling story about the working conditions and morale at Standard Gravure after the plant was sold to Mike Shea in 1986. None of this discovery material had been available at the coroner's inquest in November

1989; nor would it be revealed in full at the trial. But the lawyers' knowledge of what was contained in those stacks of sworn depositions would create a crucial background to the denials and evasions the knowledge would prompt in the course of the trial.

12

ON JULY 19, 1984, armed with an Israeli Uzi nine-millimeter carbine and a Winchester twelve-gauge shotgun, James Oliver Huberty, wearing dark glasses and camouflage pants, walked into a San Diego McDonald's and shot forty diners, killing twenty-one, before a police sniper stopped him with a bullet.

In April 1986, two Vietnam veterans dressed in military garb and armed with Ruger Mini-14 automatic rifles, shotguns, and handguns, killed two FBI agents and wounded five others in a shootout in Miami, after robbing a bank. The following year, a uniformed man nicknamed Rambo murdered three people in Texas before killing his wife, his boss, and his wife's lover. And in January 1989, in the year of the Louisville shootings, Patrick Purdy, toting an AK-47 and dressed in an army jacket, killed five children and wounded twenty-nine others in a schoolyard in Stockton, California, before shooting himself with a nine-millimeter pistol.

Focusing on Wesbecker's arsenal of weapons, his obsession with paramilitary magazines such as *Soldier of Fortune*, and parallels with the Stockton killings, James William Gibson—author of *Warrior Dreams*, published in the spring of 1994—placed the Standard Gravure incident squarely in the context of what he calls the "New War."

The "New War," according to Gibson, describes the cult of military-style violence, both in mass-culture fantasy and fact, that increased throughout the late 1970s and into the 1980s in consequence, he believes, of the humiliation of the American macho ego in Vietnam and the contemporaneous feminist challenge to male status.

Gibson cites a genre of vigilante-vengeance movies, from *Dirty Harry* (1971) to *Death Wish* (1974), *Taxi Driver* (1976) to *First Blood*

(1982), in which the lone veteran—sane or unhinged—finds meaning in life by attempting to "level the score."

By the mid-1980s, given a series of massacres in the shopping malls, campuses, and schoolyards of America, perpetrated with the panoply of combat uniform and military weaponry, the mass-culture fantasies began to merge with reality. Potential spree-killers could perfect their bloody rituals just watching the news. The February 6, 1989, issue of *Time* magazine, open at a feature headlined "Armed in America: More Guns, More Shootings, More Massacres," was found in Wesbecker's kitchen when police broke into his home on the day of the shootings.

In a keynote article, "Becoming the Armed Man," in *Public Culture* in 1991, and in his book *Warrior Dreams*, Gibson delares that the social significance of paramilitary culture—revealed in the Stockton and Louisville shootings—has been overshadowed by inconclusive debates about gun control following each incident. "Like the mercenaries, hit men, and race warriors," he writes, "the paramilitary mass murderers directly lived out the modern warrior mythology that permeated much of American culture." For Americans to have understood killers like Wesbecker and the significance of their acts, Gibson reckons, would have required understanding the social significance of paramilitary culture; but he concludes that people have been so frightened and angered by the horror of these crimes that there has been little scope for critical analysis of what led to them.

The failure of Americans to recognize the "New War" has been amply and tragically rectified in the aftermath of the Oklahoma City bombing on April 19, 1995, in which 166 people died as a result of right-wing fanaticism of the kind Gibson explores. Yet to link Wesbecker's killing spree exclusively to the "warrior culture" is to overlook its significance as an instance of one of the fastest-growing criminal trends in America: violence in the workplace.

There is a tendency to regard workplace violence as an employee-management relations problem, a failure in human-resources policies, rather than a widespread phenomenon involving society at every level. Wesbecker's killing spree was no isolated incident: it was, as Stopher's researches were revealing, a uniquely documented instance of a rapidly increasing trend.

According to the U.S. government's first comprehensive accounting of how people die at work, a total of 1,004 employees died in the workplace as a result of violence in 1992, compared with 696 such deaths in 1989. The 1992 figure represents 17 percent of U.S. workplace deaths, but, shockingly, 40 percent of *women* who die on the job are murder victims. This may well reflect the fact that women do less physically dangerous jobs than men; but it is surely significant that the first four former co-workers Wesbecker shot at Standard Gravure were women, one of whom, Jackie Miller, was reaching for her own .38 as she took three bullets.

Wesbecker's massacre, it is clear, takes its place alongside a number of hallmark workplace incidents in the late 1980s and early 1990s. In August 1986, Patrick Sherrill, a U.S. Post Office worker at Edmond, Oklahoma, arrived at work with two Colt .45-caliber pistols, a .22-caliber handgun, and hundreds of rounds of ammunition. Without speaking, he walked up to two supervisors and shot them dead. Then he went systematically through the building, shooting anyone he could find, until he finally shot himself in the head. The toll at the end of his spree was fourteen dead, besides himself, and six wounded. The day before the shootings, he had been reprimanded by a supervisor and told that he could expect an adverse performance report. Earlier he had complained to a union officer that his supervisors were picking on him.

In December 1987, David Burke, thirty-five, father of seven children, was fired from his job as a USAir agent after he was accused of stealing cash from flight-cocktail receipts. He asked for special consideration on account of his family, but his plea was denied. On a flight bound for San Francisco, Burke shot the airline customer-service manager and the pilot with a .44 magnum. The plane crashed over San Luis Obispo, killing forty-three people, including Burke. The FBI found a note, the gun, and six empty casings. The note read: "I asked for some leniency for my family . . . well, I got none. And you'll get none."

The incidents begin to describe a recurring nightmare across the United States. A former employee in San Diego returns to the plant where had worked for three years and shoots dead two executives with a shotgun. In Bennington, Vermont, a woman unhappy with how she had been treated at work shoots dead the manager at the Eveready Battery Company and tries to set the plant on fire. A dismissed post-office worker at Royal Oak, Michigan, returns to his former workplace armed with a sawed-off .22-caliber rifle and kills three supervisors and wounds six people before shooting himself in the head; six days earlier, he had lost a hearing over a grievance filed on his behalf by the union. A female social worker fired from her job with the Los Angeles County Department of Children's Services walks into her former office and shoots a supervisor who was instrumental in the decision to dismiss her. A janitor at a building maintenance company, angry over the late payment of $150, pours lighter fluid over a female bookkeeper and sets fire to her: the forty-two-year-old mother of two dies nine hours later suffering burns over 95 percent of her body.

The roll call of actual homicide represents only the tip of the iceberg. Labor experts claim that in 1994 there were 111,000 serious incidents in the workplace in the United States involving physical and emotional acts of violence. Typical checklists include: physical assault, sexual harassment, verbal abuse and intimidation, vandalism of equipment, abusive graffiti, threats by letter or telephone, damage to personal property such as slashing of tires in the parking lot, sabotage, dangerous "practical jokes." From the employees' point of view, stressors giving rise to anger and consequent violence include victimization, withdrawal of job security, late payment of wages, incomplete wages, unsafe and overstressful physical conditions, obligation to compete for one's own job, unfair demotion, unfair warnings of disciplinary action, increased working hours, aggressive supervisors, uncaring managers, drastic "downsizing" of workforce, inadequate medical and pension benefits, absence of a communal spirit, lack of break time or recreational facilities.

Human resource departments issue prevention manuals that focus instead on the huge cost of workplace violence to American business, which runs into many billions, advising that "correct personnel selection procedures are the most effective way to prevent potential problems." The authors routinely advise against acknowledging that the company, its supervisors and managers, are in any way responsible for such incidents, preferring to concentrate on "red flags and warning signs" and the telltale profiles of "employees with a grudge and a potential for violence."

"Under no circumstances should you infer," counsels Michael Mantell, author of *Ticking Bombs: Defusing Violence in the Workplace* (1994), "that we are blaming an organization for something a disturbed employee did against it. . . . The disgruntled employee, who goes home and loads his gun, is ultimately responsible for his murderous act."

Nevertheless, in advance of the Louisville trial, a remarkable portrait was emerging of volatile tensions at Standard Gravure, typical of widespread patterns of industrial and social unease in America today.

For years, Wesbecker thought that he and his co-workers were being poisoned by toxic fumes in the printing plant, and toward the end he talked of himself as being "sodomized" by the company. Whatever the literal accuracy of these assertions, a powerfully metaphorical perception of a "toxic" and "abusive" workplace haunts the story of Wesbecker's last three years at the plant.

Accounts of marathon working hours, unpredictable requests to work double shifts, night shifts, and weekends, against a background of pay cuts, hectic increases in production, and the erosion of job security, are familiar enough throughout the industrialized world. Two hundred years after Philadelphia carpenters went on strike for the ten-hour day, Wesbecker and his co-workers were routinely doing double shifts of sixteen hours a day, and working between sixty and eighty hours a week.

For the pressmen at Standard Gravure, who had known better days as skilled journeymen protected by a strong union and stroked by a paternalistic proprietor, the advent of Gannett and Mike Shea seemed sufficient reasons for the decline in working conditions and the consequent rise in stress, frustration, and anger. These volatile pressures, however, were symptomatic of something deeper and more widespread than the individual history of the Standard Gravure printing plant.

Like thousands of businesses in the late 1980s, Standard Gravure was gripped by fierce competition in a contracting market. New technologies of printing were causing massive downsizing of staffing levels, but the reductions were not deemed sufficient to keep profits buoyant in shrinking markets. The answer was an old-fashioned work speedup.

Fewer employees were obliged to work ever-longer hours for less reward. At Standard Gravure, the workforce plunged from six hundred in the mid-1980s to just eighty workers by the turn of the decade; but for individual workers "lucky" enough to retain their jobs, the hours increased and the pay was frozen or cut.

The pattern of increased working hours and increased job insecurity is endemic among both blue- and white-collar workers throughout America and Europe, as are the damaging physical and psychological consequences. According to Juliet B. Schor, author of *Overworked in America*, over the last twenty years the amount of time Americans have spent at work has risen by about nine hours a year each year, to the point where workers at all levels are spending as much time at their jobs as they did back in the 1920s.

At the same time—and Standard Gravure was an example of this— many businesses had by the late 1980s become both victims and practitioners of the predatory commercialism of the times. The style of benign paternalism practiced by the Binghams had given way to the individualistic buccaneer spirit of Mike Shea and the harsh economies-of-scale practiced by Gannett. Conglomerates, and individual entrepreneurs, survived and thrived on takeovers, mergers, and asset stripping, often acquiring valuable businesses with promissory transactions involving junk bonds, leveraged loans, and stripped assets. Mike Shea would admit in his sworn deposition that half the money for the purchase of Standard Gravure came from the workers' pension fund. He also said that the $11-million pension reversion did not go into his own pocket, but was part of the purchased assets.

The prevailing perception of workers at Standard Gravure, however, was that they had no future; that their retirement and medical benefits were worthless; that they had no job security; that they were being screwed by management and supervisors to further the ends of a business in which they had no stake.

13

By THE SPRING OF 1985, Wesbecker had sold his house on Mount Holyoke Drive for $31,000 and spent almost twice that on a low gray three-bedroom home on Nottoway Circle near Iroquois Park. He felt that this new place, a seventeen-mile drive from Standard Gravure, gave him more space and peace of mind, and asked Brenda to live with him. She moved in a few weeks later.

No sooner had he settled in than he got into another dispute with Standard Gravure, over the use of solvents. At about this time, the company began to use large amounts of toluene, a fast-drying chemical compound, to thin the yellow ink. Wesbecker believed that the workers were being poisoned by the substance. According to his uncle John Montgomery, Wesbecker's stack of material on toluene and other solvents, including documents he had sent for from Washington, D.C., stood four feet high. His aunt would testify that he was "very, very terrified about something being used in the ink."

He was making frequent visits to the plant nurse for a skin-irritation problem and complaining to anybody who would listen to him. He was trying to get co-workers to join him in a suit against Exxon, the manufacturer of toluene, because, as he told a friend: "Toluene consumes so many brain cells in such a length of time, and tears up your nervous system."

He went around the plant with a label from one of the solvent containers asking his co-workers to imagine what the fumes were doing to their lungs.

In the event, according to one pressman, Standard Gravure did not start to deal with the problem of the way they handled toluene at the plant "until men started passing out." A plant foreman later confirmed that "problems claimed by Standard Gravure employees from exposure to toluene and xylene included headaches, dizziness, disorientation, nausea, rashes, and respiratory distress."

In time, Wesbecker's complaints about the solvents merged with his distress at being put frequently on the folder. After leaving the hospital, he pressed to be treated the same as other workers who had been excused from the folder as a result of physical disability.

By July 1986, the managers and foremen at Standard Gravure had more on their minds than complaints from Wesbecker. They were going through the throes of new ownership. Having failed to complete a workers' buy-out deal, the Binghams had sold the company to Mike Shea. Believing at first that Shea would transform the fortunes of the business, people in the plant had a sense of euphoria and optimism; then morale began to plummet. The discontent focused on the terms of the purchase. Though Shea had bought Standard Gravure for over $22 million, he simultaneously stripped an important asset from the company—an offset business called Color Print in Morristown, Tennessee, and sold it for $6 million. Immediately after these transactions, Shea received $11 million from the Standard Gravure pension fund and a further $2.2 million back from the Binghams after a dispute over valuations. Workers and managers clearly felt a deep sense of grievance, since their bid to take over the company might have succeeded had they used the same tactics.

Shortly after making his purchase, Shea started laying off employees as a cost-cutting measure and increased the speed of the presses, "in order," as he explained, "to be competitive in the workplace." He also ordered daily press-machine reports, focusing on waste and output. Workers later testified that the result was more pressure and stress, and that the pressure was greatest on the folder operator.

Workers also protested that Shea knew nothing about printing plants or collective bargaining; he seemed to them to be just a businessman out to make a quick profit for himself. The union, they felt, had abandoned them, and it would not be long before Shea sold the company. Though Shea denied these allegations, he quickly acquired a reputation for telling workers one thing in a meeting and then doing the opposite. He had a catchphrase that he used to urge his employees on: "I have just two rules. Rule number one is never lose money, and rule number two is don't forget rule number one."

At this time, Wesbecker was campaigning yet again to be taken officially and permanently off the folder. He had even attempted to make representations to Shea himself. In August, he explained to the union president, Don Frazier, that he had been diagnosed as manic-depressive, that "medication helped, but the pressure of the folder seems to overcome my medication. . . . When I come in I'm fairly calm and then I begin to fall apart again, and I just really, really need to get off that folder."

Wesbecker had been prescribed lithium by his psychiatrist, Dr. Vikdam Senler, in July. He was now complaining that the drug blurred his vision. Frazier has testified that while Wesbecker imparted all this "he stared at the floor a lot, paced, and was agitated."

Despite unwritten assurances by his supervisors to employee-relations social worker Pat Lampton that Wesbecker would only be put on the folder when necessary, worksheet records show that he was put on the machine for the entirety of fifteen different shifts (from August 17 to September 20, 1986): a total of 120 hours. During this period, Wesbecker confided to a co-worker that "they were making him work on the folder just to prove they could make him do something he didn't want to do."

By November, when he consulted a new psychiatrist, Dr. David Moore, the doctor found him to be suffering "prominent" depressive symptoms and prescribed the drug Tofranil in addition to lithium. Wesbecker was still taking these powerful drugs two months later, and he was still on the folder when Moore wrote a letter to the company requesting that his patient be taken off in view of his illness.

Wesbecker was required to work on the folder only twice in the space of the next two months. But just eleven days after being on the folder the second time, his agitation was so great that his psychiatrist had him temporarily confined in Our Lady of Peace Hospital.

Back at work, Wesbecker arranged an appointment with the Human Relations Commission in Louisville and met with one of its caseworkers, Dan Mattingly, on May 14, 1987, to discuss his grievance.

Mattingly, a tall man with a priestlike, sympathetic nature according to those who know him, remembers that Wesbecker seemed high-strung and nervous at the interview, but intelligent and articulate. His grievance, said Mattingly, was that his supervisors "continued to threaten him" with the folder, and that "the threat was as harmful to him as doing the work."

Wesbecker said that the foremen made fun of him because of his mental illness, and that he had a list of fifteen pressmen qualified to work the folder who were never asked to do so. He told Mattingly that a foreman had said, "You have to learn to tough it out."

Wesbecker now filed a complaint against Standard Gravure for discrimination and unfair treatment. Union president Don Frazier consequently asked to see the company records of shift assignments, but management resolutely refused to produce them. About this time, Wesbecker phoned Mattingly to say that a message had gone up behind the Plexiglas on the foremen's noticeboard: "Problems? Call Wesbecker—585-NUTS." The supervisors, he said, were allowing the sign to remain up.

Mattingly had a meeting with Paula Warman in her office at the plant on June 16, 1987. He told her, "Before they put Mr. Wesbecker on the folder, they ought to shut the place down, because putting him on the folder is endangering his life and the lives of the people around him." Mattingly says that, although he assured her that Wesbecker could "flip out" and "anything could happen," she replied that the company could make no exceptions for him.

According to the testimony of Standard Gravure's security manager, Grady Throneberry, Mike Shea now agreed to a meeting with Wesbecker. Throneberry testified that he was asked to stand in the kitchenette of the executive suite and listen to what was taking place, to be on hand in case of trouble. According to co-workers who shared a cafeteria meal with him later, Wesbecker claimed that Shea told him he had to work even though his doctor said he couldn't, or he would lose his compensation.

Another co-worker remembers that Wesbecker, talking to him around this time, was "jittery and stuttering." Wesbecker told him that they were trying to make him pay back his disability payments for the period he had spent in the hospital, and that he was going to have to work the folder the next night. He said he was still not well, but the only reason he came back after being in the hospital was that the company had threatened to fire him if he did not turn up for work.

Mattingly remembers a conversation during this period with Don Frazier in which Frazier said that Wesbecker was very competent, and that was why the company did not want to make an exception for him on the folder.

Three weeks after Mattingly's unsuccessful attempt to intervene on his behalf, Wesbecker went with Brenda for his first consultation with Dr. Lee Coleman. Coleman found Wesbecker irritable, anxious, and pacing; he recalls that during the consultation Wesbecker mentioned having attempted suicide previously.

During his last few months at work, Wesbecker was becoming reclusive, preoccupied with weapons and with magazines featuring guns and survival. In January 1988, he bought *Soldier of Fortune* and *Full Auto Firearms*, and talked weapons and gun magazines with co-workers. On January 18, *Newsweek* published an article featuring pictures of the AK-47. This issue was found in Wesbecker's closet after his death, along with other arms magazines.

Early in January, Wesbecker bought a .25-caliber Raven semi-automatic pistol at Ray's Gun Shop in Louisville. The next month, he went back and bought a Smith and Wesson weapon. The next day, he and Brenda went target-shooting at Ray's Indoor Shooting Range. Also that month, then foreman James Popham told an associate that Wesbecker had threatened him with a gun. Wesbecker's friend Lucas told the pressroom superintendent, Don Cox, that Wesbecker had purchased a gun and was going to use it on him and other foremen and superintendents. The warnings were passed on to the security manager, Grady Throneberry, who offered to provide security at Cox's home. According to Charlie Ganote, there was a standing joke every time anyone saw Cox coming through the plant. "When Joey comes back in here, he's going to get you." Cox said that he had never done anything to Wesbecker and that he drove by his house every day. Wesbecker told a co-worker that Cox would ignore him when he drove by his house.

During February 1988, pressman Charles Metten remembers, John

Stein (whom Wesbecker shot twice on September 14, 1989) harassed Wesbecker. Metten recalls that Wesbecker cried out in a frustrated voice: "If you continue harassing me every time I come through . . . Why are you always on me?"

In April, Dr. Coleman was again writing "To Whom It May Concern" letters advising that Wesbecker's condition deteriorated when he was under heavy levels of stress, and that his overtime work should be limited to what he could handle. Coleman added that his patient's condition deteriorated under moderate levels of stress and he should not work over sixty-four hours per week.

During April and May, Wesbecker's son James exposed himself sexually in public frequently and was eventually sentenced to ninety days in the Community Corrections Center; here Wesbecker visited him every day. By June, James started threatening suicide.

Early in June 1988, Coleman took Wesbecker off Tofranil and started him on a daily course of twenty-milligram capsules of Prozac. A day or two later, Wesbecker decided to take himself off the drug, because he felt it did not suit him.

Brenda remembers that about this time Wesbecker had difficulties with his lawn mowers. She watched as he wrecked the machines with an ax and ran over them with his car. Throughout this spring and summer, Wesbecker told his son James that Brenda was refusing to have sex with him.

During the summer, according to the sworn testimony of co-worker pressman Cecil Taylor, Wesbecker was "working the folders a lot." Says Taylor, "He would just get that look. You could tell he really didn't know what he was doing. . . . He would get to moving a lot faster."

In July, Wesbecker and the industrial-relations attorney Herb Segal had a meeting in Segal's office with Standard Gravure's senior manager, Don McCall, and the firm's attorney Ivan Rich. Wesbecker asked for a written guarantee that he would not be asked to work the folder. He argued that, since the threat of going on the folder was always with him, he wanted a letter in his file stating that he would never have to work the folder again under any circumstances. McCall could not make such an assurance.

Co-workers and foremen remember Wesbecker's talking about

bombing the building with a remote-control plane, or putting a bomb beside the fifth-floor solvent-recovery tank. Their reaction at the time was that this was "just a form of speech."

In August, co-worker Charlie Ganote saw Wesbecker down in the basement of Standard Gravure and noticed that he was "shabby . . . unshaven and unkempt." On August 6, Wesbecker worked for the last time at Standard Gravure, but his dispute with the company, and his visits to the plant, were not over.

Dr. Lee Coleman wanted to get Wesbecker on long-term disability status, and he wrote to the company on August 8 recommending medical leave for his patient as of August 7. During that week, Coleman changed Wesbecker's diagnosis from "bipolar disorder" to "schizoaffective disorder" because of his tendency to be "suspicious." Wesbecker had been questioning his psychiatrist about his methods of treatment, wondering, for example, whether Coleman had been hypnotizing him; but his principal "suspicion," it seems, was that the company would move to cut his medical benefits.

Before August was over, Wesbecker purchased his nine-millimeter Sig Sauer pistol from the Archery World weapons shop: this was the gun that he would eventually use to kill himself. Six weeks later, he visited the Owen Funeral home in Louisville and paid $685 cash for his own cremation. He requested "total consumption with no ashes to be returned."

During September 1988, he deeded his Nottoway Circle house to Brenda, telling her that he did not want her to leave him again. Brenda remembers that he told her, "I really don't think I'll have need for this house if I don't beat mental illness." As they talked it through, she says, he said at last, "Well, I guess if I'm in the mental hospital, or I kill myself, or I don't make it, I guess that's the least I can do for you, is give you a roof over your head." A neighbor says that he noticed at this time that the property was looking run-down and the grass in the yard was overgrown.

Meanwhile, Wesbecker's wrangle with the company over medical claims and compensation continued. Pressman James Lucas remembers that Wesbecker came into the plant in September, and complained that

Paula Warman was a "bitch" and that his claims for psychiatric bills had not been processed. Co-worker Cecil Taylor remembers Lucas's telling him at about this time that Wesbecker had brought a gun into the plant.

In November, Brenda moved out of the Nottoway house to stay with her dying father.

The management at Standard Gravure once again had more on their minds than a truculent pressman and his quarrels over disability payments and compensation. On October 11, 1988, an explosion and fire damaged the three big presses in Area 2. As a result, the four more antiquated presses in Area 1 would be used exclusively in the future, and the pressmen faced pay cuts and layoffs. Shea, on the other hand, did not suffer any financial loss, as he would eventually collect $12 million in insurance.

Morale at the plant began to deteriorate rapidly after the fire. The security manager, Grady Throneberry, remembers that one worker said that if he was laid off he would "fix this place" before he left. Another pressman was banned from the plant after making similar threats. Rumors circulated that a restoration worker had told pressmen that the fire-damaged presses, which were to be sold off, could have been up and running in three or four months.

On the day of the explosion, Wesbecker purchased a Winchester pump shotgun at Outer Loop Gun and Pawn Shop. Two days later, he went into the burn unit at Humana Hospital to visit his friend James Lucas. Lucas remembers Wesbecker saying, "It's a damn shame the place didn't blow up."

Wesbecker's lawyer, Herb Segal, was still pressing for compensation for the discrimination complaint. In early December 1988, the company's attorney Ivan Rich had assured Segal that "any lawsuit or workers' compensation claim by Mr. Wesbecker will be vigorously contested by the company." By the end of the month, the union president, Don Frazier, was saying that he could not verify Wesbecker's complaints, since there was no evidence of embarrassment or humiliation.

The Human Relations Commission, which had been working with Segal, wrote on December 30, 1988, to Rich. Requesting an immediate settlement to the compensation suit, the commission wrote, "The Respondent [that is, Standard Gravure] does not understand how stress and resulting fear affect a person with a mental disability."

The same day, Standard Gravure replied that Wesbecker would be going on long-term disability, but if he were to return to work the company would agree to make "reasonable accommodation for any mental handicap he may have." And yet, after all the wrangles of the previous months, the company could still not make a commitment to relieve Wesbecker from working the folder should he return to work.

For Wesbecker it had been a miserable and lonely holiday season. His uncle John recalls that Wesbecker brought him a cake just before Christmas, but he did not stay long. Lucas, out of the hospital at that point, remembers that Wesbecker turned down an invitation to come around and drink an eggnog on Christmas morning. Lucas says that his conversations with Wesbecker were getting shorter and shorter, as if his friend never had time to talk. On New Year's Eve, Wesbecker called Lucas to say he hoped the coming year would be better than the last. His medication was not helping him, he said, and he felt as if "the doctors and the drugstores were in cahoots."

On the second day of the new year, 1989, Wesbecker put down a deposit on two nine-millimeter pistols at Tilford's Gun Sales. The salesman stated later to a *Courier-Journal* reporter that Wesbecker indicated the weapons he wanted by pointing to pictures in a gun magazine. The same day, he withdrew from the Communications International Union. During his conversations with a union representative, Wesbecker apparently sounded "strange."

Two weeks into January 1989, a drifter in Stockton, California, barged into an elementary school spraying bullets from an automatic rifle. He killed five children and wounded thirty others. The killings received extensive coverage on television and in the *Courier-Journal*. A little over two weeks later, *Time* magazine published an article entitled "Calendar of Senseless Shootings," recounting assaults across America, such as John Hinckley's attack on President Reagan, William Cruse's shooting of sixteen people in Florida in April 1987, Richard Farley's killing of seven computer-company employees in February 1988, Laurie Dann's shooting at an elementary school in Winnetka in May 1988, and the Stockton shootings. The AK-47 figured largely in the feature. This was the issue of the magazine found by police in Wesbecker's house.

That same week in February, Wesbecker took delivery of the two pistols from Tilford's Gun Sales. Wesbecker told his former co-worker Tommy Gosling, whom he met in a shopping mall, that he had bought weapons "in case he needed them for his bosses."

Soon after, Wesbecker was advised that his long-term disability benefits would start the following month. The letter, sent by Paula Warman in Standard Gravure's personnel office, read as follows:

> You will receive your first check on April 1, 1989 in the amount of $1,420. . . . On May 1 and continuing each month through the month of August, you will receive a check in the amount of $1,069.34. Your September check will be in the amount of $845.10. Beginning October 1, and continuing each month thereafter for the duration of your disablement until age 65 your monthly payment will be $391.21.
>
> As you know, effective January 1, 1989 we began charging medical premiums to our retired, widowed, and disabled employees. The premium for your coverage at this time is $78.00 per month. This amount will be deducted from your monthly long term disability check, unless you elect to discontinue your coverage.

Whatever Wesbecker had expected in terms of disability payments, and whatever his legal due, his perception was that he had been cheated. He told a number of people that "Standard Gravure were going to take his rights away." At the same time, he saw the premium charge on insurance coverage as further evidence that the company was heartlessly ripping him off (he was still attempting to recover medical costs relating to past illness and leave).

He swung between believing that the company was stealing his benefits, and suspecting that cuts in benefits were aimed at forcing him back to work. The company made no attempt to enumerate his rights for him, or to instruct him as to how he could make up the shortfall through Social Security claims. When he called the union, to which he had belonged for nearly thirty years, he was told by the local rep, Tommy Gosling, that he should consult his lawyer.

As it happened, his attempts to find himself legal representation were not successful, at least one lawyer believing that he would "be a pest possibly having unreasonable expectations." The only person in the world it seemed he could talk to was his old friend and co-worker, James Lucas. Lucas says Wesbecker would come over to his house but could not sit still. Sometimes he was moody and nervous, jumping from topic to topic, or he just stared through the window. Lucas says that Wesbecker had "no concept of time."

As 1989 wore on, Wesbecker's personal difficulties with Standard Gravure, and his volatile illness, necessitating a complicated trial of medications, were compounded by the unrelenting problems of his son James. Hardly a week passed without James's being arrested or attending therapy, requiring the payment of fines, consultancy fees, and medication costs. Despite the anguish he shared over James's predicament, Wesbecker seems never to have lost patience with his son. He continued to look beyond James's current difficulties to better days.

Wesbecker was encouraging his son to complete the university course he had started in economics and frequently talked with him about how this could be funded. Late in February, he discussed settling $60,000 on him for this purpose. According to James, these conversations were "online and businesslike." Wesbecker's financial records, which survive in his estate documents, reveal that he was transferring money into dependable high-yield deposit accounts. Much of his anger against Standard Gravure stemmed from his perception that the cut in disability payments would affect his capacity to help his son.

Toward the end of April, Wesbecker called Tilford's Gun Sales and asked if they would take a Norinco AK-47 in exchange for a Polytech AK-47S. Three days later, Wesbecker went into the shop and made the trade. He explained to the salesman that he wanted to use it at the Knob Creek target range. A week later, he went back to Tilford's to buy eleven hundred rounds of ammunition for $123.

By May, Wesbecker was taking six hundred milligrams of lithium a day, along with trazodone and Restoril and the tranquilizer Halcion. He had also been prescribed a drug called Soma, as a muscle relaxant. He complained that he was feeling "drugged" and "lethargic" and also noted a problem with his memory.

He told co-workers he ran into occasionally that the Standard Gravure people were watching him like a hawk to make sure he was not faking his disability.

On one occasion late at night in July, he walked into the plant and met the union president, Frazier. Wesbecker was holding the letter Paula Warman had written about his reductions in disability payments. He told Frazier in front of a witness that he "could come in and wipe the whole place out." The next day, Frazier reported this to vice-president Don McCall; according to Frazier's testimony, McCall "shrugged his shoulders and laughed."

Also in July, Brenda's father died, and a few days later Wesbecker started to stay several nights a week at the house on Blevin's Gap. Brenda remembers that there were occasional quarrels. Wesbecker complained that the house smelled, to which she responded, "I'm not the needy one, you are. You're the one that don't take a bath for a week. You're the one that pees in a can, not me." Brenda would later testify that there was a lot of anger in the relationship after their divorce in 1984. She says she stayed with him because she was a "humanitarian" and she wanted a companion.

At the end of July, Wesbecker visited his friend Lucas and told him that he could see no light at the end of the tunnel, that suicide seemed the only answer. Lucas was also depressed, and they talked about shooting each other. Lucas remembers that Wesbecker spoke about James's problems, that during the visit he could not sit still, would stare out of the window for long periods of time. He talked of "eliminating" foremen and supervisors at Standard Gravure.

On August 5, 1989, not quite six weeks before the Standard Gravure shootings, Wesbecker's grandmother Nancy, the woman he called Mother, who had been a second mother to him, died of Alzheimer's disease at the age of eighty-six. The funeral took place four days later. The immediate family of brothers and sisters (with the exception of Rosie, who had died in her thirties of cancer, and Wesbecker's uncle James, who lived in California) were together for the first time in thirty years. Someone decided to take a family picture, but Wesbecker refused to be in it, saying he was "only a nephew." According to his cousin Sheila Stoke, he appeared nervous and upset.

The day after the funeral, Wesbecker went to see his psychiatrist, Lee Coleman. He complained of memory problems and insomnia, and they discussed whether to maintain present levels of his drugs or try something new. Thinking it might alleviate Wesbecker's lethargy, Coleman suggested another trial of Prozac. He prescribed a course of twenty capsules, one daily, with gradual tapering of Desyrel (trazodone hydrochloride) over a two-to-three-week period. Coleman testified that he is uncertain whether he warned Wesbecker of the possibility of developing the manic or psychotic symptoms that had been experienced by some patients on the drug.

On August 17, seven days after his visit to Coleman, Wesbecker's prescription of twenty capsules of Prozac was filled. Wesbecker started taking them the same day.

The following week, he turned up at James Lucas's house. Sitting in the kitchen, he told Lucas: "I wish you wouldn't return to work, because I've got a plan that will result in eliminating that fucking place. . . ." The "plan" was to blow up the solvent-recovery plant, a notion he had fantasized about for years. Lucas, who believed Wesbecker was in earnest, says he replied that the scheme would involve killing a lot of innocent people, including himself, whereupon Wesbecker said he did not want to hurt Lucas and that he had an alternate plan. He had a crumpled paper in his pocket, remembers Lucas, listing seven people he would eliminate.

Why did Wesbecker go out of his way to tell his friend about the plan? How could Wesbecker count on Lucas not to inform the company? Was Wesbecker attempting to give everybody full warning of what he was about to do?

Lucas, according to his sworn testimony, told pressman Gerald Griffin about Wesbecker's plan the same day. Then he informed his supervisor the day after. Lucas's wife, who had been thoroughly shaken by Wesbecker's conversation and had confided the matter to her doctor, wrote in her diary that her husband had issued appropriate warnings. "[James] went back to work. Warned guys at work about Joe as advised by Dr. Gabbert. . . . Scared of fire scene and Joe. Joe said he wouldn't hurt Jim and would take care of him."

James Lucas would also testify under oath that on August 29, 1989, two weeks and two days before the shootings, he reported Wesbecker's threats to Grady Throneberry, head of security at Standard Gravure, and to Don McCall, executive vice-president. McCall denies receiving any such warning from Lucas. Shea, the company's owner, testified that he could not recall hearing any threats whatsoever against Standard Gravure property or persons prior to the incident.

The following week, Wesbecker told his son James about his manic-depressive condition and his fear that he might have passed on the same illness in his genes. James says his father urged him to talk it over with his psychiatrist. "He was very hyper and very fast in his speech pattern," James has said, and he complained of racing thoughts and poor concentration. Toward the end of this conversation, Wesbecker told his son that he had run out of all legal remedies and if he had to return to work he would be put back on the folder.

By now the Prozac would have been taking its full effect.

On September 2, twelve days before the shootings, Wesbecker called again at James Lucas's house. Again he spoke of blowing up the plant. When Lucas told him which shift he was currently working, Wesbecker said, "You're messing my plans up." It was at this point, says Lucas, that Wesbecker said he would go to "plan B." When Lucas asked what that meant, he said, "It does not concern you. . . . It only concerns Shea, McCall, Paula Warman, Donald Cox, Jim Popham, and the rest of the fucking office cronies." Wesbecker left information about long-term disability at Lucas's house.

On September 5, Wesbecker had a second prescription of Prozac filled. The next day, he called at Danny's Gun Repair in Louisville to have his AK-47S cleaned. According to the salesman, Wesbecker was acting strangely, so he declined his request for ammunition.

On September 9, Wesbecker went once more to Lucas's house. Acting "dazed, as if he had not slept," he said that he would not need the long-term disability information back because "after tomorrow I don't have any use for it." That night, he slept at Blevin's Gap with Brenda and, according to her testimony, had sex with her for the last time.

The next day—Sunday, September 10—Wesbecker purchased two hundred rounds of full-metal-jacket bullets from Ray's Indoor Shooting Range. That same day, both McCall and Shea received anonymous phone calls. The caller said: "Why the fuck are you sitting down?" Then hung up.

On the afternoon of Monday, September 11, 1989, three days before the shootings, Wesbecker went to his psychiatrist, Dr. Coleman, for the last time.

14

DESPITE THE SETBACKS following the hue and cry of the Scientologists, by 1993 Prozac had in public perception graduated from a highly efficacious if controversial medication for clinical depression to something approaching a general happiness pill reminiscent of "soma" in Huxley's *Brave New World.*

As Lilly's eighteen-hundred-person U.S. sales force continued to target general practitioners as well as psychiatrists, extolling the drug's efficacy for bulimia, anorexia, and general compulsive disorders, large numbers of patients who were generally low in spirits rather than clinically depressed reported a remarkable sense of well-being on Prozac; what was more, the medication had acquired a reputation for defying the "street law of drug conservation"—that what goes up must come down. Prozac, according to both Lilly and its consumers, carried neither withdrawal symptoms nor side effects. Across America, in cities and towns, in universities, in office and factory complexes, Prozac was achieving the status, according to *The New York Times*, of a "legal drug culture"; and the moral angst attending these claims was fueling the fires of publicity.

In the first cycle of media interest, the praise and the criticism of the drug had remained within the bounds of the familiar. Was Prozac the best antidepressant ever to have come onto the market? Or did it have insidious side effects, such as making people violent and suicidal? The second cycle of publicity, largely prompted by psychiatrist Peter Kramer's *Listening to Prozac*, published in the summer of 1993, raised a host of ethical and social issues relating to norms of behavior and definitions of human nature itself. Part case histories, part medical philosophy, Kramer's book deliberately set out to create a new focus for the Prozac debate across the nation and into Britain and Europe. "My own sense," he wrote, "was that the media, for all the attention they paid Prozac, had missed the main story. The transformative powers of the medicine— how it went beyond treating illness to changing personality, how it entered into our struggle to understand the self—were nowhere mentioned."

"My concern," he went on, "has been with a subset of . . . fairly healthy people who show dramatic good responses to Prozac, people who are not so much cured of illness as transformed." Here was the ultimate endorsement for a pharmaceutical product: a psychiatrist who claimed that the drug made people feel "better than normal," and without physical or psychological cost. Here, moreover, was the enthusiastic proclamation of a new vision of human identity for the twenty-first century: that personhood is a chemical-software program in the brain, and that it is now within our grasp to rewrite that program should it prove defective.

The implication, as far-reaching as it was extraordinary, was that the pharmaceutical industry, aided and abetted by the medical profession, had the authority and the ability to define, and indeed to procure, norms of psychological well-being in individuals. That implication had already found expression in the relationship between attention-deficit disorder (ADD) and the drug Ritalin, which was being taken by more than a million children at $60 a course in the United States in the early 1990s. ADD, more familiar as hyperactivity, had increasingly been ascribed to children who, in the view of their striving parents, failed to live up to certain standards of behavior and intellectual attainment. According to some researchers, 33 percent of American boys were said to be suffering the syndrome by mid-1994.

To support his thesis concerning the norms of well-being and Prozac, Kramer told some compelling stories about the drug's impact on his own patients.

Tess, the eldest of ten siblings, effectively lost both parents at the age of twelve. An aggressive survivor, she became a surrogate mother and father. Later she made a success of a business career, but her personal life was a disaster: she had a string of affairs with abusive married men and sank into depression. When she went to Kramer, she was suffering from insomnia, melancholy, loss of appetite, guilt, poor memory, and lack of concentration.

After two weeks on Prozac, says Kramer, Tess announced that for the first time in her life she knew what it felt like to have energy. "She had been depressed, it now seemed to her, her whole life. She was astonished at the sensation of being free of depression." With an unaccustomed sense of well-being, she began to cope at work, and started a new social life. "Ordinarily," says Kramer, "change comes gradually if at all. But Tess blossomed all at once."

Kramer pointed out that not all patients reacted in precisely the way Tess did. For some, the drug did nothing; for others, there was merely alleviation of depression. But he was adamant that those suffering from what he calls a "depressive temperament" were transformed in large numbers: "Prozac gives these patients the courage to do what needs to be done."

The idea that a drug could remake the personality of "normal" people gave columnists and commentators a new set of dilemmas to ponder, which in turn resulted in a renewed explosion of publicity. Did it not suggest that we are far more malleable—emotionally, psychologically, even morally—than was ever thought possible? Did it not promote a drastically determinist and reductionist view of human nature? Did it not argue, as one writer put it in *The New York Review of Books*, "that destiny itself can be changed by swallowing the right stuff"?

"He intends, or so it seems," wrote Daniel X. Freedman in *The New York Times Book Review*, "to carefully document the constraints that modern biology and pharmacology have placed on our humanistic image of the self."

For writers like David Rothman in *The New Republic,* there were profound ethical issues to consider: "After Prozac—how do we ever draw a line around the medical or psychiatric domain that will distinguish individual differences from diseases?" In other words, once we accept that we can alter nature's "given," where does it stop? "If shyness is a biologically-determined disease, then why not shortness." "Today," went on Rothman, "we stand and listen to Prozac, tomorrow we will listen to a new hormone, and the day after tomorrow, to a new genetic manipulation."

By late 1993, Prozac had become not so much a hyped pharmaceutical product as an international celebrity. Woody Allen had immortalized it in his film *Manhattan Murder Mystery*: "There's nothing wrong with you," the hero says to his agitated wife, "that can't be cured with a dose of Prozac and a bang over the head with a mallet." But although the sales expanded on the perception that Prozac had ushered in a new era of "cosmetic psychopharmacology," Lilly's reaction was decidedly ambivalent. Though not exactly disowning Peter Kramer's book, Lilly's people were distancing themselves from its more extravagant elements. As the London *Financial Times* reported, after consulting Lilly's public-relations department: "Eli Lilly has deliberately not tried to exploit some of Dr. Kramer's more dramatic claims, pointing out they are not backed by scientific trials. The company does not pretend that Prozac has miraculous qualities."

Lilly's protestations were at first sight odd, since Kramer's book and the attendant publicity had coincided with a rise in sales to $1.3 billion in 1994, a gain from the previous year of about 30 percent. By the spring of 1994, some industry statistics would be ranking it the number-two best selling drug in the world (only behind Glaxo Pharmaceuticals' ulcer-healing drug Zantac).

Lilly guessed in 1993 that the proliferating feature articles, columns, editorials, and even cartoons (like *The New Yorker*'s illustration of the householder who had given Prozac to her jovial-looking cat) could create adverse publicity. According to *The Wall Street Journal*, "Lilly officials said they worry these sound bites will deter patients with grave clinical depression from taking their disorder seriously and seeking treatment. They also worry that publicity belittling or overselling Prozac could hurt efforts to include mental illness in a national health plan."

In the spring of 1994, in an attempt to bring Prozac's "celebrity" status under control, Lilly launched an unprecedented campaign of "advertorials" in a number of top medical journals and trade publications deploring the media's role in "trivializing" the illness of depression. "Prozac is intended, as are all Lilly medicines," said the sober item of copy, "for use only where a clear medical need exists and when the scientific data have determined safety and effectiveness."

At the same time, Lilly's public-relations department distributed an article from *The Saturday Evening Post* entitled "Seeking the Wizards of Prozac," by Tracy Thompson, a writer whose thirty-year depression had been transformed by the drug. Her adulatory piece, giving Lilly's scientists the opportunity to present the drug to the reading public through authentic editorial copy, provides an interesting insight into how Lilly wished Prozac, its inventors, and its consumers to be viewed as the latest round of superhype settled down.

In her second paragraph, Thompson conjures up a metaphor characteristic of the new psychopharmacology: "Serotonin is a neurotransmitter," she writes, "the bicycle courier of the brain, shuttling electrical impulses from one nerve to another. With less serotonin being absorbed, more of it will be pedaling around up there, delivering tiny jolts of electricity from nerve to nerve. You could say this little green and white capsule [Prozac] is about to ratchet up the voltage in my head. And, in some way—no one knows precisely how—this will help me feel better. Happier. Without nameless anxiety, able to take pleasure in ordinary things. Sane."

It becomes apparent early in her article that Tracy Thompson was given a red carpet at Eli Lilly's headquarters in Indianapolis, where she toured the laboratories and met Prozac's inventors—Drs. Moody, Wong, and Fuller—who had, she notes, "a genial, pastoral demeanor—a bit like Sunday schoolteachers, or small-town family doctors." The mood and substance of this encounter, at once homespun and religious, has interesting parallels with Kramer's observation that Prozac is "transformative in the way an inspirational minister . . . can be."

Fuller had told Thompson that both he and Wong "shared a boyhood dream to become seminarians"; instead they had become priests of an altogether different kind: the dispensers of spiritual beneficence through their psychopharmacological creation. When Fuller smiles, says Thompson, it makes "him look very much like a Presbyterian minister." "Except," she goes on, "that in his theology, the soul is a collection of cells, if a dauntingly complex one. . . . Fuller quotes one of his scientific predecessors, neuroscientist Ralph Gerard: 'Behind every crooked thought, there lies a crooked molecule.' So, I ask, are we just fooling ourselves to think we are able to reason our way out of despair? Is there a chemical for every sadness?"

Fuller's answer is that every sadness *is,* undeniably, chemical. "There was an experiment," he explains, "in which damselfish were kept in a tank with only a transparent wall between some big predator fish. The damselfish had every reason to think they were about to be eaten. After a while, the serotonin levels in their brains showed a marked decrease. It's illustrative, in a crude way. Loss, anxiety, repeated rejection—things we experience do cause neurochemical changes in the brain."

Behind Lilly's initiatives to manipulate media attitudes toward Prozac was a deepening anxiety about the company's future, despite the huge volume of Prozac sales. The year 1994 saw Lilly's executives in a state of acute insecurity about the company's fiscal future. In a period in which the industry's predicted annual earnings growth was set to decelerate from an average 18 percent down to 11 percent through 1997, Lilly realized that it had become too dependent on a single product, which itself had competitors (there were at least two rival companies seeking regulatory approval for other SSRIs).

In consequence, Lilly had made the momentous decision in July 1994 to purchase PCS Inc.—the biggest pharmacy benefit manager in the United States—from the McKesson Corporation for $4 billion. The pharmacy benefit managers buy drugs at a discount, creating a buffer between the manufacturers and the physicians. They offer a variety of computerized health-plan services, from advice about weight loss to plans for exercise and stress reduction. PCS was administering some 320 million prescriptions a year and had fifty-five thousand retail pharmacies linked to its mainframe computer system, potentially permitting the implementation of sophisticated disease-management programs for millions of patients. The purchase of such a business meant that Lilly would now become in effect a customer for its own drugs (a consideration that would in time and for obvious reasons alert the antitrust watchdogs). Although the deal cost a staggering 130 times PCS's annual earnings (and resulted in a plunge of Lilly stock of 13 percent), Lilly thought it worth the gamble in order to ensure consumer selection of its products and to ward off a similar move on the part of others. The previous year, Merck and SmithKline Beecham had bought two other benefit managers for a total of $9 billion (Glaxo and Johnson & Johnson, it was rumored, had themselves been considering a joint offer for PCS in the meantime).

The purchase, which Lilly had described as its "latest and boldest" strategy (plunging the company into $2.5 billion debt), was precisely to take advantage of its new leadership of the antidepressant market while Prozac was still on the rise. According to Lilly's sales chief, Mitch Daniels, depression costs society $44 billion a year in the United States (including treatment, mortality, lost productivity, and absenteeism). By highlighting these costs through their own far-reaching disease-management program, he believed, there was a potential for a $600-million increase in the annual sales of Prozac.

In the summer of 1994, Lilly had much to lose should its reputation as a manufacturer of safe and efficacious drugs suffer a setback. The ever-present danger of adverse events was amply illustrated on May 11, 1994, when the FDA sent a warning letter to Lilly indicating that it had broken federal regulations when conducting human experiments on the drug fialuridine (FIAU). The FDA's action followed an investigation in which multiple "deviations from good . . . clinical practices" were uncovered. FIAU was tested in the early 1990s on patients suffering chronic hepatitis; the trial was stopped in 1993, five patients had died and others suffered severe illness.

As of June 11, 1994, one lawsuit against Lilly had been instigated as as result of the death of one patient, and four other suits were expected. The FIAU problem loomed with the Oraflex debacle as potential testimony in the forthcoming trial in Louisville.

As Lilly prepared to go to trial in the autumn of 1994, it seemed to stand at a crossroads in its fortunes. Projections for the sale of all its products were moving toward $6.5 billion for 1995 and beyond, with $1.7 billion accounted for by Prozac alone. Although Prozac had its rivals, the drug had become synonymous with the new range of SSRIs; in fact, Prozac was becoming synonymous with antidepressant drugs of any kind. With some ten million patients having used the drug in the United States alone (out of a national market universe estimated at fifteen million), the prospects looked rosy indeed, but the biggest rewards were still overseas, where Prozac had now won regulatory approval in seventy countries.

If Lilly had settled the Louisville case out of court, it would only have created uncertainty about the drug and emboldened the plaintiffs in other pending suits, the number of which had now swollen to 160. Lilly was therefore keen to present its case before a jury—but it was under no illusion about the risks.

Winning the case convincingly would give Lilly a powerful promotional gambit to demonstrate to the world that the drug stood vindicated by jury verdict. The consequences of a loss, on the other hand, could be catastrophic indeed; close to a third of future revenues could disappear overnight, and the hugely debt-laden company would be swamped with open-ended damages claims into the foreseeable future. Lilly, with $6.5 billion in annual earnings and twenty-eight thousand employees, could not afford to lose the Louisville Prozac case.

15

LOUISVILLIANS ARE PASSIONATE about horses: horse breeding, horse racing, and gambling. They pace their year by the track and equestrian events out on Churchill Downs—Derby weekend, the Arabian Horse Show, Breeder's Cup week.

It was about the time of the Fall's Meet in October 1994 that Louisvillians were reminded once more of the horrifying incident of September 14, 1989; alongside form notes, and autumnal announcements for the Jaycees' Octoberfest, reports began to appear in the *Courier-Journal* of the liability trial at the Old Jailhouse Building on Jefferson Square.

The plaintiffs were the twenty-seven principal survivors and relatives of the dead in the Standard Gravure shootings; and the defendant was Eli Lilly and Company, the manufacturer of Prozac (Standard Gravure, Hall Security, and Dr. Lee Coleman were not being sued for damages, but they could be accorded a percentage of liability and thus remained unrepresented defendants in the trial).

It had taken the attorneys two weeks to choose a jury of sixteen Jefferson County folk from a pool of two hundred. (The case would be decided by twelve, but alternates were of course needed.) Among these jurors, who included at least three college graduates, were several strikingly matched pairs. There were two young white men with dark hair and mustaches; two middle-aged African-American women wearing ornate glasses; two bald men in their sixties; two elderly white women with permed white hair who sat on their own in the third row like twin sisters.

One juror who stuck out from the rest was an elderly gentleman with a hearing aid who sat gazing at the proceedings with an air of bafflement, his top pocket filled with pens which he never used. By contrast, there was an inscrutable stout woman in early middle age who would scribble hour after hour on yellow legal pads, never raising her head.

All were modestly dressed; only one of the men wore a tie—Mr. Holiford, the foreman of the jury, a stern-looking fellow in his sixties who leaned heavily on a walking stick.

It was known, by reliable rumor, that among the jurors were a chemistry-laboratory technician, a teacher, a secretary, five retired women, two retired men, and a truck driver. One of the young male jurors, it later became apparent, was a gun collector and possessed every model of AK-47 ever manufactured.

The front four rows of the audience were largely occupied by the wounded, and the relatives of the dead. Angela Bowman, who wore her auburn hair in a bob, was wheeled into the building daily. She sat in one of the aisles on the side of the plaintiffs, her appealing heart-shaped face and large sorrowful eyes clearly visible to the jury and the public spectators alike. Three of the wounded pressman, John Stein, Mike Campbell, and Andrew Pointer—the only African American in the group (he always sat with his wife, away from the others)—supported themselves on canes.

There were several suited Lilly lawyers and public-relations executives among the sundry visiting attorneys in the audience, but the proceedings had attracted no journalists apart from Leslie Scanlon, court reporter for the *Courier-Journal*, and the Court TV reporter Karen Myatt, who watched from a TV monitor up on the third floor of the building.

The absence of journalists was largely explained by the media's preoccupation with the O. J. Simpson trial in Los Angeles. But the presiding judge, John Potter, and Eli Lilly were eager for the trial to remain low-profile, and had done nothing to attract attention to the proceedings and everything to discourage it. Potter said to me later, "Why are you-all so interested in this business? It's just an itsy-bitsy trial in an itsy-bitsy town." Leslie Scanlon told me, "Potter sees what's happening in Los Angeles, and he's determined that his court won't become a circus." Lilly, of course, had their own, obvious reasons for playing down the trial.

Judge John Potter, fifty-two, a rangy local with unruly sandy hair and a rubicund complexion, had been on the circuit since the age of thirty-eight. He had a reputation for being a "colorful character" given to homespun nostrums and lurid bow ties. In a chambers discussion he had told the attorneys: "I do fine on decisions if there's right or wrong or I can see a logical decision, but when it comes to discretionary decisions, I have an awfully bad habit of, if I see something is too easy or the popular way out of something, I resist it."

Early in the trial, Potter remarked: "There's a person here in Louisville who has a saying that they're frequently wrong but never in doubt. I kind of am the other way around. I'm always in doubt and I try to be wrong as infrequently as possible."

As Ed West, Lilly's head of public relations, would say with a wry smile: "We've gotten ourselves the only antiestablishment judge in the whole of Kentucky." Little did Lilly realize in October 1994 just how troublesome Judge Potter could be.

In a laconic, head-patting pep talk at the outset, Potter told the jurors: "You-all don't realize it that you-all have little antennae out to pick up absolutely every clue. . . . And you're supposed to decide the case on what happens here in the courtroom. Okay? One of things you're not supposed to do is try and read this case by what *I* do. Okay? If I come in here in a bad mood, it's not because the case is going badly or somebody didn't do well, it's because my cat got sick the night before. All right?"

The jurors appreciated Judge Potter's common touch and his humor. They had less cause to applaud his reluctance to guide them through the major issues of responsibility that would be debated in this trial.

The civil-liability trial is a peculiarly American psychodrama shaped by powerful contemporary trends. Not least is the practice of contingency arrangements in civil litigation, whereby the plaintiff's lawyer bears the risk of paying the costs, should the client lose, in exchange for the chance of earning up to 50 percent of the damages awarded, plus costs and fees, should the client win. In the American system, moreover, litigants on both sides—winners and losers—bear their own costs of bringing and defending an action; whereas in most other Western legal systems the loser not only bears his own costs but is ordered to pay the winner's costs as well.

The advantage of the "American rule" is that it removes the element of financial risk on the part of plaintiffs; but the system can lead to a great many unjustified and frivolous suits bearing little or no relation to authentic responsibility.

American lawyers justify their prodigious share of damage awards by arguing that they must be compensated not only for the cases they win, but for those they lose. Personal-injury and product-liability lawyers are thus in the business of evaluating odds and spreading the risks among a large number of cases, some of which may be extremely marginal. Many cases do not make it to court, since defendants often reckon it better to settle even though they believe themselves to be in the right. Thus the American system encourages tort (civil-wrongdoing) litigation as if it were a kind of gambling, resulting in a widespread erosion of responsibility as well as distortions in the understanding of causation.

There have, of course, been justified actions in plenty, such as the litigation against Ford Motor Company following the Kentucky school-bus crash in 1988, the Thalidomide litigation of the 1960s and '70s, and more recently the Dalkon Shield, breast-implant, and asbestosis actions, in which genuine grievances have been doggedly pursued and somewhat redressed.

By the same token, however, the courts are logjammed with frivolous and amoral suits, many of which succeed at least to the extent of out-of-court settlement. Many actions are against corporations, like the McDonald's scalding-coffee suit, but there has been a proliferation also of suits against individuals: the grandmother found liable because her son-in-law slipped and broke an ankle on her carpet; the barman sued because he gave that final drink that "made" the lush kill his wife; the parked driver faced with million-dollar damages because a careless driver suffered whiplash while ramming her from behind.

The excuse for resorting to litigation in such instances, even against friends and close relatives, is that it is "business, not personal": a notion further encouraged by the reflection that damages are paid not by individuals, and seldom even by corporations, but by the insurance companies.

The quest for a suitable target for damages following the Louisville shootings was attended by the assumption that Wesbecker himself should be excused of all responsibility for *his* actions. The tendency in America to absolve a criminal of responsibility on the grounds that another party "caused" his actions has been described by Alan Dershowitz, defense lawyer and Harvard Law School professor, as a legal tactic that is "becoming a license to kill and maim as more and more defense lawyers are employing it and more and more jurors are buying it."

A classic instance in recent American legal history, "The Twinkie Defense," has entered the national psyche as a byword for the ultimate copout. In 1978, Dan White, a former police officer, walked into City Hall in San Francisco and shot dead Mayor George Moscone and Supervisor Harvey Milk. But White was found guilty of involuntary manslaughter after the jury accepted that his actions were caused by the consumption of a large number of Twinkie cupcakes on the morning of the incident.

Similar "excuse" syndromes have become a familiar feature of American criminal trials, widely reported in the news media—their effects percolating through to corresponding civil actions. "Vietnam Syndrome," or post-traumatic combat stress—rendering a defendant incapable of distinguishing right from wrong, has been used on a number of occasions to exculpate first-degree murder. "Urban Survival Syndrome" was invoked in the 1994 Texas trial of Damian Osby, accused of murdering two brothers; the defense claimed that the violent conditions of the killer's neighborhood made him shoot the two men, and the case resulted in a mistrial. "Parental Abuse Syndrome" was used in the Menendez brothers' case, which also resulted in a mistrial, in 1994. "Multiple Personality Disorder," the fragmentation of personality as a result of sexual abuse, has frequently been invoked, most notably in 1994, when James Carlson of Arizona claimed to have eleven separate personalities, only one of which was aware of the crime of sexual assault with which he had been charged.

The legal opinion underpinning these appeals to deterministic behavior is the so-called Durham decision (District of Columbia Court of Appeals, 1954) that people can be ruled not guilty of a crime by reason of "irresistible impulse." The means by which a jury will be assisted to such a decision is the testimony of "expert witnesses," who will argue any hypothesis eloquently and with ample technical information if paid to do so.

But the willingness of lawyers to use such arguments, and of jurors to accept them, indicates a significant sea-change in American thinking about notions of responsibility. Tort litigation may well be contributing to a flight from traditional notions.

According to the psychologist Robyn Dawes, "The Durham decision recognized a change in our views. A feeling strong enough to achieve the status of an 'irresistible impulse' could in and of itself determine a behavior. Hence the person who experienced this feeling was not responsible. This change mirrored changes in our views of such problems as alcoholism, drug addiction, and crime: note that I say 'problems' not evils."

An eminent research psychologist recently observed, "There are now dozens of distinguishable theories of emotionality, hundreds of volumes devoted to that topic, and tens of thousands of articles dealing with various aspects of human affect [feeling]." A daunting reflection for jurors required to make judgments on the links between states of mind and causes of action.

The new emphasis in American society on feeling and emotion, as opposed to "reason," as suggested by Dawes, points up the contrast between the Durham decision and the traditional M'Naughten ruling originally made in the British House of Lords in 1843—and widely endorsed in the Anglo-American legal world—which held that those people who *understand* the nature of right and wrong are to be deemed responsible for their actions, whereas those who could plead a suspension of rationality are entitled to be absolved of personal responsibility.

Much would depend in this trial on arguments about Wesbecker's mental state, what caused it, and what were its consequences. The jury would hear complex arguments appealing to nature and nurture, marital problems, stress at work, personality disorders, and distinctions between psychosis and neurosis. They would hear, by the end of the trial, eloquent appeals to traditional notions about moral agency and human autonomy. More crucially, and perhaps unprecedentedly, they would hear testimony about state-of-the-art neuroscience and biology of the emotions, suggesting that the biochemistry of Wesbecker's brain could explain the disordered molecules that caused his aberrant behavior.

At the same time, they would be asked to follow, over a number of weeks, highly complex maneuvers in the clinical trials of Prozac, involving abstruse statistics and finely balanced arguments about statistical "massaging." They would be asked, in the end, whether Prozac had been a substantial cause in Wesbecker's actions on September 14, 1989, with the myriad implications that lay beneath that proposition.

The practice of deciding such a highly technical case by jury has raised serious questions about a jury's ability to exercise a sufficiently informed judgment to reach a fair verdict.

The advantage of juries in civil cases involving personal-injury liability is that jurors are supposedly more impartial than a judge. Civil cases, moreover, invariably involve the principle of how the community wishes people to behave toward each other. It was precisely this consideration that led to the ratification of the Seventh Amendment to the Constitution, guaranteeing jury trial in civil cases.

And yet, as Stephen J. Adler, legal editor of *The Wall Street Journal*, comments: "What if a jury doesn't have any idea what the lawyers are talking about? What good is a system in which jurors reach their verdicts through favoritism, prejudice, or even guesswork because they don't understand the issues? That's what many lawyers and judges, particularly those with close ties to the business community, have been wondering for the past thirty years or more."

As the Louisville jury began their duties in the trial against Eli Lilly, they were as yet unaware of the tangled web of technical material and baffling interconnections of cause and liability that would be spun in the coming weeks. Nor had Judge Potter seen fit to issue general directions as to what they might deem illegal in the various parties' actions, or what tests they must apply to decide such questions.

Should they not have been alerted, from the very outset, as to a person's or a company's duty not to harm another person? Should they not have been aware, for example, that an employer has a duty to provide adequate security in a place of work, especially after violent threats have been issued by a known person? Should they not have received direction about a pharmaceutical company's duty not to have harmed the plaintiffs by manufacturing and distributing defective drugs, or drugs with inadequate package warnings, that could result in a co-worker's running amok with an AK-47?

And in relation to Wesbecker himself, should the jurors not have been apprised of the distinction between "irresistible impulse," on the one hand, and a capacity to understand and act upon moral choices, on the other? And should they not have been advised as to the basis on which they were entitled to make judgments about that capacity or the lack of it?

"Jurors can't function effectively," comments Stephen Adler in his book *The Jury*, "if they don't understand from the very start what laws have allegedly been broken, the meaning of key terminology, and how witnesses' testimony is intended to relate to the charges. Yet court procedures dictate that jurors won't be briefed on these issues, if at all, until after all the evidence is in."

So matters stood at the outset of the Prozac trial in Louisville, Kentucky.

16

ED STOPHER LATER ADMITTED that Paul Smith's opening was the "most powerful thing I've ever heard in a courtroom: it was dynamite . . . and the presence of the plaintiffs was the most powerful thing I've ever *seen* in the courtroom."

In the first fifteen to twenty minutes, however, Smith made a rather different impression on all present.

Dressed in a navy-blue suit, a cream shirt, and a garish tie with abstract emblems, Smith started by attempting to make friends with the jurors. He informed them that, in their efforts to understand the science of the case, he and Ms. Zettler had "probably spent more time with each other than we have with our respective spouses," a reflection that may well have misfired with the more staid members of the jury.

The remark was typical of the irreverent Texan approach that would carry him through the next eleven weeks.

He began by attempting a description of Wesbecker's depression in terms of a physical disorder of the brain. "Scientists believe that the cause of this type of depression may be a result of an imbalance of the chemicals in our brain. Our brain has many chemicals and is made up of a bunch of nerves and a bunch of fibers, and apparently these chemicals help in the transmission of these thoughts from one nerve to the other. This is called neurotransmission."

As Smith reached this point, he seemed to quail at the prospect of continuing. "It's extremely complicated," he warned. "I don't understand it, and, believe me, you won't understand it when we get completely finished, so don't feel bad about that. . . ."

But the disclaimer was merely a prelude to a deeper plunge into a vulgarized description of the neurotransmitter serotonin itself.

"Serotonin is a chemical," Smith went on. "But there are specific nerve cells in the brain that make this chemical, and there are specific nerve cells in the brain that receive this chemical. Apparently, the serotonin system goes almost completely through the brain. This one neurotransmitter transmitting thought, serotonin, only picks up particular electrical nerve impulses. . . ."

At this point, just a few minutes into his exposition, Smith seemed to be going to pieces before the court's eyes. "The point is . . ." he stumbled on, "it's difficult to understand. . . . The point is . . . that this serotonin system encompasses and affects an individual's entire brain. The thought is. . . . that this clinical depression that we see so much about, that we hear so much about that . . . Joseph Wesbecker suffered from . . . is a result of an imbalance in the serotonin system in depressed individuals' brains."

With the aid of a chart, Smith now attempted to give the jurors their first lesson in the biology of the brain: how one brain cell communicates with another.

"You have a presynaptic nerve end," he started, "and you have a postsynaptic nerve end. There is in fact a space, an empty space, between the two nerve ends of the two neurons. They're called neurons. And the . . . you've got . . . It's like a bridge or a string or something and you've got a gap here. And what you have is, you have an electrical impulse with thought; thought being transmitted via electrical impulses that are picked up by these serotonin cells."

Having got, disastrously, thus far, his exposition seemed about to fall to pieces yet again. "The serotonin cells then . . ." He stopped; corrected himself: "It's not cells."

Then he started again: "The point is, is to get the thought from this side to this side, and the way serotonin does it is by traveling across. . . . The thought travels across here and it falls into a receptor site. All right?"

According to Leslie Scanlon of the *Courier-Journal*, one of Lilly's public-relations team who had been sitting behind her leaned over and whispered, "Doesn't it make you sick, the spectacle of Paul Smith blundering around trying to explain a bit of basic neuroscience?"

Smith's attempt to describe the science of the brain to the jury never got worse than this, although it would get a great deal better. More to the point, he never lost his nerve; he persevered in demonstrating to the jury what he understood to be the case in his own words, while never giving the impression that he was talking down to them from a great height—an important factor in a trial that was as much about scientific hubris as about a pharmaceutical product and mass murder.

Moving on now to the purpose of Prozac, which he described as "to stop all the serotonin being reabsorbed and lowering the level," he produced an image designed to put all this difficult science in its place. He was attempting to describe the theory underlying the lowering of serotonin levels in the brain cells of the depressed, and how Prozac can alleviate the problem:

"Now, I know this is difficult for me to explain . . ." he was saying. "It's like you have a bucket and you've got a constant stream in that bucket and you've got a hole in the bottom of the bucket. There is a smaller hole at the end, so you've always got a level of liquid in that bucket, but if you stop up the hole and have the same amount of fluid coming in, you're going to increase the level of serotonin; the theory being if you increase the level of serotonin you increase the mood."

Having stated that Prozac was an artificial substance invented and patented by Lilly ("not something that grows on trees"), Smith explained that before it could be marketed, Prozac required FDA approval—"this is what is called the clinical trials, the testing phase of Prozac."

At this point, Smith seemed to relax more, and his folksy approach to the material enabled him to communicate his basic strategy with greater clarity and emphasis: "I believed when I started this case," he said, "that FDA approval meant that a drug had been tested by the Food and Drug Administration in Washington. . . . I believed that they had actually gotten their scientists, their doctors, their chemists, and their people, the FDA people, to put this drug under the microscope. . . . I bet that you aren't any different than me in your belief that I started out with, that the FDA actually tested this drug. . . . But that's not TRUE!"

Smith was now going to the heart of the plaintiffs' case: that FDA approval is not dependent upon tests it does itself, that the FDA must take on trust the data supplied by the manufacturer.

As Smith expanded his argument, he told them he would establish that some people experience extreme agitation when started on Prozac, and that, if this effect occurs before a patient's mood improves, the patient can become violent against himself or others. This had been Joe Wesbecker's problem with Prozac, he told them.

He would demonstrate, he told them, that the German government agency that approves drugs recognized this danger. As a result, he said, the German package insert for Prozac warned doctors to observe patients closely and to consider prescribing a sedative during the initial period. No such warning, he informed them, had been given in the United States.

What Smith could not tell the jury and the court was that, in his view, the Wesbecker case recalled the Oraflex incident ten years earlier, when Lilly had pleaded guilty to twenty-five counts of misdemeanor relating to misbranding and mislabeling.

Before the trial began, Potter had ruled out the Oraflex story, on the principle that Lilly had not been called to defend their conduct in that incident and that any attempt to cite it would be unduly prejudicial.

Potter had made it understood, however, that Lilly might well open the door to the testimony should they repeatedly stress the irreproachable standards of their clinical trials. Hence, Smith and Zettler's aim was to tempt Lilly into making glowing claims for their testing procedures.

In his opening statement, Smith had already made a start on luring them into that trap. In withering short sentences, delivered with all the orotund Texan emphasis he could muster, Smith drove home the point: "The FDA itself doesn't test pharmaceutical products in this country. The FDA didn't test Prozac. The National Institute of Mental health didn't test Prozac. The Centers of Disease Control didn't test Prozac. . . . ELI LILLY AND COMPANY TESTED PROZAC. The inventor of the drug, the proponent of the application for Food and Drug [Administration] approval tested the drug. . . . Lilly set up the rules and guidelines for what people could be included in the test. The tests were conducted exclusively by Eli Lilly. The trial process was done by Lilly at their guidance, direction, and control."

Turning to the life and character of Wesbecker, Smith predicted that the defendants would attempt to attack the man himself: "What we expect Lilly to do," he said scornfully, "is not defend their drug, because we frankly think the evidence will show that this problem with this drug is indefensible. What they're going to try to do is attack the patient."

At the end of his opening argument, Smith took a little time to undermine in advance any attempt the defense might make to extend sympathy to the plaintiffs, indicating the importance of the emotional issues in the case.

"I want to tell you something real important," said Smith in confidential tones. "Mr. Stopher, the lawyer for Lilly, has talked about the sympathy factor in this case and talked about the tragedy and how he agreed that this was a tragic situation and that these were nice people. These people don't *want* your sympathy. That's not what they're here for. That's not what your job is. Fortunately, they have their own families that have given them some support."

Lilly had decided to split their opening statement: Ed Stopher tackling the question of Joe Wesbecker, and co-counsel Joe Freeman tackling the defense of Prozac.

Ed Stopher's style was more measured, more ponderous and decidedly less colorful than Paul Smith's. His opening paragraph, in fact, seemed to convey something of the enormous weight of those four hundred depositions he had been collecting for the past four years.

Stopher was a trifle stooped and heavy about the jowls; his expression was impassive and somewhat owlish in his horn-rimmed glasses. Dressed this day in a shapeless dark suit and nondescript tie (his wife, he told me later, frequently criticized his unadventurous wardrobe), Stopher introduced his strategy in sepulchral tones:

"Joseph Wesbecker's attack on Standard Gravure on September 14, 1989," he began, "was not the act of a man suddenly turned mad by Prozac. . . . It was the final chapter in a very complex life, filled with hostility, fueled by job stress. It grew out of a life twisted by insidious mental illness. It was generated out of a lifetime of estrangements and isolation, and hostile withdrawals from spouses, parents, children, friends, co-workers and bosses."

For the next hour or so, Stopher reviewed the life of Joe Wesbecker, isolating those facts that would show that "this was a premeditated massacre that Wesbecker was going to commit regardless of whether he took Prozac or not."

Wesbecker's act, he said, was "inevitable," and he painted a portrait of this inevitable killer living alone and in a state of degradation. As he worked on his description, it was reminiscent, perhaps deliberately so, of the final months of Robert de Niro's killer in *Taxi Driver*:

"That last year, he sat in his home alone with no water, no phone, with the drapes drawn, with his weapons there, and carefully planned his assault day after day and his own suicide before he ever took Prozac." Stopher went on: "He peed in a can in his bedroom, went to a restaurant to have bowel movements, and didn't shave or bathe."

Without mentioning the words "crazy" or "mad," Stopher skillfully suggested that Wesbecker had been unhinged over a period of at least twelve months: "During that last year," he said, "when he was not on Prozac, he kept the drapes drawn and he acquired written materials on mass murder, mass murderers, and assault rifles. . . ."

Wesbecker's actions on September 14, 1989, Stopher said, "were the final steps in a lifelong journey of disintegration, an extreme reflection of alienation, hostility, and mental illness which he had been fighting all of his life. . . . His intention was to kill the company."

Ed Stopher's version of Joe Wesbecker's life did not stray from any of the known facts recorded in the lengthy depositions, but his selection of the highlights harped exclusively on vengeful and violent details; on details relating to obsessive interest in guns; on spoken threats, major and minor; on intemperate outbursts at work and at home. By the same token, there was no mention of Wesbecker's redeeming qualities, or his struggles to lead a decent life, or the remarkable catalogue of workplace victimization.

Stopher's portrait of Joe Wesbecker was a classic narrative of a life wholly determined by the disastrous influences of his early upbringing and the development of a hereditary depressive disease. He made no mention of neuroscience or brain chemistry; nor did he make a link between Wesbecker's depression and Prozac.

Finally, he told the jury: "This is a painful story to everyone in this room, most especially these good people to my left, but it is a story that began long before Prozac. It is not a story that is causally related to Prozac but it is related to a man of vengeance, a man of hostility, a man of anger, and a man of deterioration not caused by the medication."

It was left to Joe Freeman to pick up the Prozac dimension and outline the defense's scientific strategy. Freeman, a man in his mid-fifties with a strong Georgia accent, was bespectacled and somewhat overweight. His brow was permanently furrowed, as if by an inner anxiety.

"Depression is a mental state," he began in a stentorian voice, "that becomes a disease, and it is so disabling and disarming that, if it were a choice between depression and a heart attack, people say they'd take the heart attack."

The brain, he told the jury, "is like a complex telephone system with lines and messages going back and forth being received and sent." Warming to his theme, he avoided the sort of single-cell description that had pitched Smith into disaster, and went for an explication of the brain in terms of numerosity.

"The brain," he said, "is made up of many neurons or what we might call major lines through which messages are sent and received by what we call neurotransmitters. Now, there are a lot of them. There are many, many, many neurons and there are many, many, many neuro-transmitters and they are of different shapes and kinds in terms of being received by the proper neuron."

He told the jury that serotonin was "used" in sending "messages," and that a low level of serotonin "causes" depression. Prozac, he said, was invented by Lilly scientists to combat the problem caused by such lower levels.

"They decided they were going to find, if they possibly could, a clean—*now, listen to this*—a clean compound and a selective compound that would affect only serotonin and bring the system of the depressed person back into balance."

Thus Freeman introduced the concept of the *selective* reuptake inhibitor. "Selective," he explained, "because if it's not selective it's just shooting all over the lot."

But what of the notion of *inhibiting*? Freeman had an extraordinary image for the jury: "Remember me talking about the pump? That I like to think about as the mother neuron or the neuron that creates the serotonin chemical that sends these messages to start with. They figured out a way to inhibit that pump from reuptake of the serotonin that was sending these messages and to balance out the system, but they left in place the sense like a mother has when the child is full, the sense that that neuron, a presynaptic neuron, had or that mother had when there was enough out there for her baby to eat or to get those messages—she stopped sending the food. She stopped sending more neurons. And over here on the other side they stopped demanding for more because there was enough there and there was a balance there and there was a help there for those people who had been so drastically sick."

It was a curiously garbled exposition for an attorney on whose performance depended the future of a $6.5-billion-per-annum company. But as Freeman turned his attention to the FDA and the clinical trials, he got increasingly testy. "Mr. Smith," he hectored the jury, "wants to make out like the FDA is a bunch of halfwits that are sitting up in Washington doing nothing, depending on what Lilly says. . . . The FDA overlook everything that you do and second-guess everything that you do. And you have to dot every 'i' and cross every 't' or they are down your throat every two or three seconds."

Freeman's peroration, when it came, was a strange digression from his theme. Abandoning the question of Prozac, he took a sudden lunge at Standard Gravure. "He [Wesbecker] was furious with these people," he said (with no explanation as to who "these people" were). "He was mad as hell, then. He had been buying weapons and everything else. When he got off it, they wrote him this mean letter, and they said not only are we going to cut you to $391, if you want to keep your insurance, we're going to take out on you $78. We don't give a dern if your grandmother just died, the only person that ever cared a thing on earth about you. You are a thing and we do not care."

Since Wesbecker's grandmother had died a full six months after the receipt of the letter Freeman was referring to, this was a strange connection; but he was suddenly back to his former theme as he uttered the final sentences of his opening argument:

"And the plaintiffs in this case I believe will not make any connection or any—make any proof that the drug was defective by way of design or manufacture but will only claim that something was wrong with the market warning or they may try to shotgun it. . . . But when you get down to it, ladies and gentlemen, I respectfully suggest to you that the verdict in this case should be 'we the jury find in favor of the defendant, Eli Lilly and Company,' and that I ask each of you so to do."

Gathering the attorneys in chambers, Judge Potter told them he had "a feeling for the case." Then he said, in his homey way, "You-all have got your battle lines drawn and each side has more than just something to sell; and I think the jury paid attention and they do, too."

The headline that was prepared that evening for the Metro Section of the next day's *Courier-Journal* under Leslie Scanlon's byline was: "Prozac Trial Opens with Focus on the Drug, Wesbecker: It's History of Killer vs. History of Antidepressant." The piece went out on the Gannett newswire, but it attracted no attention. It would take Reuters another month to get around to carrying a small item on the opening of the trial in its Business Report.

17

THOUGH THE "PROZAC TRIAL" had received scant attention in the press or on the news services, two events alarmed Paul Smith and gave him cause to raise the issue of media coverage with the judge.

On Sunday evening, October 2, there was a demonstration in Jefferson Square, before the courthouse. Scores of people who claimed they were suffering depression had turned up bearing lighted candles; several TV journalists, forewarned of the event, interviewed the participants. The demonstrators said that they were on Prozac and were there to conduct a "vigil." One of them said, "We hope that this lawsuit doesn't take our drug away."

Smith told the judge there had been TV news coverage late that night and the following morning adverse to the plaintiffs' case. Would he tell the jurors, he asked Potter, that they should not watch "any news programs at all"? Potter agreed to do so.

The second incident was the simultaneous appearance of two articles profiling the plaintiffs' star expert witness—the psychiatrist Dr. Peter Breggin, who was due to attack Lilly and Prozac vigorously in his testimony during the following weeks. One article in *The New York Times Magazine*, Smith informed the judge, had characterized the psychiatrist as an opportunist who would do anything to make money. The other, in *Time* magazine for October 10 (already available by October 3), carried a prominent article on Breggin in which a banner headline proclaimed, "His critics say that he's crazy."

Smith wanted the jury to be forbidden such reading matter. What Smith had clearly not grasped was how these items originated, and why they had appeared coincidentally at this particular time.

The ostensible reason for *Time*'s coverage of the psychiatrist was the appearance that summer of Breggin's book *Talking Back to Prozac*, a reply to Kramer's *Listening to Prozac*. But the author of the *Time* article, Christine Gorman, had unwittingly given the real game away. Buried in her piece was the information that Eli Lilly had been "deluging" journalists across America with material on Dr. Breggin in order "to discredit the maverick psychiatrist." In their attempts to find such discreditable material, Gorman informed her readers, "Lilly has combed through his old books and articles in search of anything embarrassing— just like the conservatives who used Lani Guinier's writings to scuttle her nomination to serve in the Justice Department."

What Lilly had dug up on Breggin, finessed out of earlier writings, purported to reveal that he believed in child sex and thought that American psychiatry had been invented by the Nazis.

The *Time* journalist had not appreciated, however, the coincidence of the appearance of Lilly's press kit and the beginning of the Louisville trial.

Smith's plea, as it happened, would prompt Judge Potter to tell the jury he would "expand a little bit" his usual admonition about the press. At pains not to mention the magazines by name, he gave the jurors a pep talk. "You should not only avoid reading something about this trial but avoid anything," he told them. "You know, articles on Prozac or drugs or antidepressants. . . . They range all the way from cover articles with a baby with three heads, man from Mars, those type magazines up to . . . or reputable magazines."

During the cloudless early days of October, those attending the "Prozac Trial" in Louisville's Old Jailhouse Building relived the shootings and killings of the Standard Gravure incident. The testimony seemed a necessary process of catharsis for many of the plaintiffs, who frequently wept and hugged each other as one survivor followed another onto the witness stand.

This was a particularly difficult stage of the proceedings for Lilly, with Paul Smith exploiting the testimony of each plaintiff in turn to elicit the jurors' sympathy. Ed Stopher, as he later told me, much as he was conscious that some of the plaintiffs' witnesses were aware of the persecution of Wesbecker at work, curbed his cross-examinations lest he seem callous.

On the first day of testimony—Monday, October 3—Paul Smith called Angela Bowman. Sitting in her wheelchair, dressed in a pale-blue warmup suit, she wept frequently as she vividly described how she and Sharon Needy were shot on the morning of September 14, 1989. There were few dry eyes in the court by the end of her story, and even the attorneys for the defense were visibly moved. But the jury appeared curiously indifferent.

Paul Smith told me later that he thought the jurors' faces were "like stone." When I interviewed one of them six months after the trial had ended, she told me, "We were all crying inside, but we were determined not to show what we were feeling, because we knew that we should try to look impartial. . . . Many of us cried later in the restroom."

Bowman was followed by Paula Warman, the forty-six-year-old personnel manager at the plant. Although she had been one of the severely wounded, Ed Stopher, on cross-examination, broke the cycle of sympathy by quizzing her on the lack of security in the plant despite Wesbecker's frequent threats.

Warman denied that she was aware of any threats, and Stopher did not pursue the matter. He was less mellow on the handling of Wesbecker's disability payments.

In February 1989, Paula Warman had informed Wesbecker by letter that his payments would be reduced on October 1, 1989, to $391.21. He would then be liable to pay a $78-per-month medical-insurance premium (a sum originally paid entirely by the company) should he wish his medical benefits to continue, further reducing his monthly check to $313.21. It was the understanding of the defense that Wesbecker genuinely thought, and behaved as if, the company was cheating him of his due. The implication of Stopher's questions was that Paula Warman herself was happy to give Wesbecker the impression that his entitlements had been drastically cut.

Stopher had Warman confirm that her letter made no mention that Wesbecker would be entitled to a $892 supplemental payment each month from Social Security, in addition to the company's payments. Stopher then asked her to agree that she had informed Wesbecker on the same date that the company could at any point in time decide to end the insurance policy and appropriate the amounts so far paid in.

"If the company elected to cancel the employees' medical coverage," asked Stopher, "if there was money left in that plan it didn't go to the employees; it went to the company. Correct?"

"All the benefits would have been paid and any excess money would have gone back to the company; that is correct."

"Would have gone to the company, not the employees?"

"The way the letter is written, it says it would go back to the company."

"And is that the case?"

"We never terminated the plan."

"This was a letter to Mr. Wesbecker advising him that if it was terminated that's where the money would go?"

"Yes, sir. That's what it says."

Ed Stopher had gone as far as he could to indicate that Standard Gravure had victimized Wesbecker and that Paula Warman, knowingly or unknowingly, had played a part in this. But Paul Smith was not prepared to end the day with the jurors' feeling sorry for Wesbecker.

Once again he attempted to evoke a wave of sympathy for the plaintiffs by making a dramatic roll call of the dead and wounded. All of which prompted renewed tears and sobs from the plaintiffs in the front rows.

Nor did he exclude Paula Warman herself.

"You were shot, weren't you?"

"Yes, sir; I was."

"Did you see him point any gun at you?"

"No, sir; I did not."

"Did you do anything to encourage Mr. Joseph Wesbecker to shoot you?"

"No, sir; I did not."

The following two days, Tuesday and Wednesday, Smith called to the stand nine more of Wesbecker's victims, stressing their terrible injuries and their complete innocence.

Smith wanted to establish that Wesbecker, as a result of being on Prozac, was stalking through the plant zombielike, unaware of what he was doing and whom he was shooting. He was also seeking confirmation that his witnesses were unaware of any special tension on the plant, the presence of guns, or threats uttered by Wesbecker in the preceding months or years.

Stopher, however, was keen to establish on cross-examination that Wesbecker was calm and in control, that he took time to recognize those he shot, and that he took careful aim. Aware that Wesbecker had made threats over at least five years before the shootings, Stopher was seeking testimony that the atmosphere in the plant had been deplorable; that there had been weapons around, and fights. At the same time, he was treading carefully so as not to appear to criticize the plaintiffs.

Eventually Smith seemed to have prevailed. The majority of the witnesses were able to recall for him that Wesbecker's face was "contorted," or "puffy," or "without normal expression," or "his face just looked like he wasn't there," or "he just looked through us." Few could remember Wesbecker's threats—and if they could, they declared that nobody had taken these threats seriously.

18

AFTER THE VICTIMS, it was the turn of Wesbecker's family to testify one by one in the Old Jailhouse Building. But first Paul Smith called the policeman who had taken John Stein to the hospital on the day of the shootings. Officer Joe Ball had been a boyhood friend of Wesbecker's, and Smith aimed to put some sympathetic flesh and blood on the mass murderer with his assistance.

Ball, fifty-one years of age, with a weather-beaten complexion and thick black hair, said he had known Wesbecker since sixth grade, when they attended neighboring Catholic schools.

"You would think that he was a hell-raiser," started Ball, "but he really wasn't. He would give you the shirt off his back. He was one of the Fonzies of that day. He could talk the talk but couldn't walk the walk. We were all quite small at the time and for some reason Joey grew, had big arms on him, and we kind of looked up to him."

Ball could not remember "Joey," as he liked to call him, being aggressive or violent, but he recollected being the cause of his getting into a fight. "This one fellow had been picking on me for a long time, for about three months, and I told Joey about it and Joey went over and punched him, and the guy never bothered me anymore."

Ball went on to tell the court how he would see Joey at intervals through the years, usually when he was on patrol duty about the city. "One day I ran into Joey sitting on the dock and he was eating his dinner and it was in the summertime, and that was the first time I had saw him for years. And we started talking and every two or three days I'd come by. . . . My impression was in those days he was a pretty good pressman and a pretty nice guy."

Officer Ball had been a sturdy witness. He had nothing dramatic to say about Wesbecker, except that he had once seen him with an empty banana clip in his back pocket. Before Smith let him go, he questioned him as follows:

"Up to September 14th, Officer Ball, did Joseph Wesbecker ever display any of those qualities or traits or signs that you saw in those thousands of people that you came into contact with who were violent?"

"None that I know of myself."

"Did you ever observe anything about Joseph Wesbecker up to September 14th, 1989, that would make you think he was a threat to the people of this city?"

"None, sir."

The appearance of Joe Wesbecker's mother, Martha Montgomery Wesbecker, on the witness stand created a sense of heightened expectation in the court. She was a pale, bespectacled lady, sixty-eight years of age, with a puffy face and a tendency to shake her head. Her sparse white hair was blow-dried into a halo. In a thin voice she told Paul Smith that she was suffering from "extreme high blood pressure" and that she had a "tumor" in her kidney.

As Smith worked through his questions, her answers were brief and barely audible. She told the court that she had married at fifteen after meeting her husband, Thomas Wesbecker, on a blind date. Joe's birth a year later was, she said, normal, with no complications.

Smith wanted to establish that, though Wesbecker's upbringing had been difficult following the death of his father, he had also had a reasonable amount of affection and mothering. But her answers were so noncommittal that he seemed to be putting words into her mouth. One typical exchange involved the period Wesbecker spent in an orphanage:

"Did Joe want to go to the orphanage?"

"Not particularly, no."

"Did you want to send him to the orphanage?"

"I did because the teacher said that it would be a good idea."

"Did your mom, Nancy, agree with the idea that Joe go to the orphanage?"

"No, not particularly."

"Once you put Joe in the orphanage, did you just drop him off and leave him there for nine months?"

"No."

Point by point, Smith encouraged the mother to exculpate her son for his misdemeanors. It was not Joey who had stolen gas from a truck—it was another boy, and Joey took the blame. And as for the statutory-rape charge, "The girls finally admitted that they had instigated the whole thing because they wanted to join a club and they had to have sex with a guy to. . . . The girls got the guys excited and they measured them and the largest got the job. . . ."

Smith now asked her about her son's tendency to bear grudges even within his own family—including his mother and his son Kevin. The source of this double feud, she told the court, was that Wesbecker thought Kevin was exacerbating James's sexual-exposure problem in some way. While James was staying with Martha, Wesbecker had asked her not to entertain Kevin in her home, which had brought a sharp response from her: "I just told him that I was their grandmother and he could not tell me what . . . who I could see and who I couldn't."

In an attempt to sweeten the picture of Wesbecker's obsessive feuds, Paul Smith tried to deflect some of the blame onto Martha Wesbecker herself; she seemed willing to go along with this more from lassitude than conviction:

"Are you somewhat stubborn, Ms. Wesbecker?"

"Well, I've got red hair."

"Was Joe stubborn?"

"Yes."

"Was Joe unreasonably stubborn at times?"

"Well, sometimes I thought he was."

"But, then, has anybody accused you of being unreasonably stubborn?"

"Yes, sir."

On cross-examination, Stopher attempted to go back over the whole of Wesbecker's life to show that the family had been dysfunctional and subject to mental illness. Martha Wesbecker was not an easy witness for him, but some of her answers revealed a dark side to the family history that seemed to surprise even Stopher. An example was the incident in which Wesbecker's paternal grandmother, Murrell, had been dragged off to a mental institution, watched by little Joe.

Murrell, Martha said, had not taken up residence in order to look after Joe while she herself went out to work. In fact, Murrell's son (Martha's brother-in-law) had at first put her in a nursing home, then thought better of it when he saw the bills. He began paying Martha $20 a week to look after the old woman (although Martha was out at work, and Murrell spent the day with Joe, then about six years old). When Martha asked for $5 more a week, Murrell's son went and swore out a warrant to have her put in Central State Mental Hospital rather than pay the extra amount.

The story of Martha's mother-in-law's enforced committal by her own son back in the 1940s seemed to shock the younger generation in the court. But the spectators were even more discomfited when Stopher quizzed Martha about her own mental state.

Martha appeared sick, stressed, and deeply ashamed to be sitting before the victims of her son's killing spree. Perhaps Stopher went beyond the bounds of propriety in suggesting that she had once considered suicide some forty years earlier, when she worked a fast machine at the Philip Morris cigarette factory in Louisville. "Have you ever been in a cigarette factory?" she said. "Well, when they first put you where the cigarettes come out . . . I started out as being a catcher. Well, these others were so much faster. I didn't like working that fast and it made me a little nervous."

"If I understand correctly," said Stopher, "your mother's relationship to your son created a lot of pressure and guilt in you; is that true?"

Martha denied the suggestion.

"Didn't it create so much pressure and guilt in you that you attempted to take your own life?"

"No!" she said emphatically.

The next witness was John Montgomery, Wesbecker's uncle, who had allegedly whipped Joe when he was a child. Smith wanted to dismiss this charge and at the same time attempt to undermine the idea that Wesbecker conformed to the defense's view of being hostile, paranoid, and mentally disturbed.

Now in his late sixties, with white hair and somewhat overweight, John Montgomery was as brief in his answers as his sister. Smith took his questions at a cracking pace:

"Did you ever abuse Joe Wesbecker?"

"No."

"Did you ever see anybody abuse Joe Wesbecker?"

"No."

Through a series of monosyllabic answers, Smith then extracted a "regular-guy" view of Wesbecker. He was put in the orphanage to "get an education." He married happily—"I was his best man," said Montgomery. He was a decent father to his children. He was never violent. He was a charming fellow at family gatherings. He worked hard, made a lot of money, but did not spend anything on himself. He was generous and would lend you money if ever you needed it.

When it was his turn, Stopher fared no better with John Montgomery than he had with Martha. Montgomery had a way of slipping in an extra item of information to neutralize Stopher's points. At times Stopher's patience, for all his stolidity, seemed to be wearing thin, as, for instance, during this series of questions aimed at emphasizing Wesbecker's symptoms of stress and depression.

"Did you notice that Mr. Wesbecker never stood still?"

"Nobody in the family does."

"And he never stood still; is that true?"

"No."

"Did that get worse during the 1980s?"

"I never took exception to it."

"Whether you took exception to it or not, sir, did it get worse?"

"I don't know."

19

THE LAWYERS usually had a lunch of sandwiches and cold drinks back in their office suites. Paul Smith and Nancy Zettler, wheeling boxes of documents and smoking as they went, would walk the five hundred yards to the offices of Hays, Ruben and Foley on South Street. Stopher and his colleagues took a different route, going two blocks farther, to the Providian Center on Market Street.

Some of the spectators would eat in the Sheraton Hotel rooftop restaurant, or at Wendy's on Jefferson Street. Many of the jurors and the plaintiffs would get lunch at one of the fast-food outlets in the Galleria, the glass arcade at Fourth and Muhammad Ali Boulevard.

After lunch on Thursday, October 6, Judge Potter began by taking one of the jurors to task, having spotted him in the Galleria without the red juror's label supplied by the court.

"Since we have a minute," he began in his reedy deadpan style, "I'll take a second to fuss at Mr. King. I was over having my taco fix in the Galleria and, Mr. King, I noticed you didn't have your button on. . . . And I'm just picking on you because I happened to notice you. That's really where it's important that you wear it, because somebody will come up and sit down next to you or not know. . . . I say fuss at you, but that's too strong a word. Okay?"

The incident provided a few moments of light relief before Wesbecker's elder son, Kevin, came to the witness stand, a pale thirty-one-year-old with thinning dark hair and a pencil mustache. He wore glasses and was dressed in a gray suit and red tie.

Kevin appeared smart and educated, and spoke with greater fluency than almost any of the witnesses so far. He also had a sense of reasonableness that lent integrity to his testimony.

Speaking of his early childhood, he said: "We were your typical family, had fun together, recreation together, played ball, sports, bowling, movies, went camping a few times . . . even attempted a few times of going fishing." He told the court how he had been diagnosed with scoliosis in his childhood, and about his parents' concern. His father took him to see a chiropractor, he said, and he was put into a back brace for a year.

Smith asked, "Did you feel that your dad was giving Jimmy preference over you?"

"No."

"Did you feel that your dad loved you in the early years?"

"Oh, yes. Yes, he did."

"Did you love him?"

"Yes, I did."

When Smith asked him to explain how he came to be estranged from his father for seven years, Kevin said that after graduating from high school he had enrolled in the University of Louisville, then dropped out. "He said I was medically insured through his work," Kevin went on, "and that was only if I was a full-time student, and if I wasn't a student then I was taking a chance of getting him in trouble. . . . Anyway, I refused to go back to school, so he was mad at me. We just hung up the phone and that was basically the end of the conversation."

Having shown that Wesbecker was probably on the right side in this argument, Smith wanted to demonstrate that the coldness between them was even more the fault of the son than of the father.

"Was he totally to blame in your estrangement?" Smith asked.

"Well, I was being stubborn as well . . . not listening to him. I mean, he was trying to be a parent and explain to a typical teenager about the facts of life and I wasn't prepared to listen."

Having virtually disposed of what had been characterized by the defense as a sociopathic feud instigated by Wesbecker alone, Smith now probed the story, reiterated in Ed Stopher's opening statement, that Wesbecker had lurked in a state of deranged squalor, mulling over his weapons and warrior literature without water or electricity, throughout the last twelve months of his life.

Kevin said that, in the summer of 1989, the year of the shootings, he had visited the house at least twice and found his father watching TV.

"That summer in '89, was the water turned off?" asked Smith.

"Not during the time that I was there. I used his restroom and everything seemed to work fine."

"Did your dad appear to be disheveled or unshaven or unkempt during this period of time, May or June in 1989?"

"He was in dress pants and a regular T-shirt like he always was. I mean, the house needed a woman in it. It was kind of dirty."

Cross-examining Kevin, Ed Stopher did his best to restore his original impression, in his opening statement, that Wesbecker had been violently abusive to his children. There was a hint in his questions that James's sexual-exposure problem might even have been exacerbated by Wesbecker's beatings; that he had threatened to send James to Boys Haven just as he himself had been sent to an orphanage; and that his feuds had been senseless and vicious.

Kevin remained cool throughout Stopher's inquisition, which appeared obtuse after Smith's more empathetic approach.

On redirect, Smith asked: "On those occasions where he [Wesbecker] spanked Jimmy in connection with the problem he had in exposing himself, was that in a matter of discipline or was it a matter of beating?"

"Discipline."

"As far as you know, was your dad doing everything he could to get Jimmy the psychiatric medical treatment he needed for this problem?"

"Yes, he was."

Smith then went through the close members of the family, asking Kevin whether he thought they were stubborn. In all cases, Kevin acknowledged that they were. Finally, Smith asked if Kevin felt he was at fault in his estrangement with his father.

"I believe," said Kevin, "it was being stubborn."

By the end of Kevin's testimony, Stopher's version of Wesbecker's character—a killer by nature and nurture—was beginning to look thin.

The following morning, Wesbecker's first wife, Sue Chesser, was called to the witness stand. An attractive platinum-blonde of fifty-two, she wore a pale-blue dress. She was evidently distressed and spoke in a quiet and halting voice.

Smith asked her about her early relationship with Wesbecker and encouraged her to expand on his character and what she found attractive in him. "I went to Shawnee High, and he and another of his friends used to come by and pick us up and take us to Mike's Drugstore after school and we'd all have a hamburger and Coke. . . . I guess he was kind of classified as a little on the wild side. He was a kind of daredevil. . . . He would drive a little too fast. . . . It seemed like he laughed all the time. . . . He always had something funny to say." She said that he always had friends, and she never knew him to be moody or violent.

She told the court how they had started dating seriously while Wesbecker was at the Fawcett Printing plant. After six months, they married in the local Catholic church on a Saturday morning in July 1961, both aged nineteen. They went back to work on Monday morning.

"We didn't have a lot of money back then and our friends kind of made fun of us because we didn't have a car, but we'd hop on a bus and go downtown and go to a movie. And we did a lot of walking. And we had some good times. He wanted to be successful in his job. He wanted to give his family everything he could possibly give them. He had dreams like everyone else."

Then things started going wrong. "I guess it was around 1977. He was working like twelve hours a day, seven days a week, and we didn't really get to see each other very often.

"I said, 'I need to do something.' So, anyway, I went ahead and I found a job, but he didn't like it. He told me if I didn't quit he would move out, and within about a couple months he moved out."

It was after her husband met and married Brenda, Sue told the court, that things became bitter between them. Wesbecker, she said, was convinced that she was making "terroristic threats" against his mother and Brenda. He took her to court several times and she was found guilty, although, she said, she had protested her innocence.

Then she described how he had physically attacked her.

"Joe called and told me that I had been seen at a nightclub with some guy, and he really was upset over that. And I told him I hadn't been to any nightclubs. Anyway, he hung up, and I had walked outside. And the next thing I know, he was in my driveway. And he came over and he just knocked me down and he got back in his car and went back to work. He was in his work clothes."

He asked her finally, "Did Joe up to the spring of 1989 exhibit any abnormal or unusually depressed behavior in your presence?"

"No, sir."

On cross-examination, Stopher encouraged her to remember something she claimed to have forgotten—that there was a second occasion when he came to her house and knocked her to the ground. She also acknowledged that he had kept from her the fact that he had been hospitalized on two occasions, and that he had attempted suicide.

Wesbecker's secrecy would become an important part of Stopher's case. For the time being, Stopher was satisfied merely to bring it to the attention of the jury.

Before finishing his cross-examination, he asked her about Wesbecker's fear that chemicals at the printing plant had affected his health.

"He told you that he thought the chemicals had resulted in something that his sons inherited?"

"That's right."

Stopher now moved briskly on to ask her about her knowledge of Wesbecker's complaints against Standard Gravure in relation to Jimmy's medical insurance. It appeared that Sue Chesser and Wesbecker had met at his house on Nottoway Circle just a month before the shootings to discuss a large number of James's unpaid medical bills. James had turned twenty-two, the point after which Sue and Wesbecker's insurance, which had been placed by Standard Gravure, no longer covered him. Sue acknowledged under cross-examination that this was so, and that Wesbecker had told her that Standard Gravure had "hassled" him over the medical charges.

When Smith came back for redirect, however, he was determined to counteract any impression that Wesbecker had blamed Standard Gravure for the genetic origin of his sons' conditions. "Did Mr. Wesbecker ever express concerns that some exposure to solvents at Standard Gravure could have caused, in his mind, problems with his sons?"

"No, sir. He always specified that it was Fawcett, because it would have had to have been before the kids were conceived."

20

ON MONDAY, October 10, plaintiffs' counsel set about making its case against the drug Prozac and its manufacturer, Eli Lilly. It was a long day for the jury as Paul Smith and Nancy Zettler read a highly technical deposition taken from Dr. Ray Fuller, the researcher from Eli Lilly who was coinventor of the drug.

Fuller was physically absent from the court, though he would appear several weeks later as a witness for the defense. For now, as Smith explained tortuously to the judge in chambers discussion, "We're using him basically as an educational witness to set the predicate on the serotonin system, et cetera."

Zettler added with burst of parody: "It basically is an ecology on terminology, semantic, and it just gets confusing, and if there was anything they really want him to explain, they're going to have him live to explain it."

The judge concurred; he, too, thought all this brain science was confusing, he said, and kind of tough to handle.

Dr. Ray Ward Fuller, according to his deposition, was fifty-eight years of age and a research fellow with Eli Lilly in Indianapolis. A pharmacologist by specialization, he was currently doing experiments with fluoxetine hydrochloride (Prozac) for the company. He had been leader of the Prozac research project from 1976 until the team was disbanded in 1989.

Nancy Zettler conducted the deposition, reading out her original questions while Smith provided Fuller's answers. They read rapidly and dispassionately.

She started by asking Fuller to explain the relationship between biochemistry and the mind.

"The brain," Fuller had said, "like other parts of the body, is made up of molecules. And the function of any part of the body involves molecular changes, so that when any part of the body is dysfunctional there would be some type of molecular change that would be occurring."

"Are there some personality disorders that have a biochemical basis?" Zettler asked.

"I think all personality disorders would have disordered molecular processes going on," Fuller said. "I don't think it's meaningful to use the term 'some.' . . . I don't think you can separate thought and . . . mental function and molecular changes as one causing the other; they must occur together, I think. . . . As Ralph Gerard said, 'Behind every crooked thought, there lies a crooked molecule.' "

Fuller had used this same expression when talking with Tracy Thompson for her article in *The Saturday Evening Post*; somehow it penetrated to the heart of his convictions about neuroscience.

Zettler pressed him on the meaning behind his metaphor.

"The process of thought involves molecular changes," said Fuller, "and those are simply occurring together and they can't be separated."

"So it's well recognized by you, as well as other scientists knowledgeable in the field, that our thoughts and the molecular changes in our brains are intertwined?"

"Yes."

"All right. Are you saying that a particular molecular change can cause a particular thought?"

"I believe that could occur, yes."

Having encouraged Fuller to acknowledge that schizophrenia, depression, and paranoia were the result of some "biochemical neurological change," Zettler asked him to explain a "neurotransmitter" by analogy.

"I can try to describe neurotransmitters; I don't immediately think of an analogy that would be helpful. . . . Fundamentally, the process of neurotransmission is one nerve cell or neuron releasing a substance which has an influence on an adjoining nerve cell, and that is the process by which signals are transmitted from one neuron to another."

Fuller's exposition soon expanded into a highly technical dissertation on neurotransmitter classifications. He gave his explanations patiently, but he seemed to resent being quizzed by a nonspecialist.

When Zettler asked him about his early experiments with fluoxetine, he replied: "Well, let me explain that the molecule fluoxetine was first synthesized as an oxalate salt, which has a different number, 82816, so I assume you're asking me . . . You're not trying to make a distinction between 82816 and 110140?"

Zettler persevered, gamely holding her own until she could pin him down with a specific question about the invention of Prozac.

"What was your role," she asked, "that makes you kind of a co-founder or coinventor or codeveloper of fluoxetine?"

"When Dr. Wong first found that fluoxetine, as it was later called, inhibited the uptake of radioactive serotonin by rat-brain synaptosomes in the test tube, we immediately began experiments to determine whether that compound would inhibit serotonin uptake selectively in animals, rats and mice." (When brain tissue is homogenized, the endings of nerves pinch off into little sacs called synaptosomes, which can retain many of their functions in the test tube. A synaptosome from a serotonin nerve terminal could take up serotonin.)

They discovered, he said, that fluoxetine could block serotonin uptake in a nerve cell without blocking the uptake of a related neurotransmitter, norepinephrine, a crucial factor in the avoidance of side effects, and intrinsic to the description of Prozac as a "selective" serotonin inhibitor.

As the deposition progressed along these lines, it seemed that there was a gradual increase in hostility from Fuller.

Fuller had been saying that they "administered fluoxetine initially by ingestion and in some experiments by oral gavage."

"Okay. First you injected a mouse with some fluoxetine; is that correct?"

"We injected fluoxetine into mice, I believe is the correct way of saying it," Fuller had replied.

"I may not say some things in the proper scientific way, so bear with me," snapped Zettler. "It's not my intent to confuse you; I'm probably just confusing myself, Dr. Fuller. You injected some fluoxetine into a mouse. How did you know how much fluoxetine to give to the mouse?"

Zettler seemed to be intent on familiarizing herself with ways of talking about the subject, ways of taming this specialist to accept her way of communicating about his own subject.

And as she teased out his answers, a more precise notion of the action of serotonin emerged. For example, serotonin does not actually *increase* in the brain as a whole, or even in the tissues in part, as a result of Prozac. It is the inhibition of the "reuptake" mechanism that is crucial, and this is established indirectly when the researcher measures levels of a substance called 5-HIAA, which is a metabolite of serotonin (i.e., the resulting substance when serotonin is used by the body, or metabolized). When 5-HIAA levels decrease, it is assumed that there is less reuptake of serotonin, and that therefore serotonin is more *active* in the synaptic cleft, and that this in turn, so the theory goes, improves the prospects of a patient's suffering depression.

It became clear by midafternoon that this was a difficult subject even for a bright young attorney like Zettler, let alone the jurors; Zettler, however, seemed intent not only on learning but also on exposing Fuller's ignorance of aspects of his own subject.

One example was the principle of so-called down-regulation of receptor sites. Receptor sites are molecules on the nerve cells' membrane which react to neurotransmitter substances somewhat the way a lock reacts to a key—generally, by inhibiting or exciting the activity of that cell. After taking Prozac, animal models had shown both a decrease in the number of serotonin receptor sites on nerve cells and a decline in the efficiency of the remaining receptors, leading to an eventual overall decrease in the production of serotonin.

Zettler wanted the jury to know that Prozac was capable of drastic and permanent changes in the brain that were poorly understood by the researchers themselves. She did this with a prolonged interrogation that was as discomfiting to the listeners in the courtroom as it clearly had been to Dr. Fuller. Eventually she seemed to wring from him the admission she was after:

"I'm just trying to get it clear what you mean when you say the actual number of receptors decrease. Are you talking about, for instance, as an analogy, ten receptors on a neuron and then all of a sudden there's only six as a result of down-regulation?"

"What I mean is that there are fewer receptors at the site as a result of some treatment than there had been before that treatment."

"Okay. So some of the receptors go away as a result of the treatment in that circumstance?"

"That's not the equivalent to what I said, no."

"Where am I getting it wrong, doctor?"

"There are two—at least two general ways in which the number of receptors would go down. . . . One is that receptors are disappearing at a faster rate than they had been disappearing, and the second is receptors are being made at a slower rate than they had been being made."

Despite Fuller's qualifications, the jury seemed to get her point.

As the day progressed, and Smith and Zettler neared the end of Fuller's deposition, it was clear that there was no easy means of bridging the gulf between the scientific view of the brain and the layperson's. The jury had been asked to consider various models, which tended to be simplistically mechanistic and intensely localized to the action of an ideal single cell. In her attempts to trap Fuller into admissions of ignorance about the action of serotonin and Prozac on the brain, Zettler had repeatedly required him to conform to her layperson's viewpoint, which he refused to accept.

An example of the gap between them was Zettler's unwillingness to respond to the difference between organic and mechanical systems. She had been pursuing him ("I know it's late and I'm not trying to beat a subject to death") concerning the adaptive changes in the nerve cells that occur as a result of Prozac.

In the end, Fuller expostulated: "It's a dynamic thing. Every receptor that's there wasn't there sometime back and won't be there sometime in the future. There's a dynamic nature to these receptors. They're always undergoing turnover."

Quick to seize an advantage from his frustration, she asked, "Okay, how long does it take to turn over?"

His answer then revealed in striking fashion the vulnerability of the scientist to a smart attorney.

"I don't know that that's been determined with these serotonin receptors," said Fuller.

"Has anybody tried to determine that?"

"Probably, but not that I specifically remember."

"Do you know if anybody has tried and failed?"

"No. I simply don't remember."

"Have you tried to determine that?"

"No."

"Why not?"

"Well, that's not the type of experiments that I do. I don't do radiologic receptors, which would be one way of trying to approach that. It's not a question that would help me in my research particularly."

He was being scientifically honest, but his answer came across to some as rather lame and devious.

21

THE NEXT DEPOSITION had been taken from Dr. Irwin Slater, a seventy-six-year-old New Yorker who had been an employee of Eli Lilly and Company from 1954 until his retirement at the end of 1979. He was a medical doctor who had moved early into neuropsychopharmacology as a researcher and eventually as a professor, before joining Lilly as a senior research officer.

In 1978, he said, he was asked to be responsible for the administration of clinical trials on fluoxetine (Prozac), which he had been associated with since its invention in 1972. In one of his earlier sets of experiments, he said, "we had a colony of cats with electrodes implanted in various sites in the brain and we were studying the effects of drugs on their sleep patterns."

Slater had observed that cats "which had been friendly for years" began to "growl and hiss" and became "distinctly unfriendly" while receiving "larger doses" of fluoxetine.

Smith now encouraged Slater to describe how he came to be responsible for the administration of these clinical trials in 1978. Trials on fluoxetine, Slater said, had been discontinued in 1977, because researchers thought the drug was completely ineffective. The dropping of fluoxetine had created a lot of "bitching" around the company, according to Slater. "We in pharmacology," he said, "were very unhappy, because we felt that these studies [Phase II studies, the first trials of fluoxetine on humans] had been inadequate, and we made our unhappiness known." Since he was due for retirement in a year, Slater said, he was asked by Dr. William Shedden, then vice-president in charge of medical affairs, to spend the last year of his employment making some attempt to determine whether Lilly should or should not have further interest in fluoxetine. (It was Shedden who later pleaded no contest to fifteen counts of misdemeanor in 1985 over the Oraflex drug.)

Slater had been in the habit of keeping a diary from about 1956, and Smith now asked the doctor to quote entries about Prozac's clinical trials going back to 1978–79. Portions of the diary demonstrated the pressure researchers were under to speed up the clinical trials in order to beat antidepressants being developed by rival companies.

"And you were afraid that if you took more time to examine your fragmentary evidence that the other competitive companies might get a jump on you that you would never be able to make up; is that right?"

"Right."

"And if the other product came on the market before Prozac, Prozac would be worthless?"

"Well, it would be an uphill fight, at best."

"You wrote the word 'worthless'?"

"Yes."

The deposition also revealed that, back in 1978–79, patients on clinical trials "started well on Prozac" and then faded; that there were questions as to whether antianxiety drugs like Valium should be used in combination with the substance.

Slater felt at the time that Lilly should go ahead with further trials of Prozac, but that it should be combined with other drugs. He was also worried about the ideal dosage. In June 1979, Slater wrote to a trials investigator in Nashville saying, "We know that 20 milligrams rarely works and that 60 causes lots of agitation. . . ."

He was also aware of an outside trial in which a patient became suicidal after experiencing "disordered thoughts."

As the deposition progressed, it became clear through exhibits of memoranda and letters Smith had passed to Slater for scrutiny that patients in a number of trials suffered agitation, or "excessive stimulation," while taking Prozac. Another patient "experienced psychotic worsening on active drug, which improved somewhat after it was discontinued."

Smith now wanted to know how it would be possible to determine the effect of Prozac in relation to suicidal tendencies if all suicidal patients had been excluded from the trials, or if patients were excluded as soon as they showed suicidal symptoms. This was a question for which Slater apparently had no ready answer. The importance of the suicide issue for the Wesbecker case, it emerged later, was that psychologists and psychiatrists routinely linked suicide to acts of violence. The question led to a circular argument that would continue without resolution throughout the trial: that striking side effects—like agitation and suicidal tendencies—were explained by Lilly as typical of the illness rather than the drug.

Smith now turned to the role of the Food and Drug Administration in the approval of Prozac. He read the deposition testimony of a Dr. Dorothy Dobbs, who had worked for five years with the FDA before working at Lilly from 1981 to 1985. She had left Lilly, she admitted, because she had not found her "role very satisfying."

Her duties at Lilly, she said, included liaison between the company and the FDA on fluoxetine, preparing the new-drug application, and submitting correspondence and various other documents to the FDA.

Dobbs acknowledged that she had voiced criticisms to her superiors about the volume of studies in Europe on Prozac and as a result the FDA's poor capacity to deal with the "enormous amount of incoming data." Her particular concern, she said, was lack of resources, and particularly of personnel at the FDA.

Dobbs said that the volume of clinical trial material on a drug like fluoxetine precluded proper scrutiny at the FDA.

"Would you agree that the FDA is overworked and understaffed?"

"Yes."

"And that the FDA has to rely on the sponsor, the pharmaceutical manufacturer, for some help in evaluating the safety and efficacy of a drug?"

"Yes."

"And that's based on your experience, not only as an individual who has worked with the Food and Drug Administration, but as an individual that's worked for two separate pharmaceutical firms; correct?"

"Yes."

"Additionally, the FDA system of examining a drug for safety and efficacy can only be as good as the information that it gets; correct?"

"I was hung up on your word 'system'; I'm not entirely convinced that there is one."

"Is it that disorganized?"

"Sometimes, yes."

Smith now wrung an admission from Dr. Dobbs that the FDA would play "gotcha," meaning that they would attempt to compensate for a lack of thoroughness by making spot checks. She acknowledged further that "sometimes they'll miss an area that does need inquiry," and that it was possible that "sometimes there's some area that actually could serve closer scrutiny by FDA employees that . . . doesn't get looked at."

Finally, Smith turned to the practice of allowing patients in a trial to use concomitant drugs. Allowing concomitants raises the possibility that the true effect of the drug may have been masked. This, in turn, has crucial implications for adverse-effect warnings in drug package inserts.

Dr. Dobbs had acknowledged that concomitant drugs "interfere with the anlaysis of both safety and efficacy, actually. Ideally, patients in clinical trials would be completely healthy except for whatever disease was under study and would not ingest a single aspirin."

Then she admitted that a Lilly scientist, Dr. Lee, had considered that in the earlier studies there had been "too many people on too much concomitant medication. . . ." They had used medications, she said, such as would "confound the results somewhat."

"If I'm taking a benzodiazepine and I'm depressed and I fit all the criteria, will I be allowed on the clinical trials?"

"That would depend on the wording in the protocol. The question then becomes what should the protocol say."

"All right. Do you have a recollection?"

"My recollection is that some of the studies, as I said, that had been started earlier and probably before I was there, allowed—well, this says allowed psychotropics, including benzodiazepines and chloral hydrate and—so two patients in this group get one milligram of one of them and five patients over here get ten milligrams of another for three nights and it simply fouls it up."

"It's bad?" Smith asked, referring to the practice of allowing concomitant drugs in a clinical trial.

"It's bad. It's scientifically bad."

"But it was allowed on the Prozac clinical trials?"

"As I've already acknowledged, I advised within Lilly that—before Dr. Lee did, that practice cease."

"But it didn't, did it?"

Dr. Dobbs now claimed that after she arrived she attempted to instigate a trial protocol that was "considerably cleaner" in the sense of not allowing any kind of concomitant drugs whatsoever during the tests.

Smith was ready for her.

"But none of that was ever done," he said.

Producing a trial protocol dated December 17, 1984, a full three years after Dobbs had arrived at Lilly, Smith went down through the concomitant drugs being taken by patients testing Prozac.

"My point is simply," he said, "and you're free to look at this, that you may have been under the impression that the procedure was changed where there weren't as many people receiving concomitant psychotropic medications, but it doesn't look like it looking at these tables that were dated as of December 17, 1984."

"I have to agree with you," said Dr. Dobbs.

22

ON THE MORNING of October 13, Dr. Leigh Thompson, Lilly's chief scientific officer, was called to the stand.

Stout and bespectacled, with a beak nose and graying fair hair, the fifty-six-year-old scientist acknowledged heading some four thousand researchers at the Lilly plant in Indianapolis.

Smith started by asking about the ratio between patients on Prozac and patients on placebo (a pretend drug, such as sugar water) in a typical clinical trial. "If you want to get a fairly accurate representation of head-up competition between Prozac and placebo," Smith was saying, "you generally try to put an equal amount of people on Prozac as placebo, don't you?"

"I don't want to play games," said Thompson fastidiously, "but let's be very precise. The FDA says that our fixed-dose studies of Prozac are the best that were ever done and set new standards for the industry. And in those studies . . . we had one-fourth got placebo, one-fourth got a low dose, and one-fourth got a medium dose, and one-fourth that got a high dose. . . . That's more elegant, and that's what the FDA told us."

Smith was bright with indignation.

"It seems like, Dr. Thompson, in responding to my questions, you kind of have a tendency to talk about how Lilly is the leader in these matters and things of that nature."

Immediately Stopher was on his feet, appealing to the judge. On his way to the bench, Smith said out loud to Nancy Zettler, "Mr. Stopher doesn't even let me get my question out."

"Your Honor," Stopher said when they came before Potter, "I object to Mr. Smith making these stage comments to Ms. Zettler, which he intends for the jury to hear. . . . I object to him continually making statements to Dr. Thompson about the way in which he's answering the questions. It is inappropriate for him to be commenting and making his judgments on the way in which this witness is testifying; the jury is only entitled to make that."

"This is an adverse, extremely hostile witness," Smith said angrily.

Judge Potter sustained Stopher's objection; but no sooner had tempers simmered down than Stopher was strenuously objecting again, to an exhibit Smith now wished to read to the court.

It was a five-page directive, dated April 1991, from Ed West, head of public relations at Lilly, advising Thompson how to conduct himself during TV interviews on the subject of violence and Prozac. Smith was clearly attempting to dent Thompson's easy arrogance.

Stopher added that the document was not relevant to any issue in the case. Smith responded: "The relevance is to his entire testimony. He's giving the company line. He's practiced giving this. He's coached giving this. I'm entitled to let the jury know that these questions are something that's been fielded to him before and it affects the answers that he gives."

Potter sustained the objection; but Smith went ahead and found a way to inform the court of the contents of the memo all the same.

"You've been characterized," he said to Thompson, "as a media pro by your public-relations director and your lobbying people, have you not?"

"I worked for NBC-TV for a while back, earlier, before I went to Lilly," Thompson responded blandly.

"You've been coached on how to give interviews and respond to questions concerning Prozac, haven't you?"

"They've tried."

"They have given you specific message goals to consider when you give interviews or when you speak concerning Prozac and the issue of violent, aggressive behavior and suicidality, haven't they?"

"I don't want you to go too far with that, Mr. Smith. Yes. They've provided me with their thoughts about goals. I am my own person and I speak for myself."

"Do you mean to tell this jury that no medicine for a brain disease has ever been more thoroughly researched than Prozac?"

"That is correct," said Thompson. "I will assert that. Yes."

"Do you mean to tell the jury that it's the disease, not the drug, that causes any problems that might be related to Prozac at all? . . . You've also been coached in how to give your tone, the impression to give in connection with speaking about Prozac in this issue, haven't you, Dr. Thompson?"

"Yes, sir," said Thompson with a patient smile.

"They've asked you to show compassion?"

"Yes, sir."

Finally, Smith said: "And they've told you to be friendly?"

"Actually," Thompson replied with complacent smile, "they said it comes naturally. I thought that was a great compliment."

As the cross-examination proceeded throughout the morning, the tension continued to mount, but Thompson sustained his cool aloofness. Again and again he defused Smith's questions by responding with pedantic detail.

Smith started to explore the issue of Prozac's side effects, reading in full the passage from Dr. Slater's paper on the effect of Prozac on cats, and how they began to "growl and hiss."

"Can you get the relationship from behavior from looking at cats and mice and stuff like that?" asked Smith. Then he added with a tone of sarcasm, "You certainly can't ask a cat if he's feeling depressed today, can you?"

The comment prompted smiles and titters from the gallery.

"Generally what you do," said Thompson evenly, "is you give huge doses to animals, because that may alert you to some side effect you may see in the first patients you treat. I must tell you from my own experiments, if you give various drugs to animals like cats in very high doses, you'll get all kinds of misbehavior in the animals, including the fact that you can kill them."

Which provoked a stifled laugh from the spectators, and even smiles from the jurors.

Smith now asked him what a "normal" dose of Prozac would be for a cat, and a normal level of serotonin in a human being.

Thompson had to admit that he would not even know how to study such a level in human beings.

"Are you telling me that you can't measure how much serotonin I have in my synaptic cleft?"

"I could kill you and measure it, but you probably wouldn't like that," said Thompson, again to the amusement of the court.

Thompson's complacency began to evaporate, however, as Smith focused on the relationship between known serotonin levels and depression.

Smith asked, "When the psychiatrist prescribes Prozac to increase the level of serotonin in the synaptic cleft, he doesn't even know what the level was to start with, does he?"

"That's correct."

"Much less know," went on Smith, "whether he's really depressed because of a low level of serotonin; correct?"

"The general theory since about the 1950s," Thompson began, "has been that depression is related to either too little serotonin or too little norepinephrine [a major adrenergic neurotransmitter]. There have been hundreds of studies that support the idea that depression is due to too little of one of those two. Frankly, until Prozac we didn't have a drug that would specifically work on only one of the two, so no one knew. . . . The best we can say about depression today is that, again, most people with depression have a lack of serotonin effect. But I want to be real sure that we remember that there are a third of the people that we call depressed that don't respond to any treatment that I know about, and I'm not sure what's wrong with their brains."

Smith's next question appeared to catch Thompson off-balance, exposing the remarkable gap between theory and experimental data in the field of depression. "Can you make," he asked with Texan emphasis, "any specific statement that any specific individual is specifically depressed specifically because their serotonin levels are low?"

The answer was "No, sir." Then Thompson attempted to regain his poise with a combination of flattery and charm. "That's an excellent point. And I must tell you that we have massaged the data on Prozac every way I can imagine, looking at age, obesity, sex, everything else you could find, to see if we could predict which patients would respond to it and which wouldn't. And to my knowledge, as of today, we don't have anything to distinguish the patients that will respond versus the ones that won't."

Thus Smith was granted one of the major admissions of the trial, from no less a person than Lilly's chief scientific officer himself: that nobody knows how to measure a serotonin level in the brain, either before or after giving Prozac.

Smith turned to aim a facetious smile at the plaintiffs and the jurors. Then, turning back to his witness, he said, "It's at the brain that it's important, isn't it?"

"Yes, sir."

"It's the amount available at the synaptic cleft that's important?"

"Exactly."

"And that's exactly what you can't measure."

"You're right."

"And so, if my serotonin level is a certain level, your serotonin is a certain level, the court reporter's serotonin level is a certain level, and we got—each got twenty milligrams of Prozac, what is your understanding of how much it would increase each one of our serotonin levels?"

"I don't know."

Given the importance of the link between dosage and behavior in the animal trials—for example, Slater's hissing and growling cats in the sixty-milligram range—Smith now played the point for all it was worth. "Right. When you administer Prozac, you don't know whether it's getting a twofold increase of serotonin available at the synaptic cleft or a tenfold increase of serotonin available at the synaptic cleft or a hundredfold increase of serotonin available at the synaptic cleft?"

"I probably wouldn't guess on numbers quite that high, but I agree with you, I don't know."

After the lunch break, Thompson was back on the stand. Smith read out in portions the contents of two E-mail messages that had been sent on the company's database by Thompson in February 1990 to top executives in all the international affiliates, including the medical director in the United Kingdom.

The content of the first, relating to Prozac's safety, was sufficiently sensational to transform Thompson's confidence of the morning to astute wariness.

Anything that happens in the UK can threaten this drug in the U.S. and worldwide. We are now expending enormous efforts fending off attacks because of (1) relationship to murder and, (2) inducing suicidal ideation. The appropriate level of response is indicated by Dan Masica [director of neuropsychiatry at Lilly] himself and Charles Beasley [psychiatrist in the employ of Lilly] immediately flying to Boston to talk to authors of paper on suicidal ideation [reference to findings at Harvard Medical School that Prozac induced suicide and violence in six patients, published in February 1990].

We have numerous foes. The FDA is very very skittish. . . . We must not allow one day to elapse on follow-up, flying to, investigating, et cetera, everything about Prozac. . . . Every significant event about Prozac has been a show stopper with twelfth-floor meetings. . . . There cannot be a fumble of even minor proportions on this one because political pressures and perceptions and public news, not science, could cause us to lose this one!!!!!

The second memo, also by Thompson, elucidated further the catastrophic significance of losing "this one." It was sent on the company E-mail later the same day.

I'm concerned about reports I get where UK attitude toward Prozac safety. Leber [of the FDA] suggested a few minutes ago using the CSM UK's (Committee on the Safety of Medicines) data base to compare Prozac aggression and suicidal ideation with other antidepressants in the UK. Although he [Leber] is a fan of Prozac. He believes a lot of this is garbage. He's clearly a political creature and will have to respond to pressures. I hope Patrick [Patrick P. Cechane, medical director of Lilly's affiliate in the UK] realized that Lilly can go down the tubes if we lose Prozac, and just one event in the UK can cost us that.

The occasion for both memoranda had been the dramatic international press reaction, especially in the United Kingdom, to an article in the February 1992 edition of the *American Journal of Psychiatry* by Professor Martin Teicher, co-authored by Professor Jonathan Cole (formerly a scientist at Eli Lilly who had conducted research on Prozac); both were respected psychiatrists with academic chairs at Harvard Medical School.

The article stated that six Prozac-treated patients developed "intense, violent suicidal preoccupations" within two to seven weeks of starting the drug. "None of these patients had ever experienced a similar state during treatment with any other psychotropic drug," wrote the authors. The compulsions were obsessive and emerged without reason or provocation. One of the patients put a loaded gun to her head, and another needed physical restraint to prevent self-mutilation.

Teicher and Cole estimated that between 1.9 and 7.7 percent of Prozac users would be afflicted with obsessive or violent suicidal thoughts. The authors believed that Prozac users were "at least threefold more likely to develop new suicidal ideation" than patients treated with traditional antidepressants.

Smith started by asking Thompson about the background of the two memoranda: why, for example, the anxiety about the United Kingdom? (Smith knew, of course, that some fifteen hundred damages suits had been brought in connection with Oraflex.)

"It wasn't anything that I knew specifically in the U.K.," replied Thompson, evidently rattled, "but we have far more resources in the United States for handling safety reports." This response fell below Thompson's standards of assurance and clarity.

Smith now went through the memoranda line by line, content to highlight the implicit ironies without being too specific about deeper inferences.

Eventually he focused on the apparent fact that the FDA's investigator, Dr. Leber, was a "fan of Prozac," and that Thompson and Leber had a cozy relationship. This led to an exchange in which Smith laid a bold trap in the hope of opening the door to the Oraflex story. "Well, if Paul Leber in February of 1990 was of the opinion already at this time that this was a lot of garbage, how were you going to lose Prozac? He's the head of the division that approved it, Dr. Thompson."

"Well, first of all, there are many other regulators. Remember, we market this drug in seventy-five countries that might take action against the drug, and it could be that reports would come in that would put enough pressure on the FDA that they would do something that's either right or wrong."

"Well, were there instances where the FDA had responded to pressure and done something wrong up to that point, Dr. Thompson?"

"They don't respond to pressure other than—in my opinion, other than doing a lot of investigation, having a lot of hearings. I don't think they're very responsive to pressure, but they get called up before Congress and beaten on all the time."

The question had been heavily loaded, and Thompson's answer ill-advised. Smith's face was shining with emotion; he looked as if he could hardly believe his luck. He leapt in.

"They did in connection with Oraflex, didn't they?"

"I don't really know. Did they?" responded Thompson dryly.

"Yeah. Oraflex."

Joe Freeman was on his feet. "Your Honor, you've already ruled that out."

"I don't know what you're talking about," said Potter.

The lawyers approached the bench.

Again Freeman insisted that Oraflex had been ruled out as being irrelevant to the case. Smith interrupted him, virtually inarticulate with excitement. "They were called on the carpet to testify before Congress, and he opened the door. And I called *him* on the carpet in connection with Oraflex, a Lilly drug, and adverse events that happened outside the United States."

But Potter, having now understood the full significance of the question, firmly sustained Freeman's objection.

Smith now homed in on the reflection, in the second memo, that the entire Lilly corporation could have gone under as a result of a single major adverse report on Prozac.

"I thought this was one of our three leading drugs and that if it got badly damaged that it would seriously hurt the reputation of the company," said Thompson. "I don't think I meant the company would go out of business, but it would seriously hurt us, both scientifically and financially."

"That's my question," Smith persisted. "Did you think that Eli Lilly and Company would go out of business at that time?"

"No, sir; I didn't mean that."

Smith let the matter go, and now moved on to another, more substantial issue that would reverberate through the trial: the discrepancy between German and American package warnings for Prozac.

The U.S. text offered in evidence read as follows:

The possibility of a suicide attempt is inherent in depression and may persist until significant remission occurs. Close supervision of high-risk patients should accompany initial drug therapy. Prescriptions of Prozac should be written for the smallest quantity of capsules consistent with good patient management in order to reduce the risk of overdose.

The German text read:

Until the onset of the depression-alleviating effect, the patients have to be observed adequately. In patients with suicidal risk, continuous observation and/or a generally sedating additional therapy can be necessary. In patients suffering from agitation or marked sleep disturbance, Fluctin [German trade name for Prozac] has to be used with special care.

Thompson contended that the two were only "slightly different," whereas Smith argued that "if you compare the two it's a *lot* different."

"I think the jury can read them as well as you and I can," replied Thompson loftily. "I can go into the philosophy behind them, if you'd like."

Smith commented that the German label specifically recommended the use of sedatives in connection with agitated and suicide-risk patients. Thompson's response was that only one German employee had suggested that wording, and "it doesn't say that you *ought* to do that, it says you *may*."

The Q and A now degenerated into a drawn-out squabble over whether Prozac had been found to be an "activating" drug, and what significance could be given to the notion of "activating." Citing a scientific paper offered in evidence, Smith argued that some 38 percent of patients "had been activated" by Prozac during clinical trials.

Thompson, however, continued to raise scruples about the strict significance and provenance of such data.

"Are you aware, Dr. Thompson," asked Smith at one point, that fluoxetine is activating relative to tricyclics, and tricyclics are sedating relative to fluoxetine?"

"I will be happy to address that assertion," said Thompson calmly, "but I cannot answer it yes or no without qualifying it in terms of the disease and the doses that we're speaking about, because the answer's different."

Thompson's quibbling had repeatedly broken Smith's rhythm, frustrating the attorney to the point where one could hear him hyperventilating. In his attempts to dominate Thompson, he contrived pregnant pauses, swaying and stamping, giving full vent to his Texas accent ("Prozaaark"), putting his hands up to his face in a gesture of astonishment and turning to the spectators, looking out at us pop-eyed through his horn-rimmed glasses, a facetious smile on his lips.

But just as Smith seemed to be gaining the upper hand, Thompson employed a new and astonishing weapon in his considerable armory. Smith had produced the deposition testimony of a Dr. John Greist, a psychiatrist conducting outside clinical trials for Lilly, who seemed to confirm a significant increase of violent aggressive behavior among patients on Prozac.

"Do you have any basis for disagreeing with Dr. Greist, if he has expressed the opinion that Prozac can cause violent aggressive behavior in some individuals?" asked Smith.

"Causality is very important," said Thompson. "To a scientist, I would say that almost anything is *possible,* including the possibility that this courthouse will move across the street to the park outside. In quantum mechanics, that's clearly something that's possible."

"Beg your pardon?" asked Smith incredulously. "I didn't hear what you said."

"Quantum mechanics," said Thompson, "tells us it's possible that this courthouse will move across the street to the park on the other side of the street."

"*Quantum* mechanics?" echoed Smith, turning to look out at the gallery.

"Quantum mechanics, quantum physics, will tell you that that's possible. If I flipped a coin a thousand times and it came up tails a thousand times in a row, I would tell you that it's possible that it would come up heads on the next turn; I wouldn't bet on it, but I would tell you it's possible, because, when a scientist says that, he says, 'I can't prove to you that it's impossible.' "

"Do you think Dr. Greist was talking about quantum mechanics or do you think Dr. Greist was flipping a coin when he expressed that opinion, Dr. Thompson?" asked Smith, barely keeping his composure.

"I was trying to explain how, as scientists, Dr. Greist and I would use the word 'possible,' " said Thompson reasonably. " 'And if you want to define 'can,' as 'Is it possible?,' I will agree with that, because there are very few things in life that I will tell you as a scientist are impossible."

Thompson's introduction of quantum mechanics into the argument had caused a minor sensation in the court, even startling Judge Potter, who normally remained stony-faced throughout the Q and A. In a break for bench discussion, Potter brought up the quantum reference by asking Joe Freeman whether he thought Thompson had thought of it spontaneously.

"Can I just ask something gossipy for my own satisfaction?" he said. "The moving the courthouse was an ad lib?"

"Absolutely," said Freeman.

"I couldn't even *say* 'quantum physics' or whatever it was, 'quantum mechanics,' " said one of Freeman's paralegals.

"Actually," went on Judge Potter, "I'm kind of a physics buff or whatever, and he's technically absolutely correct."

"It is correct," confirmed Ed Stopher, nodding sagely. "Yeah."

"But it was an ad lib, I tell you that," mused Potter. "I thought about that."

Potter had not seemed to grasp that Thompson had used the quantum-physics example as a piece of outrageous obfuscation, and had got away with it.

Returning to the question of dosage as he wound up his direct examination, Smith asked Thompson a series of questions about the reasons for a single-capsule dosage of twenty milligrams, and whether Prozac had a dose-related side-effect profile.

Smith reminded Thompson that he had acknowledged in a memo dated July 11, 1988, that there was "tremendous pressure from gurus and practicing psychiatrists to make ten milligrams or even five milligrams available." Then he got Thompson to admit that some psychiatrists, convinced that the manufactured dose was not safe, were dividing up the twenty-milligram pulvules down to doses as low as five milligrams and administering the compound in some kind of fruit juice. Thompson continued to insist that, despite such contentions, all Lilly's tests had supported an ideal dose of twenty milligrams per day in a single pulvule. The company nevertheless did decide after September 1989 to offer five- and ten-milligram doses, to preclude the practice (on the part of the unconverted) of breaking open the pulvule.

Smith wanted an admission from Thompson that Lilly had engineered its data in order to favor a single daily dose—a huge marketing advantage, since it obviated the complex procedure, called "titrating" (monitoring various dosage amounts to achieve an ideal dosage), that accompanies the use of most other antidepressants.

He had another E-mail to offer in evidence, dated June 11, 1991, from Thompson to Charles Sampson, director of statistical and mathematical sciences at Lilly. Thompson was asking for data on the efficacy of ten-milligram doses of Prozac to present to the Lilly board. As a result of a "Wernicke study," they had figures on five milligrams, he commented, adding that "some people have massaged those data to make 5 milligrams look not quite as good as 20 milligrams."

Smith now began to pursue Thompson on the significance of the term "massage," specifically in relation to the phrase "massaged those data to make 5 milligrams look not quite as good as 20 milligrams."

"Well," began Smith in a withering tone of disbelief, "is it the practice of Eli Lilly and Company to *massage* data?"

"Goodness gracious, I hope so," responded Thompson. "We even have a supercomputer so we can massage and look at it from every possible perspective—does it make a difference if the patient has a different age, obesity, gender, whatever."

"Dr. Wernicke [who monitored Prozac clinical trials] did the study you're talking about, didn't he?" Smith went on.

"Actually, Dr. Wernicke, Dr. Zerbe, and I designed it. Dr. Wernicke was the monitor for that study," said Thompson, persnickety as ever.

"Did you know he's [Wernicke] testified under oath in depositions taken in this case that he thinks you massage people, not data?"

The exchange was interrupted by a sudden eruption from Joe Freeman and a half-blurted answer from Thompson. Judge Potter summoned the attorneys to the bench: "Let me see you-all up here again!"

"He's now characterizing testimony that has not even been heard," Freeman told the judge.

"But is it accurate?" Potter asked.

"When we asked him [Wernicke] what it meant to massage data," Nancy Zettler intervened, "he looked at us incredulously and he said: 'You massage people, not data.' "

Potter allowed the question.

Once more Smith asked, "Were you aware that Dr. Wernicke has testified in depositions taken in this case that you massage people, not data?"

"I'm not aware of that," said Thompson, "but I don't massage anybody, but I do massage an awful lot of data. That's my hobby."

Smith left this answer hanging in the air as he switched tactics and introduced one of the potentially more damaging suggestions he would make in the trial: that Lilly had chosen not to test ten-milligram or five-milligram doses in order to enhance profits. But first he produced a Lilly executive memorandum written in June 1985 showing that the then chairman and chief executive officer, Richard Wood, had personally amended the fixed low-dose protocol for fluoxetine. "Upon his recommendations," said the memo, "we will exclude the 10 milligram fluoxetine dosage regimen."

Having drawn some sarcastic inferences in reference to Mr. Wood's lack of medical qualifications (Mr. Wood was an M.B.A.), Smith got Thompson to confirm that the ten-milligram dosage for depression had, in fact, never been studied at Lilly before the fatal day of September 14, 1989—that, in fact, it had not been tested to "this day."

Smith now produced another memo, an E-mail from Lorenzo Tallarigo of Lilly's Italian affiliate, dated December 17, 1990, to Lilly executives in Indianapolis. It asked for clinical-trial evidence for the benefit of five- and ten-milligram dosages. The message went on to warn, "We should be very careful not to suggest that these are the more appropriate dosages if we do not want to run the risk to have the higher dosages withdrawn from the market." The memo then carried a P.S. stating, "As you may imagine, our price will be half of the actual for the 10 milligrams and one-fourth for the 5 milligrams."

"When he says 'our price,' " said Smith, "he's talking about the price that Lilly would be able to charge the patient for the medication, isn't he?"

"Well, in Italy it's a strange system. I think it's a government-reimbursement price. I wasn't aware that the Italians worked this way."

"You're going to have a reduced-price profit if you sell the product in a lower dosage, correct, according to this exhibit?"

"The price will be less, yes."

"All right. And if you lower the dosage, you run the risk to have higher dosages withdrawn from the market, correct, Dr. Thompson?"

"That's what he said."

Turning his back abruptly on the witness, Smith said, "Your Honor, I think this is all I have on that subject at this time."

23

THROUGHOUT THE TRIAL, I was settled on the seventh floor of the Brown Hotel, at Broadway and Fourth, in full view of the *Louisville Courier-Journal* building, with its green curving windows and rooftop satellite dishes. The part of Standard Gravure plant not housed within the newspaper had been razed to the ground in 1992; the space it released was being used as a parking lot by newspaper personnel.

The hotel was ten minutes' walk from the Old Jailhouse Building, down Fourth Street, a pedestrian precinct with forlorn wig shops, a sports center, and a scruffy theater. I would turn up at the courthouse early each morning, hoping for a chance to talk with the lawyers or the plaintiffs before the proceedings. Many of the audience and the court officers had lunch at Wendy's, one block east, a further opportunity to make acquaintances and pick up information.

As the trial progressed, regular spectators were becoming more familiar to each other. Occasionally Judge Potter would take off his robe during the midmorning or the afternoon recess and come out front in shirtsleeves (he favored blue shirts with white cuffs and collars, to offset his lurid bow ties).

At our first encounter, he came up to ask me in his laconic fashion what I found interesting about the trial. He was moving to and fro in a strangely restless manner, as if ready to make a speedy exit should the conversation grow uncomfortable.

I began to offer the opinion that the relationship between the brain, its natural chemistry, and human behavior was surely a crucial issue for the justice system of America.

Still bobbing and weaving around me, he interrupted to say: "Do you think so? I couldn't disagree more. I've told the jury that they should treat the brain just like they'd treat any other organ of the body—

the liver or the kidney." With this he started to walk away; then he stopped and came back. "Mind you," he said, "somebody said something very interesting the other day—that for every crooked thought there's a crooked molecule. Now, that's a strange idea. . . ." Then he was gone.

At the next break, he came and found me again. "I'm still trying to work out why this case is so important to you." But this time he did not wait for an answer.

Early in the proceedings, I tried to make a date for lunch or dinner with Leslie Scanlon of the *Louisville Courier-Journal*, a tall woman in her late thirties with gray-green eyes. She told me that she had to work through her lunch breaks in the office and usually tried to get home to her daughter and husband.

Occasionally I would run into the only other journalist, Karen Myatt of Court TV, who worked up on the third floor with her backup team. Sometimes I would go up to her domain in a slow elevator along with the plaintiffs, who had a kind of cafeteria up there with soft drinks, nonstop coffee, sandwiches, and doughnuts. Karen liked to kid around with the plaintiffs; she had everybody's Christian name and background and was a mine of gossip. Her laugh could be heard from one end of the courthouse to the other. She told me with a cackle that she had been watching the Lilly lawyers carefully on her monitor and was convinced that they all had "Prozac eyes."

I was less successful at making the acquaintance of the plaintiffs, most of whom eyed me with doleful suspicion. Mike Campbell was courteous, however, and would greet me most days, as would John Stein, who had been shot in the head.

One whispered item during the break sessions involved rumors of suspected membership in the Church of Scientology. I was asked on several occasions whether I had any such affiliation. For a time, suspicion also focused on a balding young man dressed in jeans and a sweater who sat at the back of the gallery making notes in a school exercise book, and who avoided the rest of us during recess. One day I found him lunching alone at Wendy's and joined him. I learned that he was the relative of a woman who had shot both her children after being on Prozac for eight days. He described himself as "a lawyer's investigator." He was staying at the Travelodge Hotel, four blocks down from the court-house, and had no appetite for socializing.

Another Scientologist suspect was a suited Tommy Lee Jones lookalike named Bill Bass who brought a file full of notes into court each day. Eventually he invited me to lunch and told me that he was a personal-injury attorney from Houston. He had a Prozac trial of his own coming up, he said, which he called his "Thelma and Louise case," involving a mother of three who had thrown herself into the Grand Canyon after taking Prozac for two weeks. He talked at length and in gruesome detail of the injuries she had sustained on the way down.

Bass said he thought that Smith's jury selection had been faulty, that they should have run handwriting tests on the potential jurors. "I pay a top-flight handwriting expert every time I select for a jury," he told me. "And I never go wrong." He said that the Louisville jury, composed of blue-collar workers, would have no sympathy for the plaintiffs. "These people don't believe in all that liability crap. They'll think Wesbecker was a very bad man and that the rest is bullshit." He told me that there were a lot of people of German ancestry living around Louisville, and the Germans, he said, "wouldn't take kindly to people receiving a mil-lion dollars for anything." He was also convinced there were too many elderly jurors: "Everything has changed in their world; all this is new and completely unfamiliar to them."

Bass also made much of the fact that Potter's court was, in his view, "hell on earth"; he deplored the sight of exhibits strewn about the well of the courtroom. He hated the used polystyrene cups on the tables and the bundles of documents on the floor, the laptop computers, easels, and dis-play boards, the idle overhead projectors and TV screens. "It's a slum," he told me angrily, "and Potter shouldn't allow it."

Occasionally I was approached in the lobby of the courthouse by Ed West, head of public relations at Lilly. West was a well-built fellow, over six feet, always sharply dressed in a dark suit and crisp white shirt, his toe caps well polished. Exuding confidence and confidentiality, he promised to get me together with some of the top Lilly scientists. He was keen for me to drive up to Indianapolis "to meet with all the guys," and he gave me several videos on the development of Prozac and the life of Wesbecker; playing safe, he gave me this material in a format suitable for both America and Europe. They had created these videos to bolster their portrait of Wesbecker as a natural killer.

One day Ed West invited me for lunch at the deli below the Providian Tower. Over iced tea and tuna sandwiches, he told me that one key to understanding Wesbecker was the extreme significance that Thursdays had had in his life: West had a list of events in Wesbecker's life that had occurred on Thursdays, including his divorces, his grandmother's death, and the day of the shootings. Before becoming head of public relations, West had been a top salesman with Eli Lilly. He told me he had majored in psychology at college.

I tried several times to get into conversation with the plaintiffs' counsel, Paul Smith, who would rush off with Nancy Zettler after every session with huge files, a lighted cigarette between his teeth. He was always laughing and joking with his paralegals and the court officers during these frantic end-of-session departures. One evening he gave a woman marshal, an ample African American, a sudden hug, and she playfully seized one of his cases.

"Hey, I've got evidence in that!" yelled Smith.

"Good stuff?" she asked, laughing.

"You bet. Good stuff!" he said, and snatched it back.

After many pleas of enormous pressure, Smith eventually agreed to give me a brief interview one evening after the proceedings.

We met in the offices of Hays, Ruben and Foley on South Street, close to the Galleria. The design motif of the offices included a lurid Regency stripe in green, red, and yellow, with false Doric pillars and heavy mahogany furnishings. We sat in a vast empty boardroom, Smith drinking coffee from a jumbo-size cup and smoking one cigarette after another.

He told me that he was getting about four hours' sleep a night and that he would be unable to get back home to Dallas before the end of the trial. "I get up about four-thirty," he said, "shower, then begin work. I have my first meeting with Nancy at about seven, then meet with the judge at about seven-thirty. I'm rarely in bed before midnight, and Nancy works even later, because she gets up later."

Weekends, he wanted me to know, he worked from nine to seven. "You see, the trial is just the tip of the iceberg. You can't get all that work done with just two lawyers and two legal assistants. Lilly have got twelve lawyers and about forty to fifty legal assistants."

His firm back in Dallas, he told me, numbered just three lawyers. He was exclusively a trial lawyer, mostly taking referrals from other firms, and specializing in medical-negligence and personal-injury suits. Nancy, he added, was working freelance, not in a law partnership.

He wanted to assure me during this brief meeting that he was "utterly convinced" that Prozac could be dangerous for certain individuals. "I wouldn't be here now," he said, hand on heart, "unless I really believed that." The "fundamental issue," in his view, was this: "Is it always of benefit to increase the concentration of serotonin, especially when you don't know what the concentration in any individual is at any particular time?"

"In some individuals," he went on, "we don't even know whether the reason for the depression is exclusively serotonin. . . . If all three of us were to take Prozac, would the serotonin be raised in all three of us to the same amount? I mean, I think it's ludicrous to say that this will always lead to a beneficial result. But they say, definitely, one hundred percent of the time, Prozac will alter the level of serotonin. Okay, but by how much? And how much will that increase cascade on all the other brain chemicals? Secondary messengers and everything?"

Some twenty minutes into our meeting, Nancy Zettler joined us with three fresh coffees. After settling down and lighting a cigarette, she asked me, jokingly, whether I was a Scientologist.

Smith explained: "You see, what you need to understand is what Lilly had done in connection with their defending the drug. You had this group, these Scientologists, who were a fringe group opposed to any kind of psychiatric treatment, opposed to any kind of psychotropic medication. They got hold of this issue quickly, especially after this article by Dr. Teicher came out. What Lilly did was absolutely ingenious, and probably the brainchild of this guy Ed West. They said, 'This is not an issue over whether or not Prozac is safe, this is just this fringe group attacking a pharmaceutical manufacturer.' Then the Scientologists played into their hands. So Lilly was able to use them to focus all of the real issues."

"Lilly's people like to suggest that *we* are Scientologists, but it's not true," said Nancy Zettler. "We've never had anything to do with them; we've never worked for them; never even met any of them."

"They know exactly who we are," went on Smith. "We are nothing more or less than lawyers representing individuals against a corporation."

That evening, I spent an hour in the library of the *Louisville Courier-Journal* looking through back issues of the paper covering the shootings. The photographs of the body-strewn plant, the panic-frozen faces of paramedics and police, gave a sense of the profound trauma suffered by the city as a result of Wesbecker's rampage. The pages of coverage, lasting days, confirmed the cathartic role the trial must be playing, five years later.

It was already dark when I went down to the ground-floor reception area and ran into Steve Vogel, head of security at the newspaper, who offered to walk me through the part of the newspaper plant that had once been used by Standard Gravure.

Vogel, a plump, fair-haired man, told me that he had fought in Vietnam from 1969 to 1971, and that he had worked for the Louisville Police Department until 1981.

We stood in an empty space still smelling of old machine oil and solvents where the gravure presses had once thundered. Pointing up to a hole high in the wall, he showed the spot where the bullet had lodged after Wesbecker killed himself. Then he pointed to the concrete floor where they found him lying facedown. There was nothing left to see.

Carrying his walkie-talkie, he accompanied me two blocks along Broadway toward the Brown Hotel, reminiscing about the old days on the newspaper.

"I knew old man Bingham," he said. "He was very courteous; he'd always stand up when you came into the room and would give you a chair. His son Barry was like one of the boys. He'd come and have a beer with you and treat you like an equal. They were a local family, and you had a sense that they gave Louisville a feeling of togetherness. Then the company was broken up and sold off, and these Gannett people took over, and it all changed. It's all costings, and money and pressure, individuals are less important. I'm not saying that this caused Wesbecker to do what he did, but it was part of the picture. His whole world was falling apart."

When we reached the hotel, he stood outside in a chill wind as if reluctant to go. I asked him if he had been affected by the killings.

"I've seen a lot of death in Vietnam, and in the police force," he said. "I decided that I was not going to let it get to me. . . . I kind of switched off."

Then he wished me good night and walked back toward the newspaper office.

24

ON OCTOBER 17 after the weekend, Thompson was again on the witness stand, being asked about the issue of "rechallenging." Smith asked Thompson to explain to the jury how a rechallenge test worked.

"If you took penicillin and you got a rash," said Thompson, relishing the didactic role, "then you wait for a couple months and you take penicillin again, if you get another rash that looks just the same, most scientists would say that's pretty good evidence that you're allergic to penicillin and you ought to watch out. . . . It's not a hundred percent proof positive, but it's pretty good."

Smith now reminded Thompson that the FDA had suggested a rechallenge study in connection with Prozac and suicidality and violent aggressive behavior. "That had not been done in the clinical trials up to the time it was suggested by the FDA, had it?"

"It was not done," Thompson acknowledged, "and there are a whole number of reasons why, but it was not done."

"And it has not been done to date, has it?" Smith persisted.

"That's right. And there are a whole number of reasons why it hasn't been done to date."

With superlative timing, Smith now produced a correspondence between Lilly's trial scientists and a Dr. David Dunner, "an expert psychiatrist at the University of Washington." Dunner had responded to a Lilly protocol for a rechallenge on suicidality by observing, "I think the study is doable."

This led to an exchange that had Thompson dumbfounded for a change. Smith started by pursuing Dunner's statement that a rechallenge had indeed been "doable."

"But it was your testimony earlier that you couldn't get any investigator to do it," said Smith.

"We couldn't get enough investigators who would predict that they would enroll enough patients that we would get any meaningful data; that's correct."

"But he says it is doable."

"He says it's doable, but read his next sentence."

". . . But he precedes all that with saying, 'I think the study is doable,' doesn't he?"

"Yes, sir."

"He's just going to say it may be hard, it may take a while, but it's doable?"

"Yes, sir."

"But it wasn't *done,* was it, Dr. Thompson?"

"No, sir."

Approaching the end of his direct, Smith now produced evidence indicating that the FDA, as represented by Dr. Leber, had suggested in July 1990 that Lilly "put a cap" on the number of reported adverse events under Prozac, and that Lilly executives had recommended a change in the "event term 'suicide' " to "depression" in the report data. Smith's inference was that both the FDA and Lilly had deliberately manipulated the data and terminology to make the adverse events attributed to Prozac look better than they actually were.

The line of questioning provoked Thompson to some heated ripostes, including a rejoinder that Smith was "misrepresenting this completely."

But, having raised the suggestion, Smith skillfully went on to make the most of the available evidence to support his contention. One item involved a November 1990 report by the German affiliate chief, Claude Bouchy, expressing his "great concerns" in response to the request of Lilly executives that the phrase "suicidal ideation" be changed to "depression" in data on suicidality: "I do not think I could explain to the BGA [the German government's drug-regulatory body], to a judge, to a reporter, or even to my family why we would do this," the document read, "especially on the issue of—sensitive issue of suicide and suicidal ideation, at least not with the explanations that have been given our staff so far."

Thompson now found himself fighting on three fronts: for Lilly, for the FDA, and for the German affiliate, over questions of termi-

nology, language, and the subtle distinctions statisticians are required
to make.

Here was a set of issues that could run for another week without ex-
hausting the potential for further questions and mind-bending answers,
but Potter had Smith on a time constraint, and the uncomfortable inquisition was definitively stopped by the lunch recess.

After lunch, Joe Freeman at last came to question Dr. Thompson for the
defense and, in turn, to use his evidence to redeem whatever Smith had
managed to tarnish. Freeman, too, was under a time constraint, having
been warned by the judge that he could not use Thompson to "wheel-
barrow through his whole case."

Freeman, dressed in a double-breasted green suit and brown shoes,
seemingly impatient to help the witness make a good impression, started
with Thompson's background as an academic pharmacologist—which
Smith had neglected to elicit.

Thompson told the court that his wife "said she would divorce me if
I left academia and went to a drug company." Nevertheless, he had gone
to see people in Lilly in 1982 because "I thought I might want to ask
them for some money to do some research." After seeing the Indianapolis plant, he went on, he was "frankly amazed at the quantity and quality
of research." He took a job with Lilly that same year.

Skipping Thompson's major promotion in 1983 to take over the
job of William Shedden, Freeman now encouraged him to talk about
depression.

In the most detailed description of depression so far in the trial,
Thompson talked of the major symptoms of the illness—"There are nine
kinds of symptoms that you would look for to make the diagnosis of depression"—and isolated three major ones. Depressed patients, he said,
"lose the ability to find pleasure in anything"; they are also "very fatigued and just don't have the energy to get through the day"; and, typically, they have "feelings of worthlessness or inappropriate guilt."

Perorating on the agony of depression, Thompson outdid himself in
hyperbole: "These people have the most pain of any patient I have ever
seen. I have taken care of people who had the worst burns, the worst in-

juries, the worst cancer, who are in absolute agony and who are going to die in the next few days but who fight for another minute of life. And yet one out of six *depressed* people kill themselves. . . . One out of six people who have had a legitimate diagnosis of major depressive disorder will die by suicide."

Thompson's argument was that there is a high incidence of *actual* suicide among depressed patients; that some 36 percent of depressed patients will *attempt* suicide; that about "seventy percent of people are thinking, 'We haven't gotten down there yet,' but about seventy percent of people are thinking hard about suicide when they have depression."

Moving quickly on to strategies for reporting "adverse events" back to pharmaceutical companies, Thompson now explained how depression changes over time, "so that the person who looks to you at one day like they're agitated . . . might next day or the next week in fact look more like they were retarded." Thus, Thompson went on to explain, it would not be surprising to find suicidality reported as an "adverse event" even though it was not necessarily a symptom caused by the drug.

Thompson now went on to boast about Lilly's superlative "adverse-event" collection system: "The FDA has repeatedly said that we, Lilly, have the best system for collecting and analyzing and reporting adverse events, and the same thing has been said to us by foreign regulators."

Smith, not surprisingly, requested to approach the bench to object that such comments were "totally hearsay and self-serving." It was a warning shot that the defendants would not be able to continue this line of self-description with impunity.

For much of the afternoon, Thompson was encouraged to talk of the sixteen years of exhaustive studies of Prozac, not only in the United States but in seventy countries of the world. He said he would have liked to cite a long list of benefits that had been reported for Prozac—including treatment of obesity, obsessive-compulsive disease, and bulimia, cessation of smoking, alcoholism, even trichotillomania (pulling out hair), and panic attacks—but "I can't even keep up with the catalogue for all the things that people are publishing on."

He then proceeded to defend the recommended dosage of twenty milligrams daily as facilitating patient compliance: "One of the key problems in taking a chronic medicine is taking it right every day. And if you have a complicated regimen, it makes it more difficult for the patient to take."

Thompson went on to talk at length about a multitude of studies, reports, symposia, and committee and board meetings conducted to deal with the fears raised by the Teicher paper (the 1990 Harvard study alleging violent behavior, including suicidality, of patients on Prozac) and the Wesbecker affair, all leading up to a one-day advisory meeting of experts held by the FDA on September 20, 1991. The question addressed by the meeting was "Is there any especial drug or class of drugs that seem to have greater risk than the others in terms of being associated with suicidality or violent behavior?"

This meeting, Thompson said, was really called to discuss all antidepressants, but, "frankly, Lilly was the only company that agreed to appear, and virtually all the discussion or almost all the discussion was about Prozac. And what they said was that Prozac had been studied more than any other drug in this regard, so it was really the primary focus of this meeting."

According to Thompson, a vote was taken at the end of the meeting on the motion "that there was no evidence that any group of drugs or individual drug was associated with greater risk of suicide or violent behavior." The decision, he said, was unanimous among the committee members—ten to zero. Moreover, "Dr. Teicher, who was sitting there, said that those were honest votes and that he was pleased with them."

Smith was on his feet: "Your Honor, we'd object to that. It's total hearsay, it's self-serving. . . ."

Judge Potter sustained the objection.

Rounding off his questioning, Freeman asked Thompson what he meant by "credible" when he had said earlier that there was "no credible evidence" that Prozac could cause suicide or violent aggressive behavior.

"This says, looked at as a scientist, there's no credible evidence . . ."

"Did the committee look at violent hostile behavior as well?"

"Yes, sir."

"And what did they find with respect to that?"

"Well, the vote was actually the same, because it included suicidality, violent behavior, either/or, or both."

"Ten to zero?"

"Ten to zero on both votes."

25

THE WITNESS who was now called to the stand had been a leading critic of Eli Lilly and Company and its product Prozac for some years. Dr. Peter Breggin, aged fifty-eight, author of *Toxic Psychiatry* and *Talking Back to Prozac*, had devoted the last several years of his life to combating the tendency to treat mental illness, and especially depression, with pharmaceutical products rather than psychotherapy and other forms of talk therapy. Breggin has often been lumped with Thomas Szasz, who had been his mentor, and R. D. Laing as being anti-psychiatry, but he is significantly less radical than these two in his proposals.

Thomas Szasz sees psychiatric labels as pejorative social constructions that depersonalize people we do not like. By labeling people in this way, Szasz maintains, and segregating them from society, we deny the role played by society in creating mental illness.

R. D. Laing, on the other hand, claimed that schizophrenia was a result of hypocrisy in the nuclear family; he believed that parents who systematically lie emotionally to their children can produce schizophrenic behavior in them. His recommended treatment therefore involved talk therapy for the entire family.

Breggin does not go to the extreme of denying the existence of mental illness, nor does he suggest that the use of drugs is in all cases inadvisable. He claims, rather, that a wide range of pharmaceutical products are less effective and more dangerous than patients realize, and emphasizes stress in the family, community, and society as a prime cause of mental illness.

Burly, somewhat overweight, and silver-haired, Breggin gave out a strong sense of belligerence and self-confidence. He was dressed in a blue blazer, pink shirt, and light-gray pants. He said that he was married and had four children, ages fifteen to thirty-two. He had been in private practice as a psychiatrist since 1968 and was currently teaching a post-graduate program part-time at George Mason University in northern Virginia. His teaching duties involved work in "human conflict" at every level.

After twenty minutes on Breggin's background, Smith suddenly changed tack. "Why don't you tell the jury basically what psychiatrists do. I mean . . . you're a shrink. Give us generally how you set about to help people suffering from a mental disorder."

Breggin declared that he thought psychotherapy "very useful." He conceded that controversy thrived within the profession as to how useful it was with people who are diagnosed manic-depressive or schizo-phrenic, "but I find it very useful really with all diagnostic groups of people."

Breggin admitted that he sometimes prescribes drugs to his patients, but explained that he does it a little differently from most psychiatrists. "I see many people on medication because they've already been on it when they come to me, and I either let them stay on it, if that's what they want, or very frequently people come to me for help in coming off of medication. . . . I'm known as somebody who looks at and understands adverse effects of medication."

"Do you believe," Smith asked, "that Joseph Wesbecker would have benefited from any psychopharmacological treatment?"

"He wanted it," said Breggin, "and he felt it was helpful. The doctor was doing it in a rational manner, you know, and he was certainly oper-ating by standard practice. But, again, it's not how I would have ap-proached it."

Breggin said he became interested in the problems of psychiatric medication as a student back in 1954, noticing how many of the patients were being heavily sedated. It struck him that though such medication "made the hospitals quieter and the patients more subdued it was not getting the patients out and, in fact, the reduction in the state mental-hospital population doesn't begin for ten years."

Moving on from psychopharmacology, Breggin outlined the impor-tance of the brain's natural chemistry.

"An interesting way to think about it," he said, "is that we started in life as a one-celled animal and then evolved. Just one-celled animals in the ocean, and the cells got together. They aggregated, they became bodies, and the problem of the cells was how to communicate."

"Wait a minute," Smith interrupted. "Did God have any part in this?"

"I think so, but I'm not an expert on that."

"Okay. I just want to make sure we weren't turning this into some evolutionary trial."

"I'm staying within the narrow limits of science," said Breggin, "and I'm the first to acknowledge its very narrow limits. . . .

"There are many different ways that the cells in the controlling network, in the brain, talk to each other. Basically they put out some substances that are rather free-floating to communicate and they put out some that are very specific neurotransmitters calculated to tell the next cell to fire or not fire, to influence the next cell. . . . If you think of a brain cell as having an arm that reaches out to the next cell, and at the end would be like a hand, and that hand is dropping packets of chemicals, neurotransmitters, into an infinitesimally small space, the synaptic cleft, where the next hand is grabbing it . . . It's really like sparks. You think of them as sparks, but they're individualized sparks, so that the serotonin spark only is going to fire a serotonin receptor."

Each of the expositors in the trial so far had expressed the operation of the brain and central nervous system differently, both in style and in background metaphor. With his acknowledgment of evolution, of the limitations of science, of the vastness and complexity of the brain; with his handshakes and sparks, and his generally user-friendly and reassuring images, Breggin at the outset seemed the most accessible.

None of the neurotransmitters, Breggin went on, go more places in the brain than serotonin. "The nerves that are releasing serotonin, and which are affected by Prozac, reach out all over the brain and the central nervous system. . . ." Breggin stopped a moment, as if to change mental gears. "The whole organ works together. It's an orchestra, but we're sort of talking about the violins. It goes to the limbic system, associated with the emotions, color of emotions, intensity of emotions . . . into the spinal cord and the body, and particularly it has an effect on the intestines. . . . Your thyroid hormone, sexual hormones, the stress hormones are all being affected by the serotonin system, and hence by Prozac when it affects the serotonin system. . . ."

The idea behind Prozac, he went on, "is to keep the serotonin in the synaptic gap longer, so that these cells are being bombarded, or, in a sense, jacked up, just like a sense if you were flooding your carburetor, getting more in and trying to get the system to go faster. . . . Now, the nerve doesn't in a sense like that, because this is an intrusion into the metabolic processes of the brain, so the brain kicks in with . . . compensatory mechanisms. The nerve is either putting out fewer packages of serotonin or none. This is a compensatory shutdown mechanism."

Smith had ceased to question his witness, as if allowing Breggin to take over the presentation of his testimony. He was lecturing the jury, and defense counsel seemed happy to give him his head.

"But another thing happens, because the brain greets the presence of Prozac as an intrusion," Breggin continued. "The brain didn't evolve or wasn't God-given to accept Prozac. These receptors begin to disappear. . . . This is down-regulation." According to some researchers, Breggin said, people could lose up to 60 percent of their active serotonin receptors.

A full half-hour went by before Smith intervened to ask why Thompson thought all this was important—why did the effect of Prozac on the brain matter.

"Because, actually, we're only guessing as to what the overall effect is. It's not like when you give insulin and you watch the blood sugar go down, or you stop the insulin and the blood sugar goes back up. We haven't got anything tiny enough to go in there and know what the overall effect is on this system. . . ."

Smith looked at his watch. "It's five after five, Your Honor. It might be an appropriate time to stop."

26

THE FOLLOWING MORNING, Peter Breggin again took the stand to answer Smith's questions about Prozac.

After acknowledging that "we don't know how our brain relates to thought and to feeling," Breggin declared that it was generally accepted among neuroscientists that serotonin "has something to do with the regulation of impulses . . . either violent impulses toward others or toward self."

There are hundreds of articles, Breggin said, arguing that in some people the serotonin system is low, sluggish, less active when people are lacking in impulse control. On the other hand, he went on, "there's a lot of information on what happens when the system is jacked up too high." He stated that such an event was "likely to cause impulse-control problems at the other end."

Prozac's overall effect, he went on, "is to increase the output of the activity of this serotonin system, thus producing agitation, hyperactivity, overstimulation, irritability. And some people think that when the system is hyperactive it tends to produce anxiety and upset and agitation, and when it's too low it tends to produce depression. . . . We can say the consensus is this system has to do with impulse control."

Smith continued all morning to allow Breggin scope to freewheel his way through a series of generally condemnatory descriptions of Prozac. His arguments lacked shape and direction, and he was making no attempt to explain some of the inherent ambiguities in his exposition; for example, how low serotonin activity seems consistent with both criminal behavior and depression. And he frequently assured the jury that most of the claims made by the manufacturer were based on hypotheses rather than hard scientific fact, without explaining where the dividing line lay between proof and theory in science.

His argument developed sharper focus, however, when he described how high levels of hyperactivity provoked by Prozac were to be found in one out of one hundred people, according to scientific studies: "In the extreme, it produces a degree of stimulation which is psychotic in level, that is, the person loses touch with reality. They're so overstimulated they may think they're God or may think they're some incredible person."

He added that reactions to the intrusion of a drug can differ from person to person, just as with alcohol. Alluding to the fact that when Wesbecker first took Prozac in 1988 he became "fatigued," he explained that this was "almost certainly because he was taking toxic doses of lithium at the time." The patient, he pointed out, voluntarily stopped taking Prozac after a couple of days.

After an hour or so of testimony of this nature, Joe Freeman suddenly rose and asked to approach the bench, appearing both upset and determined. He wanted to make a statement to the judge and asked that the witness be absent while he did so.

After Breggin had left the courtroom, Freeman said, "Your Honor, first of all, we'd like to move to prevent this witness from giving any opinion in this case. . . . The evidence as it now stands in the case would not support him being able to give *any* opinion."

Freeman was objecting that Breggin was raising "matters that are nowhere in evidence," such as Wesbecker's medical records. More important, Freeman was appealing to the Daubert decision in U.S. federal law, which lays down criteria for qualifications and conduct on the part of expert scientific witnesses. His argument was that Breggin had been making contradictory claims about the effects of Prozac—as being, on the one hand, scientifically proved, and, on the other, purely hypothetical. "Tomorrow," Freeman suggested, "the whole premise of what I'm saying may not even be believed by anyone." Freeman's motion—to plead that Breggin was not qualified to be an expert witness—was designed merely to knock the psychiatrist off-balance. The defense had already attempted to disqualify Breggin according to the Daubert judgment before the trial began, and failed.

The arguments went back and forth for fifteen minutes or so until Judge Potter declared that Breggin was evidently qualified to form opinions about Prozac, and that Kentucky Rules of Evidence were "really very forgiving" on what he could bring as evidence.

On the point of the Daubert ruling, he said: "People tend to forget Daubert was a plaintiff's case. It was a case where the lower courts had not allowed certain testimony because it wasn't scientifically acceptable enough but the Supreme Court said they were going to permit it . . ."

Back on course, Smith asked Breggin outright his opinion as to the cause of Joseph Wesbecker's conduct on September 14, 1989.

"That Prozac was a substantial factor," responded Breggin, "a substantial cause in the events of that date in the production of violence, in the production of suicide, and that it wouldn't have happened without Prozac."

"And how did you start to come to this opinion?" asked Smith.

Breggin talked about the reports he had heard in workshops around the country and explained how he had begun to interview a number of the patients and their doctors. Then he turned to the conduct of the clinical trials. Lilly's investigators, he claimed, had been told, "if they get something that's a depression phenomenon, which would be like a suicide attempt, don't report it as a drug effect. Assume it's the depression."

"But that was what the study was supposed to decide," Breggin continued. "So we have a study that's not including heavily suicidal patients or patients like Mr. Wesbecker, who had some real suicidality in the past, not generally including them; not including people with paranoid psychoses in the past, or like Mr. Wesbecker, with manic-depressive disorder or schizoaffective disorder; it's not including all the high-risk people that this drug will eventually be given to."

Breggin now focused on the Prozac toxicology studies performed at Lilly in 1974 in which rats became "hyperirritable," and in 1978 in which dogs became "aggressive." He spoke of a report by Ray Fuller, coinventor of the drug, involving studies on humans in 1979 in which Fuller had written: "Some patients have converted from severe depression to agitation within a few days. . . . In one case the agitation was marked and the patient had to be taken off the drug. In future studies, the use of benzodiazepines to control agitation will be permitted."

According to Breggin, "very early on" Lilly "had a catastrophe" on their hands, since it seemed that they would have to use Prozac "in combination with a sedative."

Breggin now referred to a report by Dr. Richard Kapit, who had been chief medical officer at the FDA and had specific charge of writing the safety review of Prozac. Writing about Phase II (extended tests on humans) Prozac studies in 1986, Kapit reported five "serious clinical events" in the first seventy-seven patients. One involved "a paranoid psychosis," said Breggin, "and a manic psychosis ... relevant to the Wesbecker issues because Mr. Wesbecker very well may have had a drug-induced paranoid psychosis, a delusion about things being done to him at this workplace that enrages him and makes him want to take an action."

The Phase III trials (blind studies), went on Breggin, quoting from Lilly's protocol, provided that "if a patient complains of agitation the dose of the study drug should be reduced and the patient may receive a benzodiazepine at the investigator's discretion." From which Breggin concluded that "they expected the drug was doing it," and yet, he went on, "they never put it on the label."

By the afternoon, it became clear that Breggin was shaping his own offensive once more with very little prompting from Smith. Breggin spoke rapidly, sometimes repetitively, and used the attorney's questions as an opportunity to take off in his own direction, causing Freeman to complain that he was not responding to questions.

Smith told me later that he had had great difficulty with Breggin, who thought he had better ideas on how to conduct the case than the plaintiffs' attorneys.

The story Breggin had to tell about Prozac was familiar to anybody who had followed adverse press reports on Prozac during the previous four years. Listing some dozen principal citations in scientific and medical journals, Breggin mentioned the Teicher report in 1990; the work of King and Riddle at Yale "on the emergence of several destructive phenomena in children and adolescents during fluoxetine trials" (in which six of forty-two children developed "self-destructive and agitated phenomena"); a study in the spring 1992 issue of the *Journal of Analytical Toxicology*, suggesting that Prozac "may produce suicidal tendencies in some patients"; and an editorial in the *Lancet*, August 11, 1990, saying much the same thing.

The material was impressive, but Breggin's rendering of it was uneconomical and unfocused. To add to the jury's woes, the air-conditioning system had broken down, on a day when the temperature outside soared into the humid eighties.

The following morning, the judge had an admonition for the jurors. He told them that while watching coverage of the O. J. Simpson trial the evening before, he saw something that startled him. Apparently Judge Ito had told the jurors not to read a certain book, which had drawn the reflection from a TV commentator that the admonition probably "would not work."

"From that," went on Judge Potter, "you might get the idea that what I tell you every day about reading things or letting people talk to you about it is some kind of show or I'm not serious about it. I mean, when I heard them say that on TV, I thought it would be the easiest thing in the world: I simply explain to the jury, if I find out anybody is reading the book, you'll end up in jail, and it *would* work!"

Some of the jurors laughed, a little nervously; but it was clear to all present that Judge Potter would indeed throw anyone in jail who defied his orders. The moral the jurors were clearly intended to draw from Potter's warning was that things in the state of Kentucky were ordered differently from those in California.

Breggin started the morning with an impressionistic account of Wesbecker's psychological profile. Stressing his expertise in studies of "family and domestic conflict," Breggin said he thought that the early loss of his father, the estrangement of his mother, and the period Wesbecker spent in an orphanage were not sufficient to explain his psychological difficulties, let alone the killing spree. He was more inclined to believe that the impact of two divorces "played a role in his having difficulties. Like many people, when he went through separation and divorce, it was probably the most traumatic experience of his life." Even so, there was no evidence of the isolation that leads to homicide, said Breggin; in fact, even after the end of his second marriage, "he has the remarkable wherewithal to maintain the relationship with his wife."

"What's your opinion," Smith asked Breggin, "about the change in this man's condition since he began the Prozac?"

It was a crucial question for the plaintiff's expert witness.

Breggin told a hushed courtroom: "It's an abrupt change. It takes place in less than a month. It is a typical agitation reaction. It is exactly what I have documented . . . as one of the effects of Prozac, in fact, as the primary side-effect constellation of Prozac starting with the animal research through the very first Phase I and Phase II studies and right on up. He also at this point would seem to be suffering from a delusion, and Prozac can in the process of this overstimulation produce psychosis; that's been recorded again and again and is acknowledged in the labeling by the FDA."

Breggin then emphasized that Dr. Coleman had been convinced that Wesbecker's deterioration and delusion were caused by the medication. This was one of Smith's aces in the trial, and he now sought to play it for all it was worth by producing, despite considerable protest from the defense attorneys, a deposition he had taken from Coleman a year earlier.

Breggin read out Dr. Coleman's deposition, dated September 9, 1993:

"I knew that Prozac in some people could cause nervousness, could cause agitation, could cause sleep problems, plus I had started him on it three or four weeks before. When you start a new medication and something different happens, you tend to support that it's the medication that is causing it within that period of time."

Breggin commented that this was the only occasion in two years on which the psychiatrist had recommended immediate hospitalization for his patient.

This was powerful evidence for a nonspecialist jury, but Smith and Breggin had now to offer an explanation for Wesbecker's long history of threats, his purchases of guns and ammunition before he started on that course of Prozac in August 1989.

"Does this cause you to pause to reflect," asked Smith, "whether or not the purchase of these guns, and guns of this nature, indicates a plan long before Prozac to do what was done?"

". . . I think what he's trying to do," said Breggin, "as he has always done, is handle his feeling of anger, his feeling of vulnerability. He's doing it while being armed, he's doing it by having a gun, but he's handling it in a conventional, acceptable manner. . . . And then, on his last outing, the gun jams. . . . He does not fix the gun until he takes Prozac. In that agitated state he goes and gets his gun repaired."

"And what's the significance of that?" asked Smith.

"People buy a lot of guns when they feel vulnerable. But this is scary. This is a signal. . . . This man, who has been struggling on and on with his life because of impulse control but he has no major huge stressors at the moment, takes Prozac, gets agitated, and loses control of the impulses that he has struggled with on and off since at least '84."

"What else do we have concerning Mr. Wesbecker's threats after he goes on Prozac?"

". . . Brenda was interviewed by at least two police persons the day of the shooting. . . . She says clearly that there's been a change in him since the drug started. . . . The police report says, 'She stated they sleep in separate rooms because of Joe's mental condition, and the medicine that he takes causes him to be fidgety and occasionally he gets up in the middle of the night and walks around. . . .' Now, remember, Mr. Wesbecker thought Prozac was helping him and, precisely, that it had helped him remember the sex abuse, which I think is in effect saying that the medicine made him deluded, made him think he remembered the sex abuse, but he is being deluded about it, thinks it's positive. . . . That's one of the dangers of the drug. . . . We have here the police reports of Brenda really attributing his emotional upset to the drug and saying, 'I asked him to go to the doctor and get rid of this drug, but he obviously thinks it's a wonder drug.' He called it *good shit* at one point, which clearly is saying like a street drug. I mean, you say that about marijuana, speed, and things like that."

After three days of questioning, Smith finished with Breggin in the following fashion:

"Do you have an opinion whether or not Prozac as to Joseph Wesbecker was unreasonably dangerous?"

"The very fact that Mr. Wesbecker was already struggling with violent impulses—see, it's really important that here he is, he's already struggling with emotional instability, he has a diagnosis of schizo-affective disorder, he's given a drug that's never been tested on patients with these problems in its FDA approval process. It's a drug that would be expected to . . ."

"Dr. Breggin, was it unreasonably dangerous for Joseph Wesbecker?"

"It was unreasonably dangerous, particularly for Joseph Wesbecker, unreasonably dangerous."

"Did it present an unreasonable degree of harm for Joseph Wesbecker?"

"For Joseph Wesbecker and those around him it produced an unreasonable risk of harm."

"Did it produce an unreasonable risk of harm for the plaintiffs in this case?"

"Yes. Definitely."

"Do you have an opinion concerning whether or not Prozac was a substantial factor in this tragedy that occurred at Standard Gravure on September 14th, 1989?"

"Definitely, it was a very substantial factor in what he did."

With that, Judge Potter called a lunch recess until one-forty-five. But before letting the attorneys go, he held a brief conference on the subject of jurors' questions. He told them that there had been an unusual number of requests from the jury for clarification on technical and medical matters: they seemed to be coming in at the rate of two a day.

"I've never had this happen," said Freeman. "I've had one question in thirty years."

"We always get questions in Texas when the jury goes out to start deliberating," said Smith.

"We get those, too," said Potter. "And really I wouldn't have said that much about it, I normally don't mention it, but this is such a long trial."

"And it's complicated," added Smith.

"But, quite frankly, I hoped I would scare them out of doing it," went on Potter. "But when they passed our new evidence code they actually put it in the evidence code."

"They have the absolute right to do that," said Smith facetiously.

Not to be outdone in facetiousness, Potter responded, "Believe it or not, *I* have the right to ask questions and call witnesses. You want me to scare *you* to death?"

Smith laughed. "You remember the famous line from *The Verdict*, don't you," he said, "where Paul Newman was having trouble proving his medical-malpractice case and the old cranky judge hated him, just hated him? And the judge started asking questions, and Paul Newman says, 'Judge, if you're going to try my case, please don't screw it up.' "

With that, they all went to lunch.

27

DURING LUNCH RECESS, there had been much gossip in Wendy's about how Joe Freeman would handle his cross-examination of Breggin. The consensus was that the campaigning psychiatrist, used to confronting his antagonists, the psychopharmacologists, on TV talk shows, would prove a powerful adversary of Prozac when on the defensive.

Back in court, the members of the jury and the audience prepared themselves for some tough technical questions and answers ranging over clinical trials and statistics and various neuroscientific matters.

When it came, Freeman's line of questioning took everybody—not least Peter Breggin—by surprise.

After a slow beginning, with some odd questions about the meaning of the term "existential psychiatry," Freeman suddenly asked him, "Now, if I understand you, when you describe what you do in your practice, you indicated that you help people develop better principles for living?"

The innocuousness of this question seemed suspicious, but it delighted Breggin. He began to ease into his answer, became more expansive and relaxed by the minute. "That's one of the things. That's one part. See, people get bad principles, confused principles, when they grow up...." As he settled back, he began to waffle. And Freeman, nodding sagely, seemed happy to let him do so.

When Breggin at last fell silent, Freeman asked him again: "But to help people develop *better* principles of living?"

"Yes, sir," said Breggin, a look of puzzlement on his face.

"That is a direct quote, is it not?"

"Oh, it could be. It's what I believe."

Freeman paused for a moment. Then he asked: "Also, have you said and written that 'permitting children to have *sex* among themselves would go a long way toward liberating them from oppressive parental authority,' as reported in your book *The Psychology of Freedom*?"

There was an audible gasp from every quarter of the courtroom. In the moment it took Freeman to ask his question, the whole tenor of the trial seemed to have changed. The gloves were coming off. And it was abundantly clear that Breggin, Smith's star witness, along with his reputation and his opinions on Prozac, or on almost any other subject under the sun, were about to be irretrievably altered in the eyes of the decent Jefferson County folk who sat in the jury box.

Breggin, smiling nervously and shaking his head, did not handle the question well.

"That . . . if I could roll back time and roll up that sheet of paper"— he made a rolling motion with his hands—"it certainly was something I said. It's wrong. I never repeated it again. I wrote it more than fifteen years ago; it got published in 1980. I'd like to explain where I got such an idea from, but it's a wrong idea. . . ."

Breggin was falling apart before our very eyes, and Freeman had not even got started. Breggin was blathering his answers, appealing for clemency. "Could I explain where I got that idea from, what the context of the book is?"

"If they want to ask you that on cross," said Freeman, nodding toward Smith, "they certainly would."

Freeman again quoted from the book: " 'If two little children are fond of each other and if they learn to treat each other with respect, don't worry about what they are doing behind closed doors. . . .' "

Again, turning to the judge, Breggin begged to be allowed to explain.

"He can explain it," said Potter abruptly.

"I mean," started Breggin, "because it's an embarrassment; this is a dumb idea, but I'd like you to know what the context of it was. It was not an idea that played any role in my therapy ever, any role in raising kids. . . ."

Breggin was rambling, and Freeman indulged him.

When he had finished, Freeman asked him in indignant tones: "Did you accept money for putting these ideas in writing and selling them to the general public of the United States of America? Did you accept money for doing so?"

"I got a small amount of money for the book," said Breggin.

"In the same book, on the subject of religion, on page seventy, you quote the difference between believing in the divine . . ."

Smith was at last objecting. The judge called the attorneys to the bench.

"Let me hear what the quote is going to be," said Potter.

"The thrust of the quote," said Freeman, "is there's no difference in believing you're Christ and believing *in* Christ, and I think this goes to his whole credibility on principles and everything else that he says he espouses."

"This is religious premise," countered Smith, "and it is wholly inappropriate to what the man's religion is."

"This is a psychiatric principle," said Freeman.

"Let me see the book," said Potter, reaching for it.

After reading for about half a minute, he said: ". . . Mr. Smith, he's talking about mental illness."

"Don't let him characterize it as a religious philosophy, Your Honor."

"It's a quote. Go ahead."

Freeman went ahead. " 'The difference between believing in the divinity of Christ and believing in oneself as Christ is merely a difference in religious point of view': did you make that statement?"

Again Breggin was stumbling through an answer that lasted several minutes: ". . . This is something my professor, Thomas Szasz, at the university spoke about. And the point he was trying to make, and that I was trying to make, is that having a belief is not a biochemical disorder, so that the person who has gotten all enrapt in themselves and thinks they are the center of the religious universe, that they are like God, that that person in a sense . . . But at any rate, the point I was trying to make is that beliefs are not diseases of a biochemical nature. . . . There's a lot of edge in that book I'm not comfortable with. I don't hand it out."

Suddenly Freeman was bellowing in his broad Georgian accent, marching across the well of the court toward the witness. "And yet today you have been here for two days, sir," he yelled, "testifying that Mr. Joseph Wesbecker for a biochemical reason went out and did what he did on September the 14th, in the year 1989, have you not?"

Even as Breggin replied with meek assent, Smith was on his feet. "Your Honor," he shouted, "we'd object to counsel approaching the witness and screaming at the witness. That's inappropriate behavior."

"Why don't you stay back at the table? How about that?" said Potter.

"I'm sorry," said Freeman in a tone of injured righteousness. ". . . I just get a little upset. . . ."

"That's all right," said Potter with a hint of sarcasm.

Having collected his papers and suppressed his sense of outrage, Freeman launched forth again.

"Now, also, some of your scientific writings have appeared in . . . the *Penthouse* magazine; is that true or not, sir?" Freeman acted as if he found it difficult even to articulate the name of the aforementioned periodical. He held up, between thumb and forefinger, a copy of the magazine featuring a scantily clad female on the cover. Nervous giggles from the audience.

". . . And in that article you blamed English and American psychiatrists—psychiatry—for Hitler's racial programs in the extermination of the Jews, did you not? . . . In the second paragraph of the article it says, 'Without the support of English and American psychiatry, Hitler's racial programs might never have become so acceptable, and without the active efforts of German psychiatry, the extermination program would have never gotten off the ground.' Is that an accurate quote, sir?"

Breggin had meanwhile made a decision. He was going to defend the notions in the article, and he was going to do it at length.

Setting out on a confused exculpation, he tried to explain that German psychiatry under Hitler organized systematically the murder of mental patients. German psychiatrists, he said, lent themselves to this holocaust by agreeing to select patients for sterilization and eventual death. "These were biological psychiatrists," he said, a term Breggin used to mean psychiatrists who favor medication over talk. Those oriented toward a psychoanalytical and social approach, he went on, had been deported or in many cases were themselves victims of the death camps.

Breggin continued for about ten minutes. He was nervous and upset, and although much of what he said may well have been historically authentic, it came across as inappropriate.

Toward the end, he said, "Now I'll finish with perhaps the saddest part of the story, from my viewpoint as an American. In 1941, there was a debate held in the American Psychiatric Association about whether we in America should be exterminating incurable five-year-olds who were severely mentally retarded . . . and then the most grim of all things, an editorial appeared in the *American Journal of Psychiatry* in 1942, calling for the extermination of the incurably retarded."

"Are you *quite* finished?" asked Freeman.

Now it was Breggin's turn to express moral outrage. He was shouting at Freeman to take away the copy of the magazine: "Would you remove this, please? I find the cover offensive. Would you remove it, please? Would you *please* take this *back,* sir?"

Mr. Freeman, however, stood solidly behind his table.

"You can just set it on the floor," said Judge Potter, evidently amused by all this porno bathos.

But Freeman was already making moves to have photocopies of the article, including a caricature of a Nazi psychiatrist and the offensive cover, distributed among the jurors for "identification purposes."

After asking to approach the bench, Smith told Potter, "They must really be worried about Dr. Breggin if they would attach the cover of the magazine and this drawing here. . . . It's appalling to me."

"The caricature is an illustration for the article and it can come in with the front page off," ruled Potter calmly.

Suddenly Freeman changed tack. Was it true that Breggin "had been critical of psychiatrists that prescribed medication for the treatment of mental disorders?" His very tone insinuated that such a conviction was on a par with child sex and believing that American psychiatrists had caused the Nazi holocaust.

He then asked Breggin whether he was board-certified, which Breggin was not; and whether he would in any circumstances commit a dangerous patient to the hospital, which he would not. He asked him, as director of the Center for the Study of Psychiatry, how many employees he had—which Breggin was bound to admit was just a single part-timer. Then he asked how much Breggin was being paid by the plaintiffs.

Immediately Smith was on his feet, pleading prejudice. But Potter overruled him, and Breggin had to admit that he expected to receive $45,000 over a two-year period.

Then came an exchange that had Breggin, and most of the court, squirming with embarrassment.

"Is organic chemistry a cornerstone for pharmacology?" asked Freeman.

There was silence in the court for a few moments. Breggin smiled nervously at his interrogator. "I'm smiling," he said eventually, "because in deposition you found the only failing or near-failing grade I ever had in twenty years of going to school."

"Your Honor, I have a question pending," said Freeman, turning toward the bench.

"Doctor, I think you need to answer his question," said Potter.

"Biochemistry, organic chemistry, I don't know if it's a cornerstone for pharmacology, but it certainly would be a very important part of it."

"And you indicated that we somehow embarrassed you in your deposition, upon asking you about what you made on a grade in organic chemistry when you were coming here to testify against us?"

For a few moments, Breggin appeared to be beside himself with humiliation and anger. "You didn't embarrass me," he cried. "You *abused* me. Here I am, a person who has had almost straight A's his entire life, who graduated near the top of his class in high school, near the top of his class at Harvard, who never failed a subject in all of medical school, who never had any grade below C and had almost all A's, and somehow you managed to find I got a D in organic chemistry. It's astonishing. Did you also notice I graduated with honors despite that D, that I got into medical school, the best in the country?"

"We are delighted for you, sir. In spite of that grade, we're delighted that you did," said Freeman sarcastically.

"That's what the astonishment was about, sir, that you could manage . . . in such an academic career, that you could find a grade that was my senior year of college; I was already in medical school. I have to admit that, having already gotten into medical school and being in my senior year, I was not as attentive as I might have been."

But Freeman was not through.

"And having been *turned down* for the Harvard Medical School; isn't that true?"

"Yes. Probably fortunately, too," said Breggin bitterly. "I might not have been *smart* enough for Harvard Medical School. That is tough. That is tough, sir."

Changing his tactics one more, Freeman now embarked on a review of Wesbecker's entire life from birth to death. His intention was to ask Breggin, first, whether he was aware of certain specific factors in Wesbecker's biography, and, second, whether those factors were to be found in Dr. Coleman's notes.

The purpose of the exercise, which took almost two hours, was to establish a set of hereditary assumptions in relation to mental illness in Wesbecker's life, and to isolate early influences and life crises that might have led to psychopathic behavior. At the same time, Freeman wanted to show that few of these factors had been known to Wesbecker's psychiatrist Dr. Coleman, since Wesbecker had deliberately concealed them from him.

Throughout this section of Q and A, Breggin was increasingly at Freeman's mercy; he could not help playing into his hands.

"I ask you, sir," Freeman said at one point, "did you know that Joseph Wesbecker lived with Murrell Wesbecker at six years of age and that she was dragged out of the house screaming as they were taking her to the mental hospital for life as a lunatic? Did you know that, sir?"

"I don't have those details. Don't know if they're true or false."

"That would not be helpful to a young person in terms of his environment, would it, sir?"

"I don't know if he witnessed it."

"I will ask you to assume that he was there, there alone with his grandmother when this happened."

"It would be terrible."

As Freeman progressed through this highlighted history of Wesbecker's journey to homicidal disaster, Paul Smith was becoming more restless, increasingly objecting to the veracity of alleged incidents. When Freeman eventually claimed that Wesbecker's mother had attempted suicide, and that Wesbecker had tried to beat her up, Smith was on his feet. "We dispute this testimony," he declared heatedly.

Potter called them to the bench.

"Mrs. Wesbecker has testified and she mentioned nothing about that," said Smith, "and they had the opportunity to ask her about that."

". . . I'm assuming that with each of these questions," said Potter, "there's going to be evidence at the end of this case that will support a finding that they're correct."

"Our position is," responded Smith, "they're not going to be able to tie up half of this, and to do this with our expert will indelibly imprint in the jury's mind a false impression of this man's background."

Eventually Potter ruled that Freeman could seek confirmation in the form of questions from Breggin; Smith was hardly placated.

Much of the material was familiar but presented so as to show Wesbecker in the worst possible light, relating to such episodes as his estrangement from his son Kevin, his desire to send James to Boys Haven, and his various threats against Standard Gravure. The purpose was evidently to convince the jurors once again that Wesbecker's killing spree was the inevitable result of the circumstances of his whole life and influences, rather than his medication.

Freeman was not so much asking questions as promoting a particular view of Wesbecker's life. The crestfallen Breggin seemed uncomfortable throughout, and it was unlikely that he had retrieved anything of his enormously damaged prestige.

By the end of his cross-examination, Freeman had managed to question Breggin for more than two hours without a single mention of Eli Lilly.

The trial gained momentum for the plaintiffs once more on October 24, when their second expert witness was called: a supremely confident, fast-talking, youthful-looking woman named Dr. Nancy Lord, dressed in a well-cut navy-blue suit and silk turtleneck sweater. She was striking in appearance, with a wide mouth and a strong aquiline nose, her dark, naturally wavy hair worn long. For the first time, Nancy Zettler was handling the direct.

Dr. Lord admitted to being forty-two years of age, and not married "at this time." Her career had evidently taken her on an unerring path to consultancy and expert testimony. She had majored, she said, in chemistry at the University of Maryland, then attended medical school on the same campus. On becoming a doctor, she specialized for two years in pathology, then went to work at Abbott Laboratories, the pharmaceutical company, in Chicago, where she was the author of a new-drug application for a benzodiazepine called Prosom. After that she studied law, specializing in criminal and regulatory law, and became a free-lance consultant for lawyers and drug companies who were having regulatory problems with the FDA.

For about an hour, Lord explained with clarity and confidence the process of an NDA, how a new-drug application is processed for presentation to the FDA; some of the details were already known to the court, but it was clear that Zettler wanted her witness to show off her familiarity with the procedures and to establish her credentials both as a consultant and as an expert witness on the Prozac NDA.

Her testimony began to take a more lively turn, however, when she was invited to comment on Lilly's clinical-trial data, which, she said, she had scrutinized at random, making detailed spot checks in order to get a feel for its overall quality.

"When I looked at the Lilly data, I didn't find that it was adequate to study this drug," she said flatly. "The data was flawed for a number of reasons. First of all, the protocols were not well designed. . . . Not only did they permit the use of concomitant medications but they permitted the use of *psychotropic* concomitant medications that acted on the very same system of the body, the brain, that they were studying in a drug of which they had very little knowledge."

There was something about Lord's certitude, her ability to communicate freshly about the issues, that seized the attention of the court. Meanwhile, Zettler was revealing herself to be a first-class trial lawyer; her questions were well thought out and well paced. For the first time in this trial, alarm appeared to be writ large on the Lilly attorneys' faces.

"This was not the seventh or eighth benzodiazepine," Lord explained. "This was a drug that really, really was the first. And they then basically treated [that is, treated therapeutically with concomitant drugs] the adverse experiences. If somebody came on to a trial and got, say, insomnia, they couldn't sleep, or they became jumpy and agitated, instead of having them withdraw and counting that person as someone who couldn't handle the drug, they simply gave them Dalmane to go to sleep, which has a lingering anxiolytic effect during the next day."

Warming to her theme, Lord declared: "The investigators were allowed to break the blind and make a decision whether that person should go on an open-label fluoxetine long-term study, meaning, if they were doing well and were on fluoxetine, they could stay on it; if they were on imipramine and were not doing well, they could switch to fluoxetine. But by doing that, the investigator gained some knowledge by which they could have been consciously or unconsciously breaking the blind in their mind on future patients."

So she went on. Lilly did not "code adverse experiences correctly," she said, and they never "really did Phase III [studies]; they did a large Phase II." In other words, she explained, "they did the same protocol over and over; they never really opened it up and looked at different types of people that would inevitably be getting this drug once it got on the market."

She alleged that they "did some strange things"—for example, "in the way adverse experiences were coded on COSTART," the pharmaceutical industry's dictionary of precise terms. They "changed one thing to something else," she said, "and then they didn't change other things where they maybe should have." She was referring, she said, to the way in which they would routinely write down "suicidal ideation" as "depression."

Without a word of objection from the defense, who looked stunned throughout this performance, she went straight on and assigned motive to these actions, as though they were stratagems. "It looked," she said, "like they did everything possible to kind of tone down the problems with the drug rather than give them a rigorous, systematic, and comprehensive evaluation to define what the problems were and then put it in the package insert so that doctors could be warned not to use the drug in certain types of patients, or to use it more carefully."

Eventually Zettler asked, "Do you have any criticisms about the way data from overseas was gathered and reported?"

"Yes," she responded with gusto. "At one point in 1984, Eli Lilly received word from the German authorities that they were not going to approve this drug because of their concern with suicidality and agitation. They said that people became agitated before the antidepressant effects came on, and that increased the risk of suicide. They wrote a memo concerning untoward damaging effects and Lilly then went over there and looked at the data again and pulled out cases that they didn't think were suicide."

Lord let this sink in for moment. "First of all," she continued, "how are they to know? The investigator thought it was a suicide attempt. They said, well, they don't think it is. . . ." The British and the Danish, she added, were similarly concerned about safety, but Lilly reacted in a like manner.

At this point, Judge Potter called a fifteen-minute recess, and Joe Freeman at last gave voice to his dismay. At the bench he complained, "We would like for an instruction and standing objection to the witness characterizing as cover-up, intentionally misleading, or something of that kind, when she's talking about a particular act or action. This is not in the disclosure."

"I'm going to sustain the objection," said Potter. "I think your witness ought to stay away from testifying about what's inside Lilly's corporate head when she's describing any individual event. She can say they failed to report or did not disclose."

"Just don't ascribe any motive to it?" asked Zettler innocently.

"Yes."

"Okay," said Zettler. Then she headed for the lobby and a quick smoke, an exultant gleam in her eye.

After the court reconvened, Zettler again asked about the effect of concomitant medications in Prozac's clinical trials. Various witnesses had tackled this question before, but Lord's approach, loaded with qualifying detail, was devastating.

"To simply sedate them, make those things [adverse events] less of a problem and then not report them, was in my opinion improper," she said to a hushed court. She was not referring, she added, to aspirin or antibiotics. "Those sorts of things are expected. But in this case, they regularly, systematically, and in a large portion of the people used tranquilizers, sedatives, to calm people down. It happened in very high percentages of the people on the study, and it completely obscured what this product was doing to people's minds."

Next Zettler encouraged her to talk about patients who were withdrawn from the trial for whom there were no appropriate reports.

"You still at that point would get a flawed sample, because then you would be studying only those people who were able to take it without a problem. . . . To simply remove those people from the group and evaluate everybody else is skewing the data, because you've removed the people who had trouble with it."

Lord commented that Lilly had instructed the clinical investigators not to list symptoms of depression as adverse events, and that this had been pointed out by the FDA in one of their monitors' notes. The instances of this failure to report, she said, occurred "numerous, numerous times."

Then she turned to Lilly's use of the phrase "lack of efficacy" as the reason given for terminating the trial for a patient. "I found in several cases I saw reading the case-report form, it was apparent to me that the reason the person was terminated early was because they became very ill. . . . And the reason given for the termination was lack of efficacy. . . . I also saw 'The patient made a decision.' Was the decision based on not liking the way the buses ran, or was it based on feeling jumpy and jittery, like they're jumping out of their skin? We don't know. We're just told—'patient decision.' "

Lord had a way of being irreverent and highly professional in turn that lent a special quality of articulate accessibility to her presentation. And all this time, Freeman sat in silence, a look of frozen indignation on his face.

Then, concisely, well timed as ever, Zettler asked: "Let's back up just a second. . . . How would what Lilly did, in your opinion, in this case affect analysis of the data that was gathered in clinical trials?"

"It renders it *worthless*," declared Lord. "You cannot evaluate *bad* data. Statisticians can only look at the data they're given. If you have data where people are being sedated and you're looking, say, for the incidence of agitation, only the people were sedated and the agitation that was reported anyway is reported as *nervousness,* how can you possibly do a statistical analysis for agitation? . . ."

From this point on, Nancy Lord's testimony focused on a series of actual case-report forms as illustrations of the kinds of problem she had been talking about. In the course of the morning, she worked in detail through some ten cases of Prozac-trial patients in which she believed the investigators had recorded misleading reasons for discontinuing the trial. They included an outpatient who had to be hospitalized after wanting to "jump out of a window"; a man who came to the trial voluntarily and ended up on a "lockup ward" with "paranoid delusions"; a woman of sixty-four who started somewhat depressed, then, on Prozac, "really freaked out."

As the day wore on, the impression of Dr. Lord's presentation began to look like overkill. Slick, responding rapidly, forceful, she seemed to be taking Lilly's clinical trials apart single-handedly. And still the defense remained eerily silent.

Finally, when they had run out of testimony, Zettler asked her: "Are you aware of anything else —specifically with regards to violent aggressive behavior—that Lilly did in response to the issue being raised whether or not Prozac causes violent aggressive, or exacerbates violent aggressive behavior, other than this reanalysis of pre-existing data?"

"No," she said. "The only other special reanalysis—it wasn't a study—is they looked at agitated depression, how well people did who started out with agitated depression as compared with retarded depression. But they didn't do another study specifically looking for violence and aggression and they never did a study in people who were at the outset having a tendency toward violence and aggression."

And with that her direct examination was over, and she left the stand.

Potter allowed a fifteen-minute recess before Joe Freeman started his cross, during which time Nancy Zettler requested a bench discussion. If she had suspicions that Joe Freeman was planning to focus on peripheral personal issues rather than the matters raised in her testimony, they were about to be confirmed.

Zettler got as far as asking for a ban on any reference to Lord's religious or political affiliations as being prejudicial: Lord, it turned out, was a Libertarian, and as such believed in legalizing drugs.

"Your Honor," intervened Freeman scathingly, "I think I have a right to show all of the different things that this jack-of-all-trades has done in her life. She went to medical school. She dropped out of her residency, she took a psychiatric course. She dropped out of that. She went to Abbott, she dropped out of that. . . . She ran for mayor of Chicago for a political career. She ran for vice-president of the United States. . . . You would think that all she had done all of her life was make study of clinical-studies records, and that ain't so. . . ."

Zettler had been wise to raise the issue with the judge. Freeman was fighting hard for the right to expose Nancy Lord as a wacko and a Walter Mitty. The judge ruled, however, for Zettler; Freeman would not be allowed to mention Lord's political affiliation. But Zettler was left in no doubt as to his intention to destroy the witness on her curriculum vitae.

"*Mrs.* Lord," he began, as if to remind the court of her former marital status while neglecting her professional title. "I would like to get, if I might, a little bit clearer picture, so we can put it together sort of in a time line, of your background and experience."

He started by attempting to unravel her medical career, but came quickly to grief. In response to Freeman's questions, she testified that he was wrong on the dates of her medical-school attendance and that she had indeed completed school to become a qualified doctor. As for her move after four years into the pharmaceutical industry and thence into legal-consultancy work, she refused to be characterized as a "dropout" merely because she had developed her career by going from one job to another, and after four years.

Suddenly he stopped. Then he posed an extraordinary question: "Do you have any preference as to what I call you? Should I call you Nancy since you're calling me Joe, or should I call you Mrs. Lord, or what?"

"I don't recall calling you Joe," said Dr. Lord dryly.

The mystified faces in the court indicated that the majority were with her (the official record would confirm that she was correct).

"I thought I understood you to say that. Maybe I'm wishful-thinking," he said with a smile.

"No," insisted Lord, not smiling. "I will call you Mr. Freeman. You can call me Dr. Lord. That will be fine."

Joe Freeman was not doing so well this afternoon.

But, having regained something of his old equilibrium, he set about attempting to undermine her testimony of the morning, by suggesting that she had no depth of experience or background in clinical-trial procedures, and by indicating that she was a hireling primed by media training to give companies like Eli Lilly a bad time.

"Actually, where I've really learned that," she said, "is with the help of people like yourself, sir. Cross-examination is far more difficult than any television appearance."

"Were you or not hired in this case to be critical of Eli Lilly and Company and its medication fluoxetine hydrochloride?" Freeman asked eventually.

"I was hired to act as a consultant, as a technical consultant to the project, to observe what happened," she replied. "Had I not found anything wrong in the way the clinical trials were done, I would have informed my client of that."

He finished by attempting to rebut her damaging contention about the use of concomitant drugs during the trials. But his questioning actually enabled her to go out with a bold and unchallenged reiteration of her allegations.

He had put to her that the FDA itself had written to say that "concomitant medication use is not a problem in this New Drug Application [for Prozac]."

"That's what it says," she replied, unfazed.

"All right," said Freeman, as if unsure what he should say next.

Then she pounced: "Can I comment on that?"

Incredibly, he invited her to do so. "If it's responsive," he said, "I suppose so."

She was responsive all right, and eloquently so.

"That's what *they* say," she began. "They happen to be wrong. . . . We know what the profile of imipramine is; we don't know what the profile of fluoxetine is. Maybe the imipramine people would have had trouble going to sleep. Maybe the fluoxetine people would have run off and gotten on a plane for Alaska or hit their wife over the head. We just don't know, because that was the drug we were testing. And the FDA and the public deserved to know what it would do without concomitant medication."

Freeman now, with the judge's permission, conferred a few moments with Stopher. When he had finished, he turned to say, "That's all that I have at this time, Judge."

28

IN THE LAST WEEK OF OCTOBER, Wesbecker's psychiatrist, Dr. Lee Coleman, Smith's final witness, was called to testify. Since he was the last medical professional to see Wesbecker, his view of the man was crucial. He was Smith's witness, and Smith had seen him from the outset as his ace card. It was Coleman, after all, who contemporaneously put in writing that Prozac had caused the patient's final psychotic agitation.

But in the interval between Coleman's sworn deposition—generally favorable to the plaintiffs—taken in the fall of 1993, and the beginning of the trial, Smith had discovered that the psychiatrist had been in conversation with Lilly's lawyers and undergone a significant change of heart.

At eight o'clock in the morning on the day Coleman was due to give testimony, an unusual legal wrangle took place in judge's chambers in the form of a voir-dire hearing. Paul Smith had suspected Eli Lilly and Coleman of coming to some arrangement, and since he believed this could affect the doctor's evidence in court, he was determined to question the psychiatrist under oath to elicit whether his suspicions had been justified. Present in the courthouse for that early meeting were Smith, Zettler, Stopher, Freeman, Coleman, and Coleman's lawyer, Ms. Tracy Prewitt.

First, the parties argued over how to convey to the jury that Dr. Coleman had come to be dropped from the list of defendants in the case. Potter agreed that Paul Smith could ask the witness if he was no longer a defendant because of the Kentucky court ruling that "insulates" psychiatrists from claims of third parties (this had originally been ruled by Judge Potter himself). It was further agreed that Smith could seek confirmation that the issue was still on appeal, and that he might yet be an active defendant in the case.

This settled, Coleman was brought into the room with his lawyer, and for half an hour or more Smith quizzed the psychiatrist about whether he had been indemnified by Lilly; he phrased the question at least thirty different ways, and Coleman denied it in thirty different ways. Then Smith's persistence paid off.

Suddenly Coleman asked him, "You are specifically talking about indemnification?"

"*Any* kind of arrangement," said Smith.

"Well," continued the doctor, "Mr. Stopher had asked me to review his materials, and there was never any kind of formal arrangement, but my hope is that I will be reimbursed for my time. But that's not been formally agreed to."

"You've done that as a gratuity up to this point?"

"I've not been paid anything. It's just my hope that I will be reimbursed for my time."

(Smith later confessed to me he was thunderstruck by this wholly unexpected admission. "Coleman was not an expert witness, or a consultant," he commented, "he was Wesbecker's personal psychiatrist. The notion that he would accept any kind of payment for reviewing Lilly's materials changed his whole relationship to the case.")

"Have you sent Mr. Stopher a bill?" Smith asked incredulously.

"No, sir."

"How much time did you spend reviewing that material?"

"I haven't added it up; I would say probably twenty or thirty hours."

"Did you ask Mr. Stopher why he wanted you to do that?"

"Mr. Stopher informed me why he wanted me to do that . . . I think it was my last deposition when I was asked the question was it my opinion that Prozac had caused this incident. I said I didn't think I could give an informed opinion because I didn't have all the information. Mr. Stopher wanted to supply me with the information so I could make an informed opinion."

At this point Stopher intervened to protest, "Judge, we are so far away from indemnity and everything else."

"This goes to whether or not he's *designated*," exploded Smith (meaning Coleman was no longer an independent witness but a hired "expert" witness to appear on behalf of the defense).

Under further questioning, Coleman said that Lilly's lawyers had supplied him with a highlighted chronology of Wesbecker's life (based on the famous four hundred depositions) and various videos. He also admitted that he was intending to charge the lawyers $200 an hour for the time it had taken him to read and view the material.

As Smith later explained to me, it was not simply the issue of Lilly's being prepared to pay money to provide "information" to the most crucial witness in the entire trial—Wesbecker's doctor—it was the principle of the difference between straightforward witnesses and hired *expert* witnesses. Lilly, he contended, had created a confusion between the two.

After Coleman left the room, Smith gave vent to his anger and disappointment. His emotions, he confessed to me later, were not in any way simulated.

He objected to Judge Potter: "This is the most patently, manifestly unfair thing. . . . Lilly has obviously hired this man, provided this man material, and asked him specifically to render an opinion on the question of whether or not Wesbecker's conduct on September 14th, 1989, was related to the use of Prozac. By all rules of procedure, by all rules of the court, by all rules of fairness and common sense, a party cannot hire an *independent* witness during the trial, provide him material that he's never seen, both scientific data as well as factual data, and ask him to render an opinion on that without disclosing it to us, without advising us that he's going to render that opinion and the basis of that opinion. Had I not asked him that this morning, I would have never known the material that he had reviewed. I was never advised by the defendants that they had provided Dr. Coleman this information."

Judge Potter at length attempted to assuage him with the reflection that plaintiffs' counsel already had "very strong testimony [that is, from Coleman's medical notes] that Mr. Wesbecker did what he did on the 14th because of Prozac."

"I mean," Potter went on, "just a layman thinking, 'Hmm, hmm, hmm,' with their own common sense, would try and bridge that gap and bridge it in your favor. . . ."

"The problem is," wailed Smith, "this is what we have lawsuits about. This is why we hire experts, is because witnesses can be witnesses and witnesses can be *expert* witnesses. And when you go from one spot to another spot, you better comply with the rules of civil procedure, which requires specific things which this court ordered in this case."

Smith would not be mollified by the judge's comments about Prozac and causation. "His record talks about what his mental state was on September 11th, 1989, it does not speak to why he did what he did on September 14th, 1989. That requires expert testimony. . . . It is evidentiary, what Dr. Coleman put in his record on September 11th, 1989, but their entire defense in this case is not what he put in his records on September 11th, 1989 . . . but that type of action doesn't cause somebody to commit a murder of this nature. . . ."

Before long, Smith, who had now become inarticulate with indignation, had the judge sympathizing with him to the extent of saying: "What they have done, as I see it, is taken what is potentially an adverse witness and tried to woodshed him."

"And hasn't told us about it," insisted Smith. "Hasn't given us any information about that."

"That's very true," agreed Potter.

"And made this man expect to be paid for twenty or thirty hours of work that he's done. There is no distinction in this man and any other expert they have. . . ."

"No. No," Potter was saying soothingly.

"I'm sorry. It's a surprise," Smith said finally, as if to apologize for his display of high emotion.

But all along Smith's outrage had an aim in view. He wanted a ruling that Coleman could not now be asked his opinion about Wesbecker's shooting spree. It was a lot to ask of Potter, since Lilly might well use it as a basis for mistrial at a later stage.

"What do *you* say about this?" Potter asked Stopher eventually.

Now it was the defense's turn to be indignant. Stopher, a man whose emotions were always firmly under control, and who exuded a ponderous sense of rectitude on all occasions, gave a sober answer that dwelled on the fact that they had not offered information to Coleman but that he had sought it.

He ended with this solemn peroration: "The final thing that I want to remind the court of, this is a treating physician. And in every case that

I'm aware of, Your Honor, a doctor is entitled who is a treating physician to not just testify about his treatment of the patient that is under consideration; that doctor is also permitted to give opinions about the future and about the prognosis, and in this case this is no different. It would be very, very misleading to this jury to allow him to express his opinions on the 11th and not allow him to express his opinions on the 14th. It would just be devastating."

When all the arguments were through, Judge Potter, faced with two "devastated" attorneys, ruled that the defense would be allowed to ask Coleman his opinion as to whether he thought Prozac had caused Wesbecker's actions on the 14th.

Smith was beside himself. "This is just . . ." For a few moments he was speechless. Then he let rip: "We have spent hundreds and thousands of dollars preparing this case for trial," he yelled. "We have gone from Seattle to Houston to Maine to Boston, everywhere in this country, to develop the facts and the expertise in this area. They have the entire resources of Eli Lilly and Company to supply them information. We had a right to rely on what they told us about who their experts were. . . ."

"It is not a ruling I am pleased with, Mr. Smith," Potter interrupted, "but it's one that I'm not going to change. . . . Folks, I may be right, I may be wrong—I know. You know, obviously you're unhappy and I'm not particularly excited about the way this came up. But I have to rule; I've ruled; I'm not going to change it."

With this the judge offered a day's recess so that Smith could depose Coleman on what he had reviewed for Lilly; all Smith would say was "I need to take some time and compose myself."

Later he said: "We feel there's probably nothing that can really be done to cure the tragic and unjust surprise that has been visited on us at this time."

"Okay," said Judge Potter.

The court reconvened at eleven o'clock, some two hours later than usual, and Smith had Coleman to himself.

Coleman, forty-seven years of age and a citizen of Louisville, cut a strange figure, with his pure-white shock of hair and youthful face; his poor eyesight gave him a somewhat vague and distracted air.

Smith started by establishing that Coleman had been Wesbecker's psychiatrist from July 8, 1987, to September 11, 1989. He confirmed that his habit was to take notes in writing, then have those notes typed up within forty-eight hours. Smith encouraged the doctor to confirm that his notes were reliable, and that indeed his patient was honest and reliable, too. Coleman had received in full all the notes from previous doctors, psychiatrists, and various hospitalizations. He stated, moreover, that Wesbecker was not a "bad individual," or a man of "weak character." Coleman did not feel that Wesbecker was "hiding anything."

Taking Coleman through his own notes, from July 1988 through September 1989, Smith got the doctor to confirm that his patient's "anger, particularly about work, had subsided." There was no mention of hospitalizing the patient, said Smith, no reference to irritability or anger, which Coleman duly confirmed.

"Mr. Wesbecker was not going to be the type of patient that would be receptive to psychotherapy; is that right?" asked Smith.

"That's correct."

"And you felt the best way to control his mental illness was by psychopharmacology; correct?"

"That was my primary focus of treatment."

"And since it was your primary focus of treatment, wouldn't it be accurate to say that you were being careful to note the effects of the medication on Mr. Wesbecker?"

Smith now took Coleman through the two-year history of Wesbecker's medication, until they reached the point at which he put his patient on Prozac for a second time. Focusing on Wesbecker's final visit, on September 11, Smith read out Coleman's notes, with their references to the patient's "tangential thoughts," "weeping in session," the episode of "recovered memory" of "sexual abuse by co-workers."

"Tell the jury," said Smith, "what this instance of sexual abuse as related by Mr. Wesbecker was."

"Well, he had told me that he had felt like the Prozac had helped him remember . . . now I'll kind of paraphrase what he said—that he had been forced to give oral sex to one of his foremen with other co-workers watching so he could get off this machine apparently called the folder that he did not like working, and that the Prozac helped him remember that. At that point, that's when he wept in the session for a brief period of time."

A little further on, Smith asked, "Did you know at that time that Prozac had caused delusions or hallucinations in some patients?"

"I think I was aware," responded Coleman, "that Prozac, as any other antidepressant, in some people can cause delusions or hallucinations."

Having made this carefully worded admission, he then said that he had, at the time, speculated that Prozac was the probable cause of Wesbecker's false memory and general deterioration.

"You at that time felt that Prozac was the cause of Mr. Wesbecker's deterioration, didn't you?"

"I wasn't certain, but that was my feeling at the time; that is correct."

Smith now changed tack in order to achieve some damage control on what he had earlier characterized as the "tragedy" of Lilly's takeover of Coleman, who should have been a witness friendly to the plaintiffs.

"Over the last five years since this tragedy occurred," Smith began, "employees of Eli Lilly and Company had been in your office on a monthly basis, had they not?"

Coleman admitted this was so, but denied that any of these "detail people," as he described members of Lilly's sales force, said anything "substantive" to him about the trial.

Smith now moved swiftly on to the Stopher "review" episode.

". . . two or three days after this trial began, you met with Mr. Stopher and or Mr. Freeman, lawyers for Eli Lilly and Company, didn't you?"

"Mr. Stopher wanted me to review some materials that he wanted to give me for the lawsuit; yes, sir."

"And you started keeping your time in connection with that, didn't you, Dr. Coleman?"

"I started keeping my time in the hopes that they might compensate me for my time; as, if I had reviewed materials that you might have given me, I would hope you would compensate me for my time, as well."

As Smith continued to press Coleman on the details of this "review," the doctor admitted that he expected Lilly to pay him for research he did for himself using the MedLine computer databases, which can be accessed by any doctor. Coleman also acknowledged that his copies of various Lilly material had been highlighted in yellow for his convenience.

Smith clearly had two objectives. First, he wanted to give the impression that Coleman had become a Lilly hireling and could therefore not be trusted to give a reliable opinion about Prozac's effect on Wesbecker. Next, despite bitter protestations from the defense, he sought to press the main points of his case against Prozac by illustrating the gaps in Lilly's "review" material. As, for example, "Did Mr. Stopher tell you that ten years ago, five years before Joseph Wesbecker shot these people and their loved ones, that Lilly themselves were recommending to the German people that if people have problems with agitation they need to have a sedative? Did he tell you that?"

To which Coleman admitted that he did not.

"Did you know, Dr. Coleman, that people with serious suicidal risk were excluded from the Prozac clinical trials?"

"No, sir," said Coleman.

"Did you know that individuals were given concomitant sedative tranquilizers during the Prozac clinical trials?"

"No, sir."

Thus he went on, right down through every principal point made in the plaintiffs' case so far.

Then, changing tack again, he asked Coleman if he knew whether the summaries he had read in Stopher's material were "in fact the truth or not," "accurate or not"; Coleman admitted he did not.

Returning to the issue of payment for "research," Smith asked: "Do you know whether there's any plan for you to continue your work that you are keeping time on in order to bill them for this work?"

"After today I don't assume that there is; no, sir. . . ." Coleman seemed curiously unmoved about the question, laconic, as if he did not understand what the fuss was about.

"Do you intend to charge Mr. Stopher or Mr. Freeman or Eli Lilly and Company for your testimony here today, Dr. Coleman?"

"I haven't thought about that," said Coleman. "Mainly my thought was to charge them for my time. I was going to have to be here today one way or the other."

"So what's the answer? Are you going to bill them for your time here?"

"I hadn't assumed that."

"You think it might be a good idea, though, to bill them?" asked Smith.

"I don't know. This is certainly taking a lot of time."

"Okay," said Smith, ending his direct with a look of disbelief and distaste.

Ed Stopher now cross-examined Dr. Coleman.

He established that the doctor had seen his patient for about thirty minutes on each of some twenty-one visits, and throughout that time he never volunteered "that he was thinking about and even talking about killing someone else."

"Did he ever mention," Stopher asked, "during this two years and two months, sir, that he was thinking about and actually taking steps to purchase weapons and to practice with them?"

"No, sir. He never talked about weapons at all."

Stopher went on to establish through Coleman's testimony that there had in fact been a steady decline in the patient's mental health through the two-year period during which he treated him, despite trials with various medications.

"Now, sir," said Stopher, "you listed in your notes that a cause of the deterioration might be, question mark, Prozac; am I right?"

"I think 'Prozac, which might be the cause,' or 'Question from Prozac' was another thing I had written in my chart," responded Coleman.

"Now, sir, in determining the cause of the deterioration, is knowledge about Mr. Wesbecker and his life history of any significance or benefit?"

"Well, it certainly can be of benefit."

"Am I correct in understanding," went on Stopher stolidly, "that the more you know about the patient the more accurate the opinion is?"

"Correct."

Stopher had now reached a point in his cross-examination that was pivotal concerning Coleman's understanding of Wesbecker's behavior, and pivotal to the course of the entire trial. Was Wesbecker the slave or the master of his brain chemistry? Would he have been capable of resisting his undeniable homicidal fantasies and impulses had it not been for the psychopharmacological intrusion of Prozac? Did Prozac play any part in his murder spree? Or had he done it as a result of his entire life, his genetic makeup, his early and late influences, his habitual behavior?

"Dr. Coleman," Stopher asked in a sepulchral voice, "I have provided you, among other things, with information . . . about Mr. Wesbecker's ideas, statements, and actions concerning homicide, have I not, sir? . . . Empowered with that knowledge, assuming that it's accurate, sir, do you have an opinion as to whether or not Joseph Wesbecker committed multiple murders and multiple assaults on September 14, 1989, as a result of his taking Prozac?"

"My opinion," said Coleman, "is that Prozac had nothing to do with it at all."

Then he added, as if for clarification, "Now, that doesn't—you know, it's still *possible* that Prozac could have been the cause of his *deterioration. . . .*"

Stopher was gazing at the witness, his mouth slightly opened, as if with mild astonishment.

Then Coleman took another tack, contrasting Wesbecker's deterioration on the 11th with his shooting spree on the 14th. "Now," he said, "as far as the events of September the 15th, 1989, it's my opinion that that was a premeditated, planned, and executed murder. From the information you've given me, he went to dinner with his ex-wife Brenda on the 13th, he talked with his son Jimmy on the 13th. As I recall from Brenda's testimony, he didn't seem any particularly different." Then he added, to Smith's vociferous protests, "Also, reading the information that you had given me in the chronology gives a really chilling testimony to the number of threats."

And with that the judge called a halt to the day's proceedings, and the end of the plaintiffs' case.

29

DURING THE WEEK when Lilly's lawyers began their scientific defense of Prozac at the Louisville trial, thousands of researchers from all over the world were descending on the Convention Center in Miami Beach, Florida, to attend the twenty-fourth annual meeting of the American Society for Neuroscience.

The society, which had started with five hundred founder-members in 1968, boasted twenty-two thousand members by the autumn of 1994, most of whom were headed for the Florida superconference. Throughout five days, thousands of poster sites were being replaced every half-day in the vast convention halls in order to display most of the ten thousand abstracts of new research. Pressure on hotel availability was so great that delegates were sharing as many as six to a room and seeking accommodation as far away as Fort Lauderdale and downtown Miami.

Hundreds of poster sites displayed research on the serotonin system, and among these were scores of presentations devoted to fluoxetine hydrochloride, or Prozac. Here, alongside research data on dopamine and glucose metabolism, and adrenoreceptor agonists, was a poster created by Dr. Ray Fuller of Eli Lilly, who in that same week would be giving evidence in the Louisville trial. "Olanzapine compared to clozapine and haloperidol as dopamine and serotonin receptor antagonists in rats," ran his Miami presentation's headline.

Strolling along ranks of posters that disappeared into the far distance (I had traveled to Miami to spend a day at the meeting), I gained an impression of the heady prospects for brain research, especially when observing those poster sites where scientists pressed in a huddle to read the data or converse with the team responsible for the presentation.

The posters represented myriad research areas, from genetics to neuronal degeneration, from memory to neurotransmitters, from pharmacology to the visual cortex, from brain imaging to new pain therapies. Nowhere in the world would one find such a large and optimistic gathering of physiologists, psychologists, geneticists, biochemists, pharmacologists, neurologists, cell biologists, neurosurgeons, and others—all convinced that they were part of a new science on the brink of a major revolution.

Research into brain science had been gathering momentum since the mid-1980s, propelled by the expectation of remarkable breakthroughs on a wide front. As the Cold War ended, and governments pondered the peace dividends, neuroscience began to enjoy ever-higher priority as a recipient of state and corporate grant support.

Eric Kandel of Columbia University had written grandiloquently in the preface to his 1985 edition of *Principles of Neural Science* that "one of the last frontiers of science, perhaps its ultimate challenge, is to understand the biological basis of mentation." But why had the neuroscientists been so laggard in a century marked by huge strides in most other scientific and medical fields? It was the vulnerability and vast complexity of the brain itself that had kept researchers at bay. The neurophysiologists did not have the tools or techniques to enter the living cortex without devastating what they were attempting to explore.

This had not daunted the progress of those cognitive scientists who believed that real brains were as dispensable to the study of thinking as feathers are to aerodynamics. Hence the behaviorists had doggedly concentrated on input and output, ignoring the black box of the brain itself, while researchers in artificial intelligence focused on building computer models that separated the mind from its material base.

By the mid-1980s, however, the prospects for neuroscience had been transformed. Just as the invention of the telescope and the discovery of mathematical physics gave rise to new ways of understanding the universe, so rapid advances in noninvasive brain imaging, or scanning, together with ever-advancing molecular biology and genetics, had revolutionized the study of the brain. At the same time, the increased power of computers enabled researchers to test their theories with ever more sophisticated models. After a century in the doldrums, neuroscience was, in its own estimation, on a voyage to the final frontiers of science.

But the idea that the 1990s would be special to brain research was not due solely to the inspirations of academic science. A crucial impulse had come from the burgeoning biotech industry, as well as the expanding neuroscience arm of the pharmaceutical industry, whose marketing departments, aided and abetted by the media, had announced a new age of rationally designed brain drugs with cure-alls for everything from pain to Parkinson's disease. Their clinical allies in genetics and neurology, eager to explore revolutionary techniques in grafting, implanting, genetic screening, and "carrier" therapies, were not slow to advance the cause.

On January 1, 1990, the lobbyists in industry and medicine got what they wanted in the form of a joint resolution of the House and the Senate of the United States—the designation of the nineties as the "Decade of the Brain."

A principal stated reason behind the initiative had been the official estimate that some $350 billion was being lost to the U.S. economy each year through brain-related ills, including depression, Alzheimer's, and the consequences of aggressive behavior (which alone would attract grants of $500 million for neurogenetic research in 1994). This promise of major social and medical amelioration was driving the momentum and direction of investment and funding; the researchers, by a process of heliotropic survival, were following the money.

And even as the discipline was being fêted in the expectation that it would deliver a host of social and medical applications, there were growing expectations, evident in proliferating symposia and published academic papers, that neuroscience had a significant cultural role to play. Neuroscience, proclaimed a brave new constituency of philosophers, sociobiologists, and sociologists, would provide an unprecedented scientific approach to explaining the link between our physical brain states and our minds.

At a morning lecture in the Miami Beach Convention Center, Francis Crick, Nobel winner and early architect of the molecular biology that had made the neuroscience revolution possible, gave a presentation to an audience of a thousand members of the society. Neuroscientists, Crick told them, had begun to tackle the question that has fascinated philosophers for centuries: "What is consciousness?" Using a variety of modern scientific tools, he told them—from microelectrodes, which pick up electrical signals from single nerve cells, to positron emission tomography (PET), which maps broad patterns of activity in a living brain—a growing number of researchers had begun to examine the neurological mechanisms of the mind itself.

"The idea," he said, "is that our minds—the behavior of our brains— can be explained by the interactions of nerve cells and the molecules associated with them."

Crick's talk to the scientists at the Convention Center was in fact a résumé of a book he had published just a few weeks earlier, *The Astonishing Hypothesis: The Scientific Search for the Soul*, in which he had expanded his view of a neuroscientific understanding of human nature.

"The Astonishing Hypothesis," he declared, "is that you, your joys and your sorrows, your memories and your ambitions, your sense of personal identity and free will, are in fact no more than the behavior of a vast assembly of nerve cells and their associated molecules."

Then he went on to hazard that "free will" resided in a part of the brain known as the "anterior cingulate sulcus," and that "consciousness" was the effect of brain cells' oscillating globally across the neocortex at a rate of forty hertz—that is, forty cycles per second.

The significance of Crick's appearance at this annual meeting was the neat fit that was being proposed between neuroscientific research and an understanding of the mind widely referred to as "neurophilosophy." Neurophilosophy, according to Professor Patricia Churchland of the University of California at San Diego, who had in 1989 published a book of that title, envisages a "wisdom" based on neuroscientific categories. It will, she writes, overturn "folk psychology . . . that rough-hewn set of concepts, generalizations, and rules of thumb we all standardly use in explaining and predicting human behavior"—in other words, history, literature, philosophy, and the social sciences. Thus the Crick-Churchland brand of philosophical reductionism—the reduction of all explanations of human nature and behavior to patterns of molecules—claims to provide a more authentic causal explanation of human behavior than unscientific, and hence unreliable, "folk" knowledge.

The potential social and political impact of neurophilosophy is not far to seek. A view of the world that understands human beings in terms of their relationships and individual and collective histories will seek solutions to human ills in a social and communitarian context. But a philosophy that insists that the basis of all behavior lies within our individual sets of molecules will turn to neuroscience for explanations and solutions. It follows that, in a society that has begun to despair of finding communitarian remedies, the claims of pharmacological cures and antidotes will become magnified by the commercial goals of the pharmaceutical industry, and further amplified by the media.

One of the crucial byproducts of this reductionist approach to human problems has been the tendency to transform complex dynamic processes into static objects. As Professor Stephen Rose of the Open University in Britain has commented: "Violence, rather than describing an action or activity between persons, or even a person and the natural world, becomes instead a 'character'—aggression—a thing that can be abstracted from the dynamically interactive system in which it appears and is studied in isolation." The next logical step is that "aggression" becomes a single term of reference for everything from domestic violence to drive-by shootings, from mothers smacking their children to warring sides in the conflict in Bosnia. Furthermore, the term "aggression" is linked to a single neuroscientific process and location—the most popular current candidate being low activity of serotonin in the synapses of the brain; for which Lilly's neuroscientists had found an answer: fluoxetine hydrochloride, or Prozac.

The prodigality of research at the Miami neurosciences meeting left one in no doubt that neuroscience would in time transform our understanding of diseases of the brain and the central nervous system, especially in areas like schizophrenia, multiple sclerosis, Alzheimer's, bipolar depression, Huntington's disease, and Parkinson's. It was also clear that neuroscience had enormous potential to affect ideas about what it means to be human.

As Crick had shown in his talk to the delegates, the discipline had prompted a lively debate about the nature of human identity, putting new life into an ancient question: how our mental processes relate to the gray matter of the brain.

That debate, as he had acknowledged in his *Astonishing Hypothesis*, had spawned a number of of hypotheses, many of them published as trade books. For example, the American philosopher Daniel C. Dennett had made a close study of neurobiology and concluded that the brain was a "virtual machine" working on the principle of "parallel distributed processing." This means that the brain's mechanism does not tackle just a single sequence of computations, but a great many sequences simultaneously, or "in parallel." Dennett's hypothesis in his book *Consciousness Explained* was that human identity, or the self, is an illusion—no more than a series of shifting "multiple drafts" or "narratives," with no central focus or continuity.

Meanwhile, at Carnegie-Mellon University, in Pittsburgh, robotics researcher Hans Moravec was insisting that the living brain resembles nothing so much as a programmed digital computer; that within forty years it would be possible to download the contents of the mind into software in preparation for an immortal existence.

Moravec had a formidable critic in the Oxford mathematician Roger Penrose, who argued in his book *The Emperor's New Mind* that thought was an effect in the brain of quantum gravity, the strange realm of microcosmic physics; that consciousness could not be propagated by merely mechanical computation. In support of this view, Penrose appealed to neuroscientific work on cytoskeletal structures of neurons known as "microtubules," which, he believes, shrink down to a size appropriate for quantum-physical effect.

Penrose was not alone in challenging the computer-brain idea. He had found a curious ally in Switzerland in the form of Sir John Eccles, the Nobel Prize–winning neurophysiologist, who had been conducting an abrasive campaign against what he calls "promissory materialism" (the idea that the equivalence between brains and minds will one day be demonstrated scientifically).

The materialists, Eccles charged, control the world of academic appointments, funding, and publishing, thus depriving the antimaterialists of an opportunity to exert a salutary influence. Eccles had declared in his most recent book, *How the Self Controls Its Brain*, that contemporary neuroscience was entirely compatible with the existence of an immaterial soul (a viewpoint known as body-soul dualism).

It was precisely to repudiate body-soul dualism—of the kind that goes back to René Descartes, the seventeenth-century philosopher—that

Crick wrote *The Astonishing Hypothesis*. His hypothesis is that, astonishing as it may seem to many people, there is no need to posit a kind of spiritual or mental stuff to explain mental processes. The explanation lies entirely in the physical reality of the molecules themselves.

A lay reader might gain the impression from these warring theories that the identity debate prompted by neuroscience has been exclusively a contest between dualism and mechanistic reductionism; yet the discipline has also yielded a third, more complex approach, which appeals to neither tendency. Typical of the third view is the work of neuroscientists who have attempted a less computational approach to the mind-brain problem, such as Pierre Changeux, Michael Gazzaniga, and most notably Gerald Edelman.

Edelman, who has written a famously inaccessible trilogy on his theory, believes that the way the brain works has more in common with a vast jungle or ecological habitat than a computational system. His contribution to the mind-body debate is a hypothesis he calls "Neuronal Group Selection," which argues that the brain develops, before and after birth, by a process not unlike natural selection in evolution. As a model, or a metaphor, nothing could be further from the Crick brand of computational neuroscience.

Edelman stresses the dynamism, the ceaseless novelty and creativity of mental processes, and draws striking contrasts between the machines of our own devising and the brain's predicament as an evolved living and dying organism. He concludes that, though evolutionary theory can elucidate the problem of higher-order human consciousness, including free will, no reductionist scientific explanation of a human individual is possible.

It is significant that Edelman argues for a clear distinction between reductionist method and a reductionist philosophy. "To reduce a theory of human behavior to a theory of molecular interactions is simply silly," he writes, "made clear when one considers how many different levels of physical, biological and social interactions must be put into place before higher order consciousness emerges." Quoting Diderot, he reminds his readers that "to be human is to go beyond physics."

As with Crick, Edelman's thinking has attracted some distinguished supporters from neighboring scientific disciplines, including the writer-neurologist Oliver Sacks, who believes that Neuronal Group Selection is ideally suited to his own holistic approach to clinical neurology. Just as Crick's view of the mind espouses a radically reductionist, determinist, and individualist view of human nature, so the appeal of Edelman's theory is its scope to foster an imaginative, free, and yet communitarian identity.

As the neuroscientists met in Miami at the midpoint of the "Decade of the Brain," it seemed clear that the discipline could be exploited to underpin several models of human identity. Much as it seemed to go against the tide of science itself, some neuroscientific theories were reconfirming a dualistic view of the person as a spiritual-material divide: a popular notion among an assortment of New Ageists, evangelicals, and members of the New Right, keen to espouse a spiritual moral agency as a token of radical individualism essentially detached from both biology and society. On the other hand, the discipline could espouse the narrow reductionism of a Francis Crick, who, like Marvin Minsky, saw the brain as a "meat machine," opening up the hubristic prospect that human behavior could in time be explained and hence controlled. In all respects, the Crickian view inherits the computer metaphors employed by artificial-intelligence researchers like Moravec, and by eliminative materialist philosophers like Dennett.

Finally, neuroscience has shown itself capable of yielding to the softer, nondualist, yet nonmechanistic and nonreductionist approach of Edelman and Sacks, with their invitation to see human identity as an open rather than a closed system, with an emphasis on human beings as social animals with imagination and a measure of freedom. Such a view proclaims the possibility of confirming a human identity that does violence neither to modern science nor to traditional ideas about the soul.

At the heart of the mind-brain debate, in which scientists like Moravec, Crick, Dennett, Penrose, Eccles, and Edelman are at loggerheads, is an issue that lay at the heart of the Louisville trial: What is the link between brain states and human behavior? And how do people resolve such a question?

Much depends, it is clear, on the influence of popular exposition in publishing and the media. As R. C. Lewontin shrewdly remarks in his

Biology as Ideology: The Doctrine of DNA: "A simple and dramatic theory that explains everything makes good press, good radio, good TV, and best-selling books. Anyone with academic authority, a halfway decent writing style, and a simple and powerful idea has easy entry to the public consciousness." By the same token, complex, open-ended ideas receive less prominence in the media unless they are vulgarized and distorted out of recognition.

New ideas about human identity also find their way into mass culture via the testimony and verdicts of the courts of law. As it happened, Lilly's view of identity was in all respects identical to Francis Crick's. Lilly's account of the mind-brain relationship, as promoted in the publicity and marketing material on Prozac throughout the world, had effectively argued that the mind is a chemical-software program running in the brain. In unfortunate individuals, so their argument goes, the program develops faults—"Behind every crooked thought, there lies a crooked molecule"—as when reuptake mechanisms create low levels of serotonin, resulting in depression, compulsive disorders, and aggression. Lilly's solution is essentially a rewrite program in the form of a selective serotonin reuptake inhibitor—Prozac.

Paul Smith had bought this chemical-software version of the human mind and presented it in his case for the plaintiffs, believing that the battle would be fought on such neuroscientifically correct grounds. The only difference between his position and Lilly's, he argued, was that Prozac had signally failed as a rewrite program in precisely the type of fault it was designed to correct. Moreover, by raising the level of serotonin to unpredictably high levels, the drug had destroyed Wesbecker's impulse-control mechanisms, thereby robbing him of his autonomy. Hence Smith's emphasis on testimony that likened Wesbecker's behavior to that of a zombie as he stalked the Standard Gravure plant.

The defense had now to demolish plaintiffs' counsel's allegations that Prozac was defective and the company negligent in its trials and package warnings. But how should they deal with Wesbecker's status as the ultimate cause of the shootings at Standard Gravure?

One of the deep ironies of this case had been that Ed Stopher had avoided neuroscientific arguments in his diagnosis of Wesbecker. Although arguments about crooked molecules suited the sound bites of pharmaceutical marketing, Lilly's lawyers readily changed their tune when it came to influencing the Louisville jury.

Instead, on cross-examination of the plaintiffs' witnesses, Stopher had pursued a more "folk-psychological" argument: that Wesbecker's actions had been determined by his disadvantaged nature and deprived nurture. He had attempted to test this argument by delving into the childhood and youth of Wesbecker. But Smith had expertly undermined the impact of that approach by establishing Wesbecker, through the testimony of many witnesses, as a humane and reasonable man, and, for part of his life at least, a caring father.

The defense was therefore left with a double task in relation to Wesbecker himself. They would need a strategy to explain why Prozac had not worked with this particular individual. And in the light of their failure to pull off the nature-and-nurture argument, they would have to offer an alternative explanation, credible to this jury of Louisville folk, as to why Wesbecker had done his terrible deeds.

But to begin with, the defense team called on Dr. Ray Fuller himself to rehearse the story of the neuroscience revolution, the rapid advances in psychopharmacology, and Prozac's part in it.

30

A PALE, BESPECTACLED, clerical-looking man, Ray Fuller seemed tired and somewhat stricken. Dressed conservatively in muted colors, he was questioned by John McGoldrick, a lean, ascetic-looking man in gold-rimmed glasses from Newark, New Jersey, who had now assumed the role of scientific counsel for the defense. Freeman, meanwhile, remained in court, situated to the left of the witness stand and in full sight of the jury, his face running through a gamut of indignant emotions, from outrage to scorn, at almost any question posed by the plaintiffs' counsel.

McGoldrick, who looked considerably fitter than Freeman, and who had a way of staring provocatively out at the plaintiffs in the gallery, took Fuller through a lengthy direct examination of his background and credentials.

Next McGoldrick encouraged Fuller to describe the neuroscience revolution and how it had affected knowledge about the brain. This was the first overview of the discipline offered during the trial, and Fuller handled the questions evenly and unadventurously.

"I think we've probably made more rapid progress during recent years in understanding the brain than any other part of the body, partly because we have probably lagged behind prior to that in understanding the brain."

Asked to be more specific, Fuller focused first on the discovery of multiple neurotransmitter substances, the brain's natural chemicals. Then he talked about the growing army of scientists engaged in uncovering the secrets of the brain and the central nervous system.

Neuroscience, and its byproduct Prozac, Fuller said, had to do with the unfolding symphony of scientific progress; with a revolution in knowledge about ourselves that would dominate the third millennium; with the alleviation of mental illness and crime, especially crimes of violence; and it had been approved by presidents of the United States on both sides of the political divide.

Fuller now recounted the story of depression, serotonin, and the discovery of fluoxetine hydrochloride. A large body of scientific data, he was saying, showed "that serotonin is an important neurotransmitter in modulating aggressive behavior."

"What's modulating mean?" asked McGoldrick sharply.

"Affecting, controlling, that sort of thing," Fuller replied. "And these studies as a whole have shown that increasing serotonin function by whatever means, by means of Prozac or by means of some other kind of drug, causes a decrease in aggressive behavior. . . . Studies showed, without exception, that any treatment which . . . decreased serotonin function increased aggressive behavior."

When Smith came to cross-examine this quiet, understated expert, he tried at first to dent his scientific hubris by inviting him to confirm that the brain was extremely complex, that there was a great deal *not* known about it.

Fuller stonewalled the question.

Then Smith attempted to move from the complexity of the whole brain to the complexity of the serotonin system by asking him about the thirteen different kinds of known serotonin receptors on a typical neuronal cell. He was trying to tempt the neuroscientist into an admission of ignorance; but his own description of the complexity of neuroscience and the mysterious link between physical and mental states fell ludicrously short of scientific realities. For instance, Smith could not grasp the difference between "secondary messengers" in technical language, meaning one chemical reaction in response to another, and "message" in common parlance.

As the Q and A developed, it betrayed Smith's tendency to reduce moods and behavior to molecular objects, a misunderstanding perhaps prompted by much of the expert testimony in the trial, especially Fuller's own statement that "for every crooked thought there's a crooked molecule." Yet Smith's difficulties eventually proved instructive.

"These thirteen different program receptors are activated by different concentrations of serotonin. Is that right?" asked Smith.

"Yes, sir."

"Okay, is this serotonin carrying a certain message?"

"I honestly don't know what you mean by that question."

"Okay. Well, we think that serotonin is implicated in depression, do we not?"

"Yes, sir."

"All right. And so would depression or elevation of mood be one of these thirteen separate programmed serotonin receptors?"

"No," responded Fuller with mild frustration. ". . . A receptor is a discrete molecule with which serotonin reacts. A receptor is not a function like a mood or appetite or something like that."

"But serotonin affects those feelings, doesn't it?"

"Serotonin affects those functions via its action on specific receptors."

"Okay. Is that the way to say it?"

"Yes, sir."

"In other words, there might be a specific receptor that is *associated* with mood; right?"

"Yes, sir."

As morning wore into afternoon, Smith covered the now familiar ground of the aggressive behavior of animals on fluoxetine in early trials, and the use of concomitant sedatives in clinical trials. Smith's lay instincts about the science of Prozac seemed to have convinced him that the researchers really did not understand a fraction of what they pretended to know. But how could he tempt Fuller into acknowledging this? At length, it was obvious he was not succeeding, yet something else was happening: Fuller had none of the overweening certitude of Leigh Thompson, but as question followed question he appeared to reveal a condescension bordering on contempt. Again and again Fuller rephrased Smith's questions as if determined not to give a scintilla of credence to the attorney's grasp of the science. Then, in an unguarded moment, Fuller allowed himself the indulgence of a laugh at Smith's expense.

The incident occurred in a sequence of questions about a report of animal aggression during trials.

"Turn to the second page, where it's talking about Dog Two; under observations, it said, 'Marked aggressive behavior. Technician bit, attempting dosing.' Right?"

Fuller's shoulders were gently heaving with mirth.

"Is that funny?" snapped Smith.

Joe Freeman, who had also been laughing at the quotation, suddenly looked alarmed.

"Well, it honestly sounds a little bit like the technician did the biting," said Fuller, a wan smile still playing about his lips. "But I don't think that's what was intended."

"You never *thought* that was what was intended, did you?" said Smith severely.

"No, I wouldn't seriously think that was intended," replied the crestfallen Fuller.

Smith now turned his attention to dosage and efficacy, and was attempting to expose the gap between the theory of Prozac and actual evidence of what it did to serotonin in the synaptic gap. The more he pressed, the more Fuller became uncomfortable and obstructive; but by sheer persistence Smith eventually brought the witness to the admission he wanted.

"Prozac is used to treat depression," said Fuller at last. "You don't diagnose depression by measuring anything in the blood. You don't measure blood sugar. You don't measure blood serotonin. You diagnose depression by measuring depressive symptoms, and that's what you look to treat, and that's what you look to to see if it's better."

"But you can't tell whether or not that Prozac is lowering or raising a particular individual's level of serotonin by virtue of a blood test, can you?"

"A psychiatrist isn't interested in whether the serotonin level has changed; it's whether the depressive symptoms are improved," said Fuller.

Turning to the judge, Smith said: "We'd object to that answer as being nonresponsive, Your Honor."

"Yes, you can," said Fuller. "It is straightforward to measure serotonin concentration in the blood. And as a matter of fact, that has been measured after Prozac or fluoxetine in lots of patients."

"Be clear with us, Dr. Fuller," went on Smith sharply. "Levels of serotonin in the blood are not relevant to levels of serotonin in the brain, are they, at the synaptic cleft?"

"That's correct."

"It can't be measured, can it?"

"That's correct."

Fuller had not enjoyed being questioned on his own discipline by a nonspecialist, and he had allowed his annoyance and disdain to show. He had consistently thwarted Smith's questions and disrupted his flow, a situation apparently much relished by Freeman.

After Smith had finished and the lawyers went up to the bench, Nancy Zettler complained to Judge Potter.

"One of our plaintiffs said she saw Mr. Freeman smiling and winking at the jury," she told him. "I didn't see anything yesterday, but I was watching today and there was just some interaction going on. We would ask that the court caution Mr. Freeman not to wink at them and smile at them."

"Just be pleasant," Potter said soothingly to them both.

"I certainly haven't intended to, Judge," said Freeman.

"Maybe it's just his Southern ways," Potter remarked, attempting to defuse what could turn into a verbal brawl at any moment.

"But there's no *reason* for him to sit over there, Judge," went on Zettler.

"That's *right,* Mr. Freeman," said the judge.

But when court reconvened, Joe Freeman was back at his vantage point.

The next Lilly witness to take the stand was a Dr. Joachim Wernicke, who had worked as moderator on Prozac trials from 1984 to 1990. Dressed in an ill-fitting blue suit, Wernicke had a dark shank of hair brushed across a balding head. He spoke in a strong German accent.

Speaking of his background, he told the court that he had come to the United States at the age of nine and that his parents had been political refugees from East Berlin. He was now forty-seven years old. Wernicke, who looked every inch the popular image of a scientist, said that he nowadays worked for a small company called Cyberonics.

As if to counteract the forbidding aura exuding from his witness, McGoldrick encouraged him to tell the court that he was married with two daughters and that they owned a chocolate Labrador. This did little, however, to dispel the faintly sinister account of the special device his current employers made for the treatment of epilepsy: "It's implanted in the chest with a generator," he was saying in his thickly guttural voice. "The electrodes are planted in the neck, where one feels the pulse in the neck next to the carotid artery. It's totally implanted. And then it can be changed with a computer program in a programming system that we've also developed to deliver these stimuli to the brain."

McGoldrick wanted Wernicke to describe the painstaking process of the human clinical trials, the relationship between the FDA and the pharmaceutical company, the rules laid down for investigating and approving new drugs.

Accordingly, Wernicke stressed the "methodical" and "systematic" nature of Lilly's trials, the company's obsessive attention to safety. He explained the role of protocols laid down by outside institutional bodies, including the FDA. "A protocol," he said, "is like a road map or the cookbook for the study. It tells you what to do, when to do it, how many patients, what you're going to measure, when you're going to measure it, how you're going to analyze the data."

Yet another exhaustive description of Lilly's trial procedures with congratulatory embellishments contributed a picture of Lilly's self-image as a scrupulous drug company, and helped spread the share of responsibility for clinical trials with associated university departments and the FDA.

Smith rose to cross-examine after two days of Wernicke's reassuring defense testimony, spry and confident. He was through with the science of the brain and was about to concentrate on what he was best at—elucidating the bureaucracy and internal politics of a major pharmaceutical company.

He came straight to the point.

"Dr. Wernicke, is it your position that Eli Lilly and Company fully and completely disclosed to the United States Food and Drug Administration what the German government meant by 'unacceptable damaging effects'?"

"Yes," said Wernicke without hesitation.

Smith's question alluded to an issue of major significance. Had

Lilly's scientific officers given the FDA a false impression of the concern about Prozac among the German regulatory body (BGA)?

According to Smith, the BGA had raised a question about "unacceptable damaging effects" in relation to suicidality and Prozac just a few days before the FDA was about to issue its preliminary approval. When Lilly passed on the BGA's concern to the FDA, Smith said, the impression had been given that the Germans were worried about "organ damage," not increased risk of suicide on Prozac.

Unlike Leigh Thompson and Ray Fuller, Wernicke was a deferential witness. As Smith cross-examined him on the basis of a series of letters and memoranda exchanged in 1984, Wernicke insisted that the impression of false reporting had been the "result of a confusion."

"I am responsible for this confusion," he said dolefully, "and I understand now how I was confused, because I never saw those words 'unacceptable damage' in that context, and in my mind that was all the same issue."

But Smith would not accept his excuse; he continued to harry the scientist until Wernicke acquiesced in what looked like an admission of culpability.

Quoting from the symptom-definition code used by the BGA in its original query, Smith got Wernicke to admit that he was aware that the Germans were referring to a code expressed as 2.1, indicating that their concern was about suicide on Prozac and not organ damage. Then Smith quoted from another BGA document on suicide risk: " 'The use of the preparation seems objectionable as the increase in agitating effect occurs earlier than the mood-elevating effect and, therefore, an increased risk of suicide exists.' Correct, sir?"

"Yes," said Wernicke.

"And that's important, isn't it?"

"Yes . . ."

Wernicke now insisted that the FDA itself should have realized the significance of the 2.1 code, as if seeking to mitigate somewhat the damage that was being done to Lilly's defense by widening the onus of responsibility.

"You said the Germans didn't define it?" Smith asked at last.

"I don't believe that I needed to point the FDA to that," said the lugubrious Wernicke.

"You don't think so, when *they* were calling you and asking you a specific question about a specific item?"

"No. I don't feel that I need to point to that," said Wernicke, his English tense structure collapsing under pressure. "What I felt and still do need to do is to tell them what my opinion and information was on that issue at the time."

"That was wrong, wasn't it, at best?"

"I don't think it was wrong."

"It was either a mistake on your part or it was misrepresentation on your part, wasn't it?" cried Smith, his face full of emotion.

"The most of it was that I had not seen those words 'damaging effects' and thought that it was all the same. . . ." Suddenly Wernicke was blathering, taking a circular route back to his starting point.

As Smith's interrogation proceeded, and the pressure increased, the jury witnessed the phenomenon of vanishing responsibility. For example, Wernicke pleaded that he had no responsibility, or even knowledge, of a memorandum sent to the BGA informing them that there should be "no doubt on fluoxetine's positive benefit/risk" if the drug were administered to suicidal and agitated patients with an accompanying sedative. When Smith pointed to his name among the "copies to," Wernicke again pleaded that he had no memory of it, that his inclusion was a formality, that any responsibility for the memorandum lay with a colleague.

Then Smith returned to the fact that German package warnings, as recommended by September 14, 1989, had contained a clear directive that patients should be offered "an additional sedative" in cases of extreme sleep disturbances or excitability, a warning, he inferred, that was omitted from American package warnings. Linking the German package warning to the recommendations about "positive benefit/risk" in the memorandum, Smith seemed to have made a palpable point.

He followed it up by bringing into evidence a curious E-mail, the minutes of a meeting that was convened at Lilly's headquarters just five hours after the Wesbecker shootings. The document was later circulated to the group of top clinical executives who had attended. The subject, Smith declared, was "mortality in the Prozac depression database."

"Let's read it together," Smith said. "It says, 'All attendees were in agreement as to the importance of Medical being able to proactively provide information to whatever source, FDA, consumer groups, et cetera, on adverse events as well as mortality in the clinical trial database.... Charles [Beasley] indicated that these results would be used in a PR document developed by a person or persons unknown at this time.' "

Smith later told me that this item was a typical example of the serendipitous isolation of evidence when two lawyers were attempting to process two and a half million pages of documents: "Nancy had come across it by chance and had been trying to push it under my nose for a week, and I kept saying, 'Give me a break!' Then I found it on the kitchen table in my apartment one morning and it hit me between the eyes."

At first it was not clear what advantage Smith was attempting to extract from these minutes other than making Lilly appear manipulative and cynical. And yet here was Dr. Joachim Wernicke more or less conceding the point.

"You had just learned that Joseph Wesbecker was on Prozac and had committed this act, hadn't you?"

"I do not remember that in conjunction with this meeting," said Wernicke apologetically. "I don't remember this meeting exactly. That may well be, but I don't remember whether that's the case."

"It may well be that you were having a meeting about this five hours after it happened, mightn't it, sir?"

"That could well be," said Wernicke lamely.

"Well, is it your testimony that you heard about this incident, you guys up here at Lilly got together with the statisticians and with the computer people and said, 'Gosh, we don't know how many people have been killed. We don't know how much mortality there is in our U.S. clinical-trial database.' Is that what you're telling this jury?"

Wernicke was floundering. "It may well have been," he said at length. "But I just don't know."

Smith's interrogation now shifted to the abstruse science of statistics, the facts and figures, the rationale, behind Lilly's analysis of deaths associated with Prozac. Wernicke was vague about what he knew and did not know about the mortality figures, and as Smith pursued him he began to distance himself from responsibility for such information. But Smith allowed him little leeway. "You had a number of deaths all along but you hadn't analyzed your database to know what number of deaths you had and how to analyze the statistics on those deaths; is that what you're telling this jury?"

At length, Wernicke tried to bring the questions to a conclusion with a final plea of justified ignorance: "As time went by, my responsibilities shifted to a number of other projects, and some of the psychiatrists took over more and more of the fluoxetine—Prozac—work."

But Smith brought the discussion back to the meeting on September 14, 1989, the day of the Wesbecker shootings. He had not finished with what he evidently saw as its sinister and cynical aims.

Reading again from the memorandum of the meeting, he noted, " 'Charles [Dr. Charles Beasley] indicated that these results [analyses of deaths on Prozac asked for at the meeting] would be used in a PR document developed by a person or persons unknown at this time.' So all this stuff you're doing is going to be turned into a public-relations document," said Smith.

"My view of the way this is handled," said Wernicke, "is that I analyze the data, I provide the answers. If people want to use it, then I hand it over, then how people use it, that's up to them. . . ."

Throughout the rest of the day, Smith questioned Wernicke about clinical-trial procedures.

"There were no Prozac studies on individuals with schizophrenia, were there?" he asked eventually.

"That's correct, to my knowledge."

"There were no Prozac studies with patients with depressive paranoid depression, psychotic depression, were there?" went on Smith.

"Not specifically as an inclusion criterion," said Wernicke. "That's right."

"There were no Prozac clinical trials to examine the effect of Prozac on individuals with schizoaffective disorder, were there, sir?"

"To my knowledge, that's correct."

Then came the payoff—a twist of the thread that recalled the last ten years of Wesbecker's life, with its evident episodes of paranoia, and Lee Coleman's prescribing of Prozac. "Let me ask you this, Dr. Wernicke: were any Prozac clinical trials done on individuals suffering from psychotic depression?"

"Not to my knowledge."

"Were there any Prozac clinical trials done on individuals suffering from schizoaffective disorder?"

"Not that I'm aware of, no."

"Is Prozac contraindicated in the package insert for individuals suffering from psychotic depression? . . . Schizoaffective disorder?"

In both cases the witness answered, "No."

The hapless Wernicke was looking pale and haunted—as well he might, for he appeared at that moment to be carrying the reputation of Eli Lilly and Company on his shoulders. But there was worse to come.

After asking whether Lilly had adequately warned the FDA of the German BGA's misgivings about Prozac, Smith turned to a memorandum he had cited in his direct examination of Leigh Thompson. The document referred to a request for efficacy data on ten-milligram doses of Prozac, containing the comment that "Some people have *massaged* [my italics] those data to make 5 milligrams look not quite as good as 20 milligrams." The document had been brought in evidence earlier during Leigh Thompson's testimony, when Smith had drawn the inference that Lilly had settled on twenty milligrams for a better patient-compliance profile, and in order to make higher profits overseas.

"Now, when you gave your deposition in this case," went on Smith, "you told me that you were not aware that anybody had massaged the data in your trial to make five milligrams look not quite as good as twenty milligrams; correct, sir?"

"That's correct," Wernicke replied.

"Have you ever massaged data, Dr. Wernicke?"

"I don't know what that means. You have to put that in a context of . . ."

"You told me in your deposition that you massaged *people,* didn't you?" went on Smith.

"That's what one does, not that that's what I do. But that's the correct use of that term."

"Well, you hadn't ordinarily seen the term 'massage' used in connection with a statistical analysis, had you?"

"Well, except by Dr. Thompson. He uses words like that; he has a very flowery language, and I might have heard it."

"Well, you told me in your deposition in Houston that you had never heard Dr. Thompson use such a word in connection with statistics, didn't you?"

Wernicke continued to stall through several questions, until Smith raised the stakes by accusing him of discussing the use of the term with Lilly's attorneys.

Finally, Smith said: "When I took your deposition, you told me 'massage' has a bad connotation with statistics, didn't you? . . . Were you aware of any massaging of this data that you collected to make five milligrams look not as good as twenty milligrams, Dr. Wernicke?"

"No," said the doctor. "I'm not aware of any such manipulation."

"Manipulation!" shouted Smith, turning gleefully toward the public gallery. "You use the term 'manipulation.' Isn't that really what you're talking about when you say 'massage'? You're talking about manipulating data to make the five-milligram look not quite as good as the twenty?"

"If it were done with the intent of showing some outcome and, in this case, making one dose look worse than another, I would call that manipulating."

"And that's what was done, according to Dr. Thompson, in this memo; correct?"

To a hushed court, and a horrified row of Lilly attorneys, Wernicke conceded the allegation.

"According to Dr. Thompson," said Wernicke, "he seemed to imply that that may have been done."

31

THERE WAS A BREAK of almost a week, and the bright fall skies gave way to dismal days of mist and rain as the trial continued on into the middle of November.

As one defense witness followed another, Lilly seemed to be attempting to force the jury into submission by burying them under a mountain of information. A troop of medical doctors, professors, neuroscientists gave testimony in turn, each extolling the rigor of Lilly's scientific programs and its unimpeachable testing methods. Each came laden with degrees, honors, prizes, and a large measure of certitude. In the midst of this information overload, Smith had to satisfy himself with finding an occasional chink in the heavy armor of professional hubris.

On November 15, his painstaking eye for detail was rewarded when one of Lilly's biggest guns, Dr. John Greist from Indianapolis, took the stand. During direct examination, this clean-cut fifty-five-year-old with iron-gray hair had expatiated with mounting confidence on his medical and scientific credentials. Greist had run a series of Prozac clinical trials in his hospital department at Wisconsin, and he had a position at a medical-education foundation called the Dean Trust.

In testifying that Wesbecker had been the victim of what he called a "malignant" depression (meaning a chronic, worsening condition) ever since the early 1980s, Greist had cited a psychiatric assessment (Minnesota Multiphasic Personality Inventory, or MMPI) made in 1983, based on a patient questionnaire. Greist claimed that a series of critical questions in Wesbecker's MMPI had revealed key symptoms of aggression, paranoia, mental confusion, suicidal ideation, and antisocial behavior.

Greist had based this opinion not on Wesbecker's original answer sheet but on the document supplied by Lilly that copied Wesbecker's true-or-false answers alongside the interpretations of the assessing doctor ["Dr. Butcher of Minnesota"].

In one of the most powerful cross-examinations of the trial, Smith now produced the copied assessments and showed that, in the "critical" questions selected by Greist, Wesbecker's answers did not match the original. Going backward and forward, from the original to Dr. Butcher's assessment, Smith played the advantage for all it was worth.

"All right. Let's see," Smith started. "You have checked Item 43 as being particularly appropriate?"

"Well, it's one of the items that I checked; correct."

"It says, 'My sleep is fitful and disturbed.' "

"Yes."

"It says 'true' there; right?"

"Uh-huh. Yes."

"Go back, doctor, and look at the actual answer on the answer sheet."

"Yes. It's different. It says 'false.' "

"It's *false*?" Smith cried in an amazed voice, looking out toward the gallery.

"Yep," said Greist, staring at the sheet in front of him.

"Okay. Mistake there, huh?" asked Smith, sarcastically.

"That's correct. Something is wrong here, that is for sure."

Point by point—without a single objection from Lilly's lawyers, who sat with frozen faces throughout—Smith went on down through items marked on the original and compared his answers with those on the "critical" sheet provided by Lilly. In the 1983 MMPI test, Wesbecker had denied that he felt constantly anxious, incapable of controlling his life, aggressive, prone to "peculiar experiences," mentally confused, incapable of concentrating, persecuted, suspicious. But on Lilly's sheet, used in evidence earlier in Greist's testimony under direct examination, each of these questions had been marked in the affirmative.

"Now let's look at something that you marked 'really critical,' " Smith said at last. " 'When someone does me wrong I feel I should pay him back if I can, just for the principle of the thing.' The form marks this as true; right?"

"Yep."

"What's the actual answer that Joseph T. Wesbecker gave?"

"False. That's what the form says."

"But his actual answer was *false*?" echoed Smith, his eyes stretched wide as he gazed around the court.

"That's correct."

"In that he *didn't* feel like when someone did him wrong he should pay them back?"

"That would be correct."

"There are some more in here that are wrong?"

"I trust we'll learn that," said Greist, his face gray with shock and humiliation.

"The whole thing is worthless? Isn't it?"

"This particular instrument, unless it is explained—I would throw out any interpretation based on it at this point," said Greist grimly. Then he muttered as if to himself: ". . . there's something really wrong here. There's no question about *that*."

"Something really wrong here, isn't there?" echoed Smith.

"That's right," said Greist finally.

As Smith let the echo of this exchange hang in the silent court for a few moments, the inference he hoped to convey was obvious. For all its army of highly paid lawyers and paralegals, Lilly's defense team had shown themselves incapable of running a simple check on two crucial and accessible documents. More important, as Greist had intimated in his testimony under direct examination, and as Stopher had claimed in his opening statement at the beginning of the trial, the MMPI test had been crucial to the view that Wesbecker had been prone to harm himself and others for years, not just in the summer of 1989.

As the end of the trial came into sight, Smith and Zettler were looking good, despite their evident exhaustion. The feeling among the spectators was that Smith had succeeded in establishing at least the impression that Lilly had cut corners in its testing and marketing of Prozac. And despite the solemn façade of Ed Stopher and the expert witnesses, an impression of ineptness and lack of candor hovered over Lilly's discovery and testimony. Yet this did not add up to anything like a verdict in the plaintiff's favor. Even if the defense could persuade the jury that Lilly had been negligent in testing and marketing Prozac, it would not indicate that they had been knowingly and irresponsibly negligent—a crucial factor for significant punitive damages in such a case (unless, of course, the Oraflex evidence were allowed). And in any case, the real nub of the trial was not Lilly's negligence (damaging as that might be to the company's reputation and fortunes) but whether the jury could be convinced that Prozac had been a substantial cause of Wesbecker's actions.

The question—whether there would be a case for punitive damages, should the plaintiffs prevail—had been argued before the judge in chambers on the evening before Greist's testimony.

Joe Freeman started by referring to the "ridiculous claims" of the plaintiffs, and appealing to the "very high standard" the state of Kentucky had established in connection "with even the submission of punitive damages." He was seeking to persuade Judge Potter that punitive damages would be an issue only if the plaintiffs could show that Lilly either "acted with malice" or was "flagrantly indifferent to the rights of the plaintiff, that is . . . what it was doing will result in human death or bodily harm."

Freeman now listed what he deemed to be the leading allegations made by the plaintiffs' counsel in the trial, and how, in his view, he believed those allegations had been answered. His list of the plaintiffs' claims included: the "growling and hissing dogs and cats," the stimulant effect of Prozac on humans during clinical trials, the prior exclusion of suicidal patients from trials, the use of concomitant sedatives with Prozac, the "culling out" of suicide attempts during the clinical trials from the trial data, failure to perform clinical trials that would better define the patient population most likely to become violent on Prozac. On each point, Freeman sought to persuade the judge that even if the matter were proved (which of course he was not conceding) there was no case to cite malice or flagrant behavior.

Freeman's last point raised the Oraflex issue directly. Referring to the plaintiffs' claim that Lilly had failed to report "adverse events" from its own databases, Freeman reminded the judge that all those adverse events were to be reported "by law."

"Failure to report these adverse events," went on Freeman, "is a felony." Then he checked himself and said, "Lilly was found guilty of a misdemeanor for not failing to report but reporting late ten events in connection with Oraflex, and one other misdemeanor. It was not ever found guilty of any felony."

The comment was no doubt intended to anticipate and defuse any further attempt to introduce the Oraflex evidence.

When it was his turn to speak, Smith graciously conceded that Freeman had "done a pretty good job in setting out for the court what the facts are and the contentions are from both sides," but he was now going to "recap" his position in his own words, from his own point of view, and with particular reference to punitive damages.

He began by insisting that Lilly had known very early on in animal studies and very early in human studies that the drug agitated some patients. But the company "had done nothing but try to cover up that profile in a number of ways."

He then listed the plaintiffs' allegations more or less as Freeman had done, except that he put new emphasis on Lilly's attempted manipulation of the regulating bodies.

"When the German government raised the issue [of agitation and suicidality on Prozac] I believe we've shown not only that Lilly did not inform the FDA but they did everything they could by contacting directly and indirectly members of the German government to try to manipulate them and to try to convince them, or somehow get them to approve this drug without contraindications, like the BGA originally wanted." Smith went on to claim that he believed Lilly was successful in this "because of this influence—undue influence on government officials in the BGA."

His final point was that, "if they hadn't tested this drug in schizoaffective patients, which they knew had the underlying depressive condition, they should have contraindicated the use of that drug in the package insert. What is even worse in this case, Judge, is that the drug was not only not tested, very early on they had some bad experiences with these types of patients. They never tested it specifically. They never told the FDA about their suspicions, and then they used concomitant medications that under their protocol should not have been let in."

In conclusion, he told Potter, "Frankly, we don't concede that there was no subjective awareness that the conduct would result in death and bodily harm."

Then Nancy Zettler intervened to make a point about Oraflex. The plaintiffs were not going to concede subjectivity, she said, because Lilly had a history of this kind of conduct.

"In fact," she said, "before or actually during the same time that this drug and its new-drug application was being filed was when they got caught not reporting deaths that occurred with their drug Oraflex. In that case they did exactly what they're doing here. They said it was part of the underlying disease process or it was something that was related to the underlying condition of the patients that were getting Oraflex."

She went on to say that "the FDA has redone their regulations to require stricter reporting of adverse events, and stricter because of Lilly's conduct, specifically because of the conduct of Lilly." The plaintiffs, she went on, would show "that this is a company with a history of flagrant disregard for the safety of the potential patients that are getting their drugs."

Judge Potter merely responded that he would get back to them with a judgment in due course. But, as Potter would have cause to remember later, he had once again been left in no doubt as to the explosive potential of the Oraflex story.

32

WHEN THE DEFENSE turned back to the character and mind-set of Joe Wesbecker, Ed Stopher again took charge of the case.

His first witness was Brenda Camp, Wesbecker's second ex-wife, a woman in her mid-forties with cascading black hair, doleful eyes, and plentiful makeup. She was wearing a broad-shouldered royal-blue dress with spangled epaulettes, and heavy beaded earrings.

Stopher's aim was to establish that Wesbecker had a deep-seated personality disorder—in contrast to the impression given by Sue Chesser, his first wife, that he had many redeeming qualities.

Speaking in laid-back Southern style, Brenda Camp told how she met Wesbecker at a Parents Without Partners dance in November 1980 and began to date him about three weeks later. She was then separated from her husband, and residing in her marital home with two young children. Wesbecker was living alone in a house on Mount Holyoke Drive. They married— "privately," she said, in a house in Indiana—in August 1981.

They had what she described as a "prenuptial contract," which kept their earnings separate, "other than we gave each other gifts." Since her marital home was going into foreclosure, she had moved in with him on Mount Holyoke with her two children; his two boys, James and Kevin, who lived with Wesbecker's first ex-wife, visited occasionally.

Talking of the early days of their marriage, she began to weep. "He tried to help me with my kids. He couldn't have been a nicer man at first—we dated and lived together a year before we married, and if it hadn't been for him, I don't know how I would have made it."

Asked about Wesbecker's threats to kill her first husband, Dr. Beasley, she responded: "Yes. He threatened to kill him three times. . . .

He said one time he would wait at his office and when he left he would roll down the window and blow his brains out."

She denied that he had physically abused her, but she recalled his abnormal moods. "The only form of abuse," she continued, "he would become extremely quiet and recluse. He might go three weeks without talking to you."

By November 1984, they had divorced.

"He lied to me and I didn't know he had been ill prior to us meeting. . . . I could no longer cope with having my children around him when he wouldn't speak, the emotional impact; I could no longer be around that man who wanted to murder the father of my children. . . . I thought, for safety, my children did not need to be around that. After he threatened to kill my daughter, that was enough."

In the most damaging testimony to the plaintiffs' case so far, Brenda Camp went on to describe Wesbecker's behavior toward her daughter Melissa, who had reached her early twenties by the time of killings in 1989.

On New Year's Eve 1983, they were driving, just the two of them, down Bardstown Road on their way to the movies. "By that stoplight right beside the Steak N Shake, he looked right at me and said, 'You know, it would be easy for me to blow your daughter's brains out, and then I wouldn't have to look at her. I wouldn't have to see her and I wouldn't have to be jealous of yours and her relationship.' So I hit him. I got out of the car and I walked Bardstown Road at about—I don't know—ten-thirty at night. We didn't go to no movies."

"Had your daughter done anything to incite him or to make him mad?"

"No, sir," she replied promptly. "Melissa made attempts to speak to the man. She did it thinking she could make a difference. She just couldn't see where that wasn't okay. . . . On the day we put his remains to rest, she carried them. In that bizarre moment, she said, 'Mom, I just have to carry them.' So I guess she was looking for normality, too, and there wasn't any."

"Ms. Camp, did he ever talk about death to you?" asked Stopher.

"He had a morbid sense of humor. He had an infatuation with death. He didn't fear it. One morning I woke up, it was a pretty morning, and I remember him beside me. He tapped me like that and said, 'How would you like to die today?' "

"Did he ever talk of his own death?" asked the lawyer.

"I was sleeping in a separate bedroom from him. We didn't always sleep together. . . . Two in the morning, I heard the sound of pulling duct tape in the living room and the car running. . . . I let a couple of hours go by. So I get up. I went in, and he was in the hallway on the floor, bleeding on the mouth, duct tape all masked around him. There was a hose outside the window coming down."

"All right, Ms. Camp," went on Stopher, would you tell us about the second suicide attempt?"

"I come home from work. And he was running up and down the road. He was out of his head and he's banging on my car. And I pull in the driveway and I'm, like, 'Oh, Lord.' And he had beat the front door of the house. He had tore up stuff in the living room. He had tore stuff out of his wallet. He had threw stuff out of the cabinet. He was delirious, like he didn't know where he was at. He was talking out of his head, like, 'Where am I?' Running up and down the road . . . I call EMS. He had overdosed on pills. Either he had saved up some of his medicine—I seen over-the-counter stuff ripped and tore . . . Funny things. Let water running. Just bizarre, crazy things. Toilet paper just—I mean, I don't know how to describe it. Rolls of toilet paper hanging from the kitchen thing."

Then Stopher encouraged her to talk about Wesbecker's difficulties at work.

"His biggest thing he wanted was a less-stressful job so he could continue to work. . . . You can tease people, but I can remember walking in the plant and some of them would make fun of him. And they'd say vulgarities to me."

Stopher asked her about his interest in guns.

"Early 1988, Joe bought me a gun for my birthday. I made a vacation trip with my two children alone. He was determined I was going to have a gun for protection going to Myrtle Beach. He always believed I ought to have a gun as a woman. He took me out to this shooting range, it didn't last long. I shot a few times, took the earplugs off, we had a severe argument, and I left."

Toward the end of her testimony, she told how Wesbecker had deeded to her his house on Nottoway Circle on September 27, 1988. At that time, she explained, they were getting ready to separate again. "He did not want the relationship to end. I did not want him to progressively become more mentally ill. . . . There is no palimony in the state of Kentucky. If he would have ended up in a mental institute, I would have been put out of the home again after all the money I had paid out in the eight-year relationship." She presented him, she said, with the alternatives of giving her a cash settlement or deeding the house solely in her name.

Wesbecker, she said, saw a further advantage in this settlement: he feared that, if the house remained in his name and he was institutionalized, the property would be taken to cover his medical bills.

In the year following the gift of the house, she went on, Wesbecker expected her to pay the bills for electricity, garbage collection, water, and telephone. "I cut that off," she said, "because I got tired of paying the bills."

Her testimony about the reasons for and consequences of that decision then became increasingly garbled. "He'd pee in a can, urinate," she said. "He would—I don't know. Sometimes I let him take a bath at my father's home. Sometimes I helped him wash his clothes. Sometimes I think he went without taking a bath."

Smith's witnesses had succeeded in contradicting the portrait of Wesbecker's domestic squalor established by Stopher in his opening statement. But Brenda Camp, despite the contradictions in her testimony, had now done much to reinstate Stopher's version. And now, as she finished her testimony, a strange ambiguity hung over Wesbecker's financial affairs, the gift of his house, and just how much she had known about his intentions.

All she would say was: "I would have never put Joe out. We were too good of friends. He could have lived there for a lot of years, and then I would have had to make a decision."

33

THE FOLLOWING WEEK, a troop of former employees, union members, and foremen at Standard Gravure lined up to testify.

Mostly fatigued and overweight men in late middle age, they talked of the stresses at the plant, and in particular the tyranny of the folder machine. One foreman maintained that there was no company policy recognizing mental illness as a handicap. Another spoke of the increase in fumes in the pressroom after Mike Shea bought the company: "Especially in Area 2 . . . in the pressroom itself, it just kind of knocked you down when you walked in."

Don Cox, the pressroom superintendent, said that Wesbecker was not the only stressed-out person on the plant, "because there was a lot of stress in the building at the time." He singled out the fact that "it had been a long time since people had gotten a pay raise; there was a lot of rumors about the company closing, business was not very good, just numerous things."

Don Frazier, the union president at the plant, spoke of the stress following the news that the new owner, Shea, had "sold or converted the pension plan in a company out in California." He said the perception was that "he was able to restructure this pension plan so that he had several million dollars that he could get out to put in his own pocket."

Shea, Frazier said, was a "hard bargainer"; one of the first things he did was to revoke the company "philosophy" of reviewing the pensions of retirees according to a cost-of-living index. But the principal change in the actual functioning of the presses, said Frazier, involved increasing the speed of the machines. "It creates a great deal more tension and you have to pay more attention to detail. There's more web breaks, more work. It's a tense situation. The higher speeds, especially with the older presses that we had, created a great deal of stress. . . . The crew or man in charge who didn't meet the running speed would have a rather unpleasant time."

Some of the former employees testified that Wesbecker believed toluene was injuring their health. "He was going to try to get it taken out of the plant," said one witness. "He collected a lot of data from the government on the chemical and showed it to his doctor."

A pressman named Danny Lee West confirmed that they called Wesbecker names, such as "Sexbecker," and they said he was "going crazy or *was* crazy." He testified about the graffiti on the walls ridiculing Wesbecker, but added that there was a whole variety of obscene and aggressive graffiti around the plant, such as "Cox Sucks," and a picture referring to Shea in which "somebody mimeographed an airplane and showed a picture of a plane blowing up. Another one was the plane looked like a penis and it was blowing up." He said that it was routine to find "hit lists" of managers' names written up on the wall.

A foreman named Roger Coffey related a typical clash he had with Wesbecker. He called Wesbecker at home on one occasion to ask him to volunteer for a shift. Coffey failed to get Wesbecker and spoke to Brenda instead.

The next evening, Wesbecker telephoned Coffey's household a number of times through the night, saying, "This is Joe Wesbecker, and when Roger gets up you tell him that I've called. And I'm going to call you every half-hour from now till he gets up." When Coffey's wife asked if Wesbecker wanted her to wake him, he replied, "No. I just want you to let him know if he can call me at my house then I can call him at his."

Most of the witnesses could testify to Wesbecker's increasing fascination with guns, AK-47s, gun magazines, and weapons catalogues. Another spoke of his interest in "paint" missile target practice. Frazier mentioned how Wesbecker started to make "exotic" and "crazy" statements. "He would have a confrontation and he'd say something like, 'Well, you know, maybe that person should be blowed away.' " His co-workers also recall his threats to blow up the plant with the use of a guided model plane.

"He really hated being off from work," said Frazier. "He expressed that to me on more than one occasion. He just did not want to be retired. He didn't think it was fair. He didn't think it was right. He thought it was totally wrong, and in a way I agreed with the man."

Throughout his questioning, Ed Stopher had not been averse to implying that Wesbecker's mental state had been partly exacerbated by the general state of affairs at Standard Gravure, but was careful to stop short of casting aspersions on the co-worker plaintiffs. He also emphasized the lack of security arrangements at Standard Gravure, implying a strong element of responsibility on the part of company officers and the outside firm, Hall Security Service Inc., for the lack of effective systems and practices to protect employees.

Meanwhile, Paul Smith, who was handling cross-examination for the plaintiffs, was seeking confirmation that Wesbecker's threats were neither serious nor taken seriously. Smith was at pains to keep the focus on Wesbecker's illness and Prozac, and in his determination to silence testimony about workplace stress he occasionally hectored his witnesses.

But the tactic failed when he harried union chief Don Frazier.

"The problem Joe was having was . . . that by virtue of his mental illness he couldn't handle the stress of the folder; correct?" asked Smith.

"Nerves, mental illness, I guess whatever you're calling it."

"And what Joe wanted was to be taken off the folder?"

"That's correct."

"But the reason he couldn't work the folder was because of his underlying mental illness, wasn't it?"

"I think you've asked me that three times and I keep saying yes, nerves, mental illness, emotional problems, whatever."

"It wasn't Standard Gravure that caused him to be mentally ill, was it?"

"I certainly think they contributed to his problems, along with all the rest of us that worked there."

"Did Standard Gravure cause Mr. Joseph Wesbecker to be manic-depressive, bipolar?"

"I don't think I'm qualified to answer that."

"Well, in your opinion?"

"I think they had a lot to do with it. They certainly disturbed *me*."

"Are you suffering from some mental illness, sir?"

"I think, like, a lot of people down there have emotional disturbance from that to this day, yes."

"Have you heard about the theory or belief that mental illness of major depressive disorder is a result of an imbalance in the serotonin system? Know anything about that?"

"Only what I read," said Frazier skeptically.

In a week when Stopher consistently attempted to divert attention toward the conduct of the company and its security system, his most telling direct examination was of Grady Throneberry, safety-and-security manager at Standard Gravure during the time of the shootings.

Throneberry was a lean, laconic individual, fit-looking, and sharply dressed. He testified that he had once been "a police officer in a small city," and before that he had sold cars. He admitted that in the mid-1980s he had operated a group called Business Security, which provided guard service for various companies, including Standard Gravure and WHAS Radio. At the same time, he said, he had also operated a hot-tub company called Good Clean Fun.

Throneberry admitted that while he was security manager at Standard Gravure he retained a financial interest in the security-guard service that was supplying the security at the printing plant.

With vociferous objections from Smith, Stopher doggedly argued that "the relevance is that it influenced his judgment to give the contract to the company that got it that was not qualified, to the opinions of the plaintiffs' own expert."

Judge Potter overruled Smith's objection, and Stopher continued.

Throneberry then testified that over a period of eighteen months prior to the shootings at Standard Gravure he had earned a sum of $25,000 from Hall Security, to which he had sold out his own security company, and which had assumed the Standard Gravure security contract.

"Did you select Hall Security?" Stopher asked.

"No, I didn't select Hall Security," Throneberry responded.

"Did you recommend Hall Security?"

"Yeah, I suppose so."

"Was there competitive bidding?"

"No, there was not."

After suggesting conflict of interest, which Throneberry denied, Stopher sought to demonstrate that the company and the security group had failed in their duty to protect the employees of Standard Gravure.

The question that had constantly been raised about security standards at the plant since September 14, 1989, was simply: why did no one in management react to Wesbecker's many threats? Senior management at the plant had denied being informed of any such threats; Throneberry said that he knew about the threats, but unfortunately his files on the subject were missing.

Stopher sought to infer that there was something amiss here, since there was no lack of documentation relating to other hazards at the plant. The security "problems" Stopher listed as coming within the responsibility of Throneberry included "loan-sharking muscle work, intimidation by collecting debts on loan-sharking, drugs, alcohol, and the like."

In an attempt to rebut testimony that nobody took Wesbecker's threats seriously, Stopher encouraged Throneberry to admit that he had once secreted himself in an adjacent kitchenette while Shea had a meeting with Wesbecker.

This incident evidently worried Smith. In his cross-examination, he returned to it in a facetious run of questions.

"Mr. Shea wasn't sitting behind bulletproof glass or anything?" asked Smith.

"No."

"You didn't hear Shea screaming or yelling?"

"No."

"You didn't hear any doors slamming?"

"No."

"You didn't hear anybody pounding on any desk or pounding on any doors, did you?"

"No."

"Would you agree with me, sir, that if Mr. Wesbecker was going to do violence to Mr. Shea he could very well have done it right then and there?"

"Well, he could have."

"But he didn't, did he?"

Try as he might, however, Smith could not eradicate the impression that Wesbecker's threats had been neglected by Standard Gravure's managers.

34

As THE TRIAL drew to a close, the defense began to turn, belatedly, to alternative sources of liability and responsibility. Ed Stopher's direct examination attempted to show that Standard Gravure, although it was not
a defendant in the case, must shoulder a portion of the blame for Wesbecker's actions.

On November 17, Dan Mattingly was called to the stand. Although
it was warm in the courtroom, this tall, balding, soft-spoken man continued to wear his raincoat. A local investigator for the Human Relations
Commission, Mattingly got involved in Wesbecker's case during the
pressman's final years at Standard Gravure. Mattingly said he had
warned Paula Warman, the plant's personnel manager, that "the company should shut down rather than force Wesbecker to work on the
folder."

Mattingly said that Wesbecker had frequently claimed his mental
condition made working the folder too stressful. "He described himself
as a safety hazard in a stressful situation, because he was on a lot of
heavy medication."

Even if the company didn't often assign Wesbecker to work on the
folder during his final months of work, Mattingly maintained, the threat
that they might was almost as bad. "He would go home and worry about
that and stew and fret. It became a problem even when he was away
from the job."

The court then saw a videotaped deposition by Mike Shea, Standard
Gravure's owner since 1986. The broad-shouldered, youthful Shea said
he was not aware of threats Wesbecker made against the company, and
went on to declare that he doubted whether there would have been a way
to stop him once he decided to kill.

"Do I wish we had figured out some way to prevent this—the man from going over the breaking point and doing what he did? I wish we would've. . . . Still, I'm not sure there was a way to stop a man who was coming in with death on his mind."

Throughout the deposition, Ed Stopher had hammered away, but Shea had denied that he was aware of any concerns raised about a lack of security, and said he never knew of any employees' bringing guns into the plant. He repeatedly declined to confirm that managers at the plant had acted irresponsibly after Wesbecker's threats. "It's my understanding," he said, "that Mr. Wesbecker was constantly in that type of joking mode, or that there were many instances where he would make casual remarks like that. So, whether or not he had cried wolf so long that no one believed him, I just don't know."

The following day, Stopher returned to Wesbecker's life and character, the principal thrust of Lilly's case.

First he called Wesbecker's younger son, James, to the stand. Like his elder brother, Kevin, James looked remarkably like his father. Pale in the face, bespectacled, and with tight curly hair, James T. Wesbecker, now aged twenty-seven, was dressed in a sober blue suit and conservative tie. He said that he was living with his mother, Sue Chesser, Wesbecker's first ex-wife, and was currently unemployed. He had graduated in economics from the University of Louisville, but had failed to complete a postgraduate course at North Carolina State.

Stopher was relying on James to confirm the main outline of the defense argument that Wesbecker had been on a path to homicidal mania all of his life. For two and a half hours, Stopher questioned him about Wesbecker's history of mental illness, his periodic estrangements from members of the family, and his belief that toluene had damaged his health.

James was quietly spoken and nervous; his reluctant testimony finally turned into an ordeal when he was obliged to describe to the jury his sexual-exposure problem and how this affected his father's emotional difficulties. Yet, much as he acknowledged Wesbecker's occasional anger and depressive behavior in the last ten years of his life, James gave moving testimony to his father's patience and support over his problem.

As Stopher took him through the story of his father's life, it became clear that James was not going to help the defense case. An example was James's account of Wesbecker's coldness toward his stepdaughter, Melissa. As far as James was concerned, they had merely "drifted apart."

"She had gotten older," he said, "and was going out more and would come in and wake him up. And Dad didn't like to be waked up in the middle of the night, because he may not go back to sleep, so he got kind of irritated with her."

When Stopher asked what he meant by "irritated," he said, "He told Brenda she needed to deal with her daughter . . . to take care of it."

As he began his cross-examination, Smith wanted it known that neither he nor Nancy Zettler had ever spoken to the witness before. Then he began his questioning.

"Did you love your dad?"

"Very much so."

"Did he act as a loving father to you?"

"Yes, sir."

"What type of things would you and he do together before you were eight or nine years old?"

"Have snowball fights, build a snowman in the snow, or he taught me how to build igloos and stuff when we had big snowdrifts. He taught me how to play sports, especially football, make friends, ride a bike, numerous things."

"Did you-all have friends over to your house?"

"Yes, sir; we did."

"And did your friends enjoy coming over, as far as you know?"

"Yes, sir."

Smith's cross-examination elicited the son's view that Wesbecker had eventually succeeded in getting over his estrangements and difficulties, both with his mother and with Kevin. He said his father had never done anything violent or evil. "As far as I was concerned," he said, "he was incapable of that kind of act."

According to James, however, in the final days of Wesbecker's life, after he had begun the course of Prozac, "he wasn't really the same person." His father was drastically altered in those last three weeks, he said.

"His hair wasn't combed. Wore a T-shirt and blue jeans—that was good enough. Dad was never like that."

It had been a grueling day for James Wesbecker, and a qualified success for the plaintiffs. Yet there had been one item of information gleaned by Ed Stopher on redirect that presumably explained why the defense had called him to the stand. James Wesbecker, it seemed, had himself filed a compensation suit against Eli Lilly for his father's death, and thus (along with all the other members of his family) had every motive to shape his testimony accordingly.

It was the afternoon of Friday, November 18, and when the judge addressed the jury he announced a ten-day recess for Thanksgiving in the following week. After giving his usual list of admonitions, he wished the jurors a "Happy Turkey Day" and dismissed them.

35

AFTER THANKSGIVING RECESS, Ed Stopher began to wind up his case by offering testimony on Wesbecker's personality and his mental journey to mass murder.

First he presented the deposition of Morton Leventhal, the clinical psychologist who had submitted Wesbecker to a battery of psychological tests in 1984. Leventhal had described Wesbecker then as a "passive-dependent, rather paranoid, somewhat schizoid man who perceives the world as threatening and harbors a great deal of anger at what 'they' have done to him."

The most scientific Leventhal got was to claim that Wesbecker's IQ was above average—in the range of 110 to 120—but that he suffered from an impairment of "visual motor ability" that would have created unusual stress in any work involving manual skill. Back in 1984, Leventhal had written that "Wesbecker shows signs of a longstanding perceptual handicap which he has striven mightily to hide but which has undoubtedly been a stress factor for a long time."

Leventhal's final overview on Wesbecker was that he was angry because he lacked control over his life, but reluctant to express that anger; as a result, the danger had turned inward. "I think he will be a difficult person to treat," Leventhal had written in 1984, "because he really doesn't trust anyone enough to engage in a psychotherapeutic relationship, the only possible vehicle for getting at the personality disorder."

It was left to an expert witness who had never met Wesbecker to present a final analysis of his character and history, and to explain from the defense point of view why he shot twenty people on September 14, 1989.

Dr. Robert Granacher, Jr., from Lexington, Kentucky, was called to the stand on the morning of Thursday, December 1. Granacher was a tall, slim fifty-three-year-old, with dark, deep-set eyes, evenly tanned face and bald head, and pure-white hair on the sides. He wore a well-cut dark suit and red polka-dotted tie.

Granacher said he spent half his time treating private patients but was also a trained forensic psychiatrist. "The way I use the word, it means medical-legal analysis, and I'm one of 263 psychiatrists in North America that is board-certified to do that kind of work."

He said that in the course of his career he had made some four thousand depositions on issues related to mental competency and sanity in various criminal cases—including "murder, kidnapping, armed robbery, rape, various kinds of assault and battery." He had worked with police, and sheriffs, and in jails; in murder cases, he had worked both for defendants and for the prosecution.

Encouraged by Ed Stopher, he told the court that he charged $350 an hour for his time ($450 an hour for depositions) and that he had sent a bill to Eli Lilly for some $50,000 for his work to date. His rate for a single day in court was $4,500.

In the course of the previous year, he went on, he had completed what he called a "psychiatric autopsy" for the defense; "the purpose of my evaluation," he said, "is to try to understand the mind of Joseph Wesbecker from early in life until September 14, 1989."

"Was that an easy task?" asked Stopher.

"No, sir. It's the largest task I have undertaken in my career in forensic psychiatry. It's the largest amount of information I've ever had to deal with, the largest number of depositions I've ever had to deal with, the largest case that I personally have ever seen in my career."

As he began his testimony, something about the dogmatism of Granacher's delivery and tone of voice was clearly grating on many of the plaintiffs, who could be heard sighing and gasping with exasperation in the gallery. It was grating on Smith, too. Ill with the flu, sitting at his table dabbing one tissue after another at his streaming eyes and sore nostrils, he frequently shook his head and glared up at the witness.

Granacher began to speak early in his testimony of Wesbecker's "intentions," first in relation to his purchase of guns, and then as a *cause* of his disturbed behavior independent of other factors, such as his state of mind or outside influences.

"Wesbecker began to form the *intent* to harm people at Standard Gravure around 1983," said Granacher, "which clearly is six years before this act took place. By 'form the intent,' I mean that he began to consciously think of individuals that he wanted to kill, the reasons he wanted to kill them. He put that in his mind, and he slowly evolved a plan which he carried out on September 14th, 1989."

Granacher told the jury that he was confident about Wesbecker's "intent" because the killer "left little bread crumbs all over the place. He would drop a bread crumb for one person, bread crumb for his wife, bread crumb for his son, bread crumb for someone else. No one ever had all the bread crumbs so that they could follow the trail, but they were all out there."

The intrusion of anything so folk-psychological as "intention"—the argument that Wesbecker did what he did because he alone *wanted* to—was about to throw the judge and plaintiffs' counsel into an intellectual free-fall. Yet it was an argument that might well have appeal for a jury overwhelmed by complex technical and psychiatric arguments and the conflicting testimonies of ninety or so witnesses.

"On the day he met with Dr. Coleman," Granacher had been saying, "Joseph Wesbecker had the *intent* to do what he did in his mind as he sat with Dr. Coleman in his office. That explains to me the intense level of distress Dr. Coleman noted; unknown to Dr. Coleman, these ideas were in Joseph Wesbecker's *head*. How do I know that? Because on the very same day he told his son James, 'I have a plan.' "

Stopher further emphasized this line of argument by asking him, "With regard to Wesbecker's actions on September 14, 1989, do you have an opinion, sir, as to whether or not those actions were intentional or whether they were unintentional?"

Smith was on his feet before the question was finished, requesting to approach the bench. He objected that "intention" was pure speculation, and that the witness was no better able to know what Wesbecker had intended than was any other witness.

"Any psychiatrist is able to give an opinion based upon whatever facts and information he may have as to the state of mind of the patient," countered Stopher. "That's what insanity and sanity are all about. This witness has qualified himself that he's experienced to do it, and has already in this case."

Potter was at first inclined to sustain Smith's objection, on the basis that he did not think it was a "topic on which an expert witness will be helpful to this jury."

But Stopher immediately appealed: "The other side has taken the position that he didn't intend to do this, that Prozac *made* him do it."

Potter was clearly in a quandary. After all the scientific and technical arguments, after all those hundreds of depositions on Wesbecker's life, the case notes on his mental illness, Stopher and his witness had brought the case down to a simple issue of individual agency versus chemical determinism.

Potter thought for a few moments, then made a stab at a compromise. "I understand their position that Prozac made him do it, just the way this guy's testified that the mother's death made him do it. If he's just going to say this guy was . . . not some kind of drug person on a rip . . . a competent person doing what he intended to do, I think the jury can hear . . . they've heard the evidence, they can make up their mind. But I'm going to sustain the objection to him talking about what his intent was on September 14."

Potter seemed happier with the notion of *both* sides' proposing deterministic arguments from their separate points of view. Was it fair at this stage, he seemed to be saying, to introduce the notion of free will by allowing the proposition that Wesbecker was a sane, competent individual, fully in control of his actions, even if disordered in his God-given personality?

But Stopher was not inclined to withdraw. As far as the defense was concerned, he told Potter, the judge had only to decide whether Dr. Granacher was entitled as a psychiatrist to make such determinations.

"Your Honor," said the attorney solemnly, "I would like for you to hear his answer to that, because that is essential to my case that this gentleman has an opinion as an expert about what motivated [Wesbecker]. . . . And keeping that out, even though the jury may already have that conclusion in mind and even though it may be obvious, this gentleman, I think, as an expert witness is entitled to say that."

But Potter was still unhappy.

After pondering the matter for another minute or two, he said he would send out the jury and hear the witness's answers for himself before deciding whether to allow the question.

After the jury had departed, Stopher put his question to Granacher once more.

"Do you have an opinion as to whether or not Mr. Wesbecker's actions on September 14, 1989, were intentional or unintentional?"

Granacher's answer was long and detailed. He spoke of the purchases of guns, and threats to kill personnel at Standard Gravure, going back to April 1987. He spoke of further purchases in August 1988 and the arrangements Wesbecker made for his own funeral. He spoke of Wesbecker's systematic moves to divest himself of property in the fall of 1988; his purchase of more guns around the time of the Stockton massacre in California; his target shooting; his journey to the gunsmith to have his AK-47 cleaned; his talk of a "plan" with his son; the careful route he took through the printing plant, and his ability to pick and choose whom he shot. All of which, Granacher told Stopher, he would use as the basis of his arguments in any question with regard to "intent versus unintentional and sane versus insane."

Invited to comment on Granacher's argument, Smith said angrily, "We've gone from the sublime to the ridiculous in the witness's answer. He's no more qualified to render that opinion than any jury is."

"I'm going to sustain the objection," said Potter finally. "I really think he's getting into an area where the jurors are as qualified to sort out these fact things themselves and then draw their conclusion as well as he can."

Stopher appeared to have lost the argument, but by the time he resumed his direct examination he had found another way of introducing the issue of Wesbecker's autonomous intention. More perhaps from weariness than strategy, Smith and the judge acquiesced.

"Dr. Granacher, would you explain, first of all, your understanding of the term 'impulse control'?"

"That term is a term of art in psychiatry that deals with certain disorders that have an impulsive element to them, implying there's some problem with controlling impulse."

Under Stopher's guidance, Granacher once again embarked on the detailed narrative of Wesbecker's consciously planned path to the killings on September 14—a process that involved no out-of-control or impulsive element, according to Granacher. For will, intention, moral agency, he had merely substituted "impulse control"—the behavior associated with active serotonin in the synapses.

Of all the witnesses who had taken the stand, none, not even Nancy Lord, had exhibited such confidence as Granacher.

It was his opinion, he now declared with certitude, that Prozac could in no sense have "caused" Wesbecker to lose impulse control on September 14. Wesbecker, he said, had displayed a "homicidal intent that he carried in his mind almost on a daily basis towards other people." This "personality disorder," which Granacher characterized as "adult aggression," had been a pattern for many years. The symptoms, he said, were frequent references to killing, fixing, blowing people away.

Stopher asked, "In connection with the elements of this schizoid half of [Wesbecker's] diagnosis, is that a personality disorder or is that a mental illness?"

"In Joseph Wesbecker's case," said Granacher, "in my opinion it was a personality disorder, a schizoid-type personality disorder with paranoid features. . . . "

"Can you clear me up at least, sir," asked Stopher, "what's the difference between a mental illness and a personality disorder?"

"Well, there are two very different conditions," said Granacher. "A mental illness, for the most part, is a disease of the brain, depression, panic disorder, anxiety, schizophrenia; that's why we use medicines to treat them. There's something chemically wrong in the brain."

Granacher paused for a few moments as if to prepare for a statement of considerable gravity. "A personality disorder, on the other hand, is where our normal . . . " Suddenly he was at a loss for words, and he paused. "All of us have a personality," he said fervently. "It's *God*-given, everybody is born with a personality. It's there. . . . "

After weeks of exposition about neurotransmitters and receptor sites, about depression and schizoaffective disorders, and crooked thoughts relating to crooked molecules, this was a startling culmination to Lilly's case.

Professor Granacher was telling the jury that Wesbecker was of course mentally ill, but the reason he killed lay beyond the compass of neuroscience entirely; it lay even beyond the ambit of the story of his life and relationships, his "nature and nurture."

At this moment in the trial, two versions of Wesbecker's actions stood in dramatic contradiction. One, proposed by the defense, was that Wesbecker understood the nature of right and wrong and was entirely responsible for his own actions as a matter of conscious choice. The other, proposed by the plaintiffs, was that Wesbecker could not be deemed responsible for an action that had been prompted by "irresistible impulse."

The two versions of Wesbecker's actions now on offer to the jury appealed to two very different accounts of the human person: on the one hand, a view of the individual as a kind of chemical software running in the brain; on the other, a view of the self as an overriding Cartesian controller—the "intentional" moral agent, in total charge of unbidden impulses. On the one hand, reductive physicalism; on the other, body-soul dualism. Neither of these stark alternatives, representing two leading interpretations of human identity in contemporary America, left room for the complexities of Wesbecker's history. In consequence, in this closing stage of the trial, there seemed little scope for the jury to ponder the social dimension of the trial testimony.

And how should the jury choose between the two accounts?

The problem, as Judge D. L. Bazelon had pointed out when making the Durham decision in 1954, was in ascertaining the nature of "irresistible." When the Durham rule is invoked, it is common for attorneys to call upon psychiatric "experts." But since the "experts" naturally tend to promote the view of whoever is paying them, their opinions are clearly of little value in arriving at the truth.

Stopher now led Granacher through a series of assertions about Prozac, agitation, and violence.

"There is not a single medical article in the world literature of the advanced nations," he declared ponderously, "that shows any antide-pressant has ever caused homicides in any human being on this planet, not a single medical article."

Next Granacher put the argument the other way around: "In the medical textbooks—I'm going to give you a big word here—on the psychopharmacology of aggression, the pharmacology that deals with drugs that affect behavior, there's one finding that we know about anti-depressants. Every antidepressant ever developed to be used in a human being uniformly reduces aggression, and in particular, predatory aggres-sion—going after someone."

Here was Granacher's belt-and-suspenders defense. Wesbecker did what he did not because of his brain chemistry, but because he wanted to do it and could have done differently had he so chosen. But even if one granted the argument that brain chemistry could affect violence and aggres-sion, Granacher was saying, it is inconceivable that Prozac could have been a cause of such aggression, since its whole point is to *reduce* aggression.

Taking the point about aggression and agitation a step further, Granacher now declared that as Wesbecker stalked the plant on that fateful day, "he was not agitated, and since he wasn't agitated, his agita-tion played no part in what he did."

"He had a goal," Granacher went on. "He was goal-directed. He was on a tunnel vision to do what he intended to do, going from specific goal to specific goal. . . . He was not a deranged Rambo wild man, screaming and yelling, running through the plant spraying rounds everywhere. There were very few rounds that missed a target. . . . Mr. Wesbecker was not agitated on September 14th, 1989, when he killed those people in Standard Gravure."

After eleven weeks of complex argument and testimony, the jurors had been given at the last minute a simple map of human identity, one that any child could understand: Joe Wesbecker did what he did because he was a bad man; this in no way altered the fact that he did what he did because he alone was in control and responsible for his actions.

The plaintiffs were not happy with Dr. Granacher. During the morning recess, word had got to Ed Stopher that there had even been rumors of threatened violence to the witness.

"Judge," said Ed Stopher at the bench, "it was reported to me by somebody who's in the courtroom that Mr. Scherer was overheard saying to Mr. Pointer that he wanted to borrow his cane so that he could use it on somebody in the courtroom. I'd assume that this was a joke, but I would like to request one more time that people be warned not to say those kinds of things in the courtroom—even in the audience, out of the presence of, obviously, the jury. But those kinds of things in this can be taken the wrong way." Gordon Scherer had been one of Wesbecker's victims, shot in the break room; he still walked with a limp.

Judge Potter asked Paul Smith to instruct his paralegals to talk to the plaintiffs.

36

WHEN PAUL SMITH stood up to cross-examine Granacher, it was evident that he was running a high temperature. He could hardly speak, and his face was covered with scarlet blotches. He coughed for a while, then croaked that he would try to make his questions as understandable as possible.

Smith started by asking the psychiatrist to confirm once again that he had billed his client, Lilly, $50,000; then he went on to quote a speech Granacher had made at a convention for forensic psychiatrists that had met in San Antonio in 1993. Granacher had told the delegates, Smith informed the court, "Stabilize your cash flow, do not take cases for which you do not have a retainer. If you can't get a retainer, don't take the case. Now, this is my rule, as I told you before we started."

In this and other ways, Smith attempted to humiliate the witness for some twenty minutes; but Granacher remained unabashed, answering evenly and unapologetically.

Granacher was less sanguine, however, when Smith applied some arithmetic to the number of depositions he did a year (two hundred at $450 an hour, almost one every workday), and the number of private patients he claimed to have on his books—more than two thousand. As he probed the conduct of the psychiatrist's practice, it was clear that Smith wanted to undermine the witness's claim to have become an expert on Wesbecker and Prozac.

Granacher happily admitted that he did not know anything about the development of the drug.

"It wasn't interesting to you as to who was used in the clinical trials, what group of patients were used?" asked Smith.

"No, sir. It's an FDA-approved drug. I don't need to know that."

"You base your blind faith on the FDA?"

"They've forgotten more about approving drugs than I ever knew, sir."

"And your blind faith in Lilly's character and reputation in reporting the accuracy of their trials to the FDA?"

"I don't have any opinion about Lilly. I have an opinion about what the FDA said about Lilly's product and whether or not it was acceptable to use in humans. And if the FDA approved it, that's good enough for me."

As far as Smith was concerned, Granacher had just opened a crucial door. During the next bench discussion, Smith made his intention plain. He told Potter that Granacher "said, 'If it's good enough for the FDA, it's good enough for me.' And I intend to stick that right in front of him concerning, number one, he said the FDA doesn't make any mistakes; number two, he says that Lilly does good testing of their drugs. So I think this is the time that I should use the Oraflex."

Judge Potter decided to hear the Oraflex arguments that evening in chambers after the evening recess.

Paul Smith having lost his voice entirely, Nancy Zettler spoke for the plaintiffs; Ed Stopher spoke for the defense.

"Lilly has opened the door for this evidence," began Zettler. "Its purpose is to rebut their constant—with just about every witness they've put on who's not a layperson—injection of testimony as to Lilly's glowing reputation within the scientific community as well as with the FDA."

She added that she also wished to bring into evidence the case of Lilly's drug fialuridine, FIAU, manufactured for the treatment of hepatitis B. This drug, she said, "prompted five deaths during clinical trials."

Ed Stopher responded by citing legal precedent and the rule in Kentucky law that insists that evidence can only be brought in from a previous offense if the witness has been jailed or sentenced to death.

Potter was unmoved. So Stopher went to his next tactic: "I must confess to Your Honor that, if this is allowed in, we have no choice but to move for a mistrial of the case. We think the prejudice to us is extraordinary."

"If it's prejudicial for us to put this in," Zettler replied, "it's prejudicial for them to say things like . . . I mean, constantly, with every Lilly witness and every expert, they've gotten out some sort of gratuitous evidence that this company is the best in the business; it's got the best researchers; it's got the best this, the most ethical that, the most upstanding, the world-class type of people over and over and over again. . . . We believe we have the right to rebut this evidence that they are not in fact holier than thou . . . with getting things reported and complying with FDA regulations. A lot of this stuff with Oraflex is the exact type of thing that happened in this case: that they had things from outside the United States that they just simply did not report to the FDA until they were caught."

Judge Potter turned to Ed Stopher: "I mean, everything you say is true, but when a person gets on the stand and says, 'I've never run a red light; I've never had a traffic ticket; I'm the world's safest driver,' probably shouldn't have said it. But once they get up there and say it, can't people say: 'Isn't it true, ma'am, that you've been arrested for drunken driving or you've got a speeding ticket,' or whatever it happens to be?"

"No, sir," said Stopher. "The answer to that is that, if that person was not convicted of a felony, that that information does not come in."

So the arguments went back and forth through the evening, until Smith made a tactical concession: "If the court wants to think about it overnight, we'd certainly accommodate the court in that regard."

"All right," said Judge Potter, and he told them to be back in his chambers at eight-fifty-five the following morning.

37

AT 8:55 A.M. on a wet and gloomy day, Wednesday, December 7, 1994, the lawyers in the Fentress trial met in Judge Potter's chambers. He had decided, at last, to allow the plaintiffs to produce documents that would tell the highly damaging story of the Oraflex debacle to the jury.

"Lilly has injected the issue into the trial," Potter told them bluntly. "I guess the phrase, if I had to, that would be used is that Lilly 'opened the door' to this kind of testimony when they put in that kind of evidence. What that really means is, I think, that something is now relevant which would have otherwise not been relevant."

Ed Stopher, in his most sepulchral mood so far, moved immediately for a mistrial. "We think the prejudice to us from this is extraordinary and should be kept out."

Potter was not moved. Referring to the glowing praise Dr. Leigh Thompson repeatedly heaped on Lilly's clinical-trial procedures, he said, "I wonder if the jury wouldn't view his accolades for Lilly differently if they realized that, shortly after he came there, Lilly was the subject of an investigation by the Justice Department and then later pleaded guilty, and he may well have gotten his promotion because his predecessor was looking at thirteen years in jail."

Then Stopher told the judge, "I think that we want to consider taking a writ of mandamus [a ruling from a higher court] on this issue, because we think that if the trial does progress that the error here is so prejudicial and so irreparable that we'd like to consider getting a ruling from the Court of Appeals or the Supreme Court before this matter proceeds any further."

Potter agreed that he would allow some time for Stopher to deliberate about such a writ, and that in the meantime he would put a temporary embargo on the Oraflex evidence.

For the spectators, the day started like all the others in the previous ten weeks. There was some rebuttal evidence in progress in the morning, focusing on whether or not Mike Campbell and Bill Hoffman had spoken to the police about Wesbecker from their hospital beds. But it soon became obvious that the lawyers' minds were on other matters. A recess that was supposed to last fifteen minutes seemed to continue indefinitely.

Out in the lobby, there were huddles of excited attorneys and plaintiffs. The plaintiffs' individual lawyers, twenty in all, were beginning to arrive from all over Louisville.

Karen Myatt of Court TV came up to Leslie Scanlon of the *Louisville Courier-Journal* in the lobby. Myatt said, "If it walks like a duck, and talks like a duck, it's a duck!"

"What's going on, Karen?" asked Leslie.

"It's the 's' word," said Myatt. Settlement.

Bill Bass, the Houston lawyer with the "Thelma and Louise case," ran into me in the corridor of the court and whispered that he thought they had done a "high-low," meaning an agreement that, win or lose, Lilly would agree upon a fixed sum in damages, no matter what higher damages might subsequently be awarded. "There's been some sort of deal," he said, shaking his head.

At lunchtime, Myatt, Scanlon, and I were eating in the delicatessen below the Providian Tower and saw one of Smith's paralegals entering the building. "If it walks like a duck . . ." said Myatt, laughing.

The lawyers finally convened with the judge at three in the afternoon, but all they could tell Potter was that they had agreed not to meet until two o'clock the next day.

Referring to the excitement outside the court and the repeated questions of the three journalists who had seen the trial through, Potter said: "The newspaper people have asked me what's going on. And I have told them honestly that, you know, that you-all asked for additional time and I gave it to you because—and I don't know what's going on. I would just suggest for your point of view . . . whatever's going on, I would keep it confidential because, I mean, they're out there, sniff, sniff, sniff, sniff."

"Boy, are they," Smith said, laughing. "I think the reporter just saw two hundred lawyers all of a sudden appear and—"

"Well, I don't know," Potter said. "They're the ones that mentioned the 's' word."

The fact was, Potter had no idea what was going on.

On the morning of Thursday, December 8, the meetings and huddles continued in and out of the courthouse, until at noon Judge Potter again met with the attorneys from both sides.

"Okay," Potter began. "Why don't you tell me anything you want to tell me?"

"Judge," said Paul Smith, "after a great deal of consideration, the plaintiffs, in an effort to facilitate getting this case to the jury as rapidly and expeditiously as possible, are going to close the evidence without the introduction of any further evidence and reserve the offering of the Oraflex documents for admission into the punitive-damages phase, if any, instead of offering it in the liability-only phase, with permission of the court, of course."

Joe Freeman added that since the Oraflex evidence was not to be offered there would be no need for surrebuttal evidence.

At this point, Judge Potter requested that they continue their discussion off the record. It was a decision he would later regret.

Potter later stated, "I was taken by surprise by the decision not to introduce the Oraflex evidence. I asked the parties [after they had gone off the record] if 'money had changed hands.' In response I was told by the attorney for one side (with the other side present) or by both sides that money had not changed hands. Both sides then stated that a 'justiciable' controversy remained."

Which was their explanation for continuing with the trial to a jury verdict.

The fact was, as emerged almost six months later, the two parties had made a strictly secret deal arguably unprecedented in any Western court. According to Judge Potter, in exchange for substantial sums of money awarded to each of the plaintiffs ("It is a tremendous amount—it boggles the mind," said one knowledgeable attorney who represented a plaintiff in another matter), the plaintiffs had agreed not to bring in the potentially damaging Oraflex evidence. They had agreed, further, not to appeal the verdict, whichever side won, and not to go to a punitive-damages phase of the litigation. The payments would be paid in three parts over three years, indicating that should any party divulge details of the agreement, that party, or possibly all parties on the plaintiffs' side, could forfeit payments.

Lilly had clearly believed that the Oraflex evidence would put the trial at risk for them, with far-reaching consequences for Prozac and the reputation of the company and its products. Not only would sales of Prozac be badly hit in the United States and around the world, but the long-buried issue of Oraflex would once again be resurrected, fueling further bad publicity.

But why not simply make a deal to settle and end the trial? The facts indicate that Lilly wanted it both ways. They wanted to quash the Oraflex evidence and, at the same time, badly wanted the vindication of a jury verdict in their favor. A mere settlement would only indicate that there was indeed a problem with Prozac, and embolden the other 160-odd suits in the pipeline.

Secret agreements between litigating parties to withhold specific evidence is not uncommon. What was unprecedented about this settlement, in the view of many legal experts, was the apparent decision, according to Judge Potter himself later on, to keep it from the judge.

Exactly why the plaintiffs' counsel decided not to go ahead with the Oraflex evidence may never be known. Paul Smith told me six months later, when he was still denying the deal itself, that the introduction of Oraflex might have resulted in a mistrial or endless legal maneuvers on the part of Lilly, at unbearable cost to the plaintiffs. Still, at this stage, in May 1995, he was insisting that he had reserved the right to bring in the Oraflex evidence at the punitive-damages stage of the litigation. But, as it later became apparent, Smith knew all along that, win or lose, there was not to be a punitive-damages phase.

The plaintiffs, it is clear, were not willing to gamble further and decided to take what Lilly offered, despite the fact that a jury verdict against them would greatly affect the fate of other plaintiffs following in their train; despite the fact, too, that Prozac's reputation would be considerably enhanced by a jury verdict in Lilly's favor.

Both sides had much to win by coming to this secret arrangement. Both sides came to it because they had too much to lose.

Later, on the evening of December 8, the lawyers trooped back to Potter's chambers and introduced several motions, including a request for a defense verdict on punitive damages.

The issue of punitive damages would be raised again the following morning, when the lawyers met Potter to discuss other matters. Paul Smith told Potter that he was not aiming to refer to any potential punitive-damages phase in his closing argument: "I'm assuming that would be highly objectionable, to mention anything of that nature."

"Absolutely," said Stopher.

"We would certainly object highly," said McGoldrick.

"Okay," said Potter at last, "neither side is going to talk about any potential ramifications of their verdict."

All these business-as-usual exchanges would be seen in retrospect as a tactic to cover the traces of the secret agreement.

38

ON THE MORNING of Friday, December 9, the public gallery in the Old Jailhouse courtroom had filled by eight-thirty, and the marshals allowed people to sit in the aisles to accommodate the spectators. A cluster of Lilly executives had gathered in the vicinity of Ed West and the in-house counsel team, and there were sundry lawyers at the back of the gallery, obvious because of their stacks of files and dark suits. A few journalists, mainly from wire services, had flown in from out of town, and half a dozen TV reporters were watching proceedings on the Court TV monitor up on the third floor.

At nine o'clock, McGoldrick began the closing arguments for the defense.

"Let me start with how I think you should end this case," he told the jury. "Prozac is a safe medicine. It helps or even cures people of a terrible disease. It is very important that you vindicate this good medicine against the false charge that it had anything whatsoever to do with what Joe Wesbecker did in his murders."

He was reminding the jurors that a verdict against Prozac would deprive millions of depressed people of a cure for depression, driving home the implication that they would bear a heavy responsibility for adding to the total of human misery in the world. "We're proud of this product," he said. "We're proud that it's safe and works to help people. We're proud of the men and women who invented it."

There were no surprises in much of McGoldrick's crisp speech, which harped on Lilly's defense of the Prozac animal and clinical trials; but his presentation took a more dramatic turn when he finally focused on the plaintiffs' expert witness, Dr. Peter Breggin.

In just two sentences, he evoked the acute discomfiture of the psychiatrist's cross-examination by Joe Freeman a month earlier. "I just don't know what to make—I *truly* don't know what to make of all that business about Dr. Breggin having written that it's good for little children to have sex with each other and the article in *Penthouse* magazine about how American psychiatry caused the holocaust. I'll leave that up to you to measure that stuff."

The real point about Breggin, he told them, was that this plaintiffs' witness was "on the fringe," he was "not in the mainstream," and he was therefore "no match" for the defense expert witness, Dr. Ray Fuller.

"Compare Dr. Breggin for a minute with someone like Dr. Ray Fuller," he went on. "Dr. Ray Fuller, he's really an extraordinary man, I think. As a young man, he worked, you recall, in the wards in the state mental hospital. Before they had medicines to help these folks, it was kind of a bedlam. He dedicated his life to trying to find medicines that would help people like this. Unlike a lot of us, he succeeded. He really has done it. . . ."

Here was a rehearsal of the missionary-zeal argument: Fuller the "seminarian," flitting by night through the wards of the insane "bedlam"; Fuller the dedicated "Presbyterian minister," the savior and the healer. So different from this "fringe" character put up by the plaintiffs.

It was left to Stopher to propound the principal case for the defense. Taking his time, his voice mournful and occasionally quivering with emotion, he attempted to empathize with the plaintiffs.

"I want to tell you," he intoned with a catch in his throat, "that I feel deeply for the victims of the terrible, awful crimes that occurred on September 14, 1989. Every time I'm reminded of it, it drives a stake through my heart. . . . Not one hair on their heads should have been disturbed by Joseph Wesbecker. I remember precisely where I was when I heard it on the radio that day, just like the day that President Kennedy was shot."

The message, with its mawkish and Biblical overtones, was that the defense, in Stopher's person, stood for solidarity with local community—something the Texan personal-injury lawyer Paul Smith would never understand.

The main substance of his closing argument, however, was the issue of "cause," he told them. And with this he returned to the testimony of

Dr. Granacher, the final expert witness, that Wesbecker was an autonomous agent, who murdered because he chose to, not because he had been programmed or determined in any way.

This defense argument, he told them, was supported by the judge himself, referring to brief instruction sheets that had been distributed to the jury that morning. "Judge Potter has already instructed you . . . that Joseph Wesbecker had a duty not to hurt these people, and he violated that duty and he is at fault."

The issue, Stopher went on, was not whether Wesbecker's acts were justified and whether the injuries sustained by the plaintiffs were deserved. The issue, he said, was "did he do these things because he wanted to . . . or did he act involuntarily, not knowing where he was and what he was doing, out of control, agitated or anxious?"

Having weighed the reaction of the jury to Granacher's testimony and judged it favorable, Stopher was going for the simple catchall safety-net argument: the moral agent versus the robot, free will versus determinism, individual culpability versus a species of the "Twinkie Defense."

"If he did what he intended to do," said Stopher, "or what he wanted to do, then Prozac is not the cause; *he* is the *only* cause. If he knew what he was doing and wanted to do it, then he alone should be held responsible for what he did."

He now added a curious clause aimed at addressing a possible scruple about the state of Wesbecker's reason: "That doesn't mean that his intention makes any sense—all murders are without a rational basis—or that his actions were justified; most assuredly, they were not. But from *his* point of view, if he did what he desired to do, then he alone should be held accountable for what he did do."

What was impressive about this claim for Wesbecker's culpability, in this final stage of the trial, was its power to challenge deterministic notions based on brain chemistry. It indicated that the notion of the killer, even a mentally sick killer like Wesbecker, as an autonomous "moral agent" still had the potential to compete with powerful determinist explanations from science. More important, it revealed that Lilly had decided to abandon its original strategy of explaining Wesbecker's actions on the basis of a mix of inherited weaknesses, personal relationships, family and communitarian history.

But he had more to say about the philosophy of cause, which he expounded to the jury in the form of a parable.

"When I was three years old, there was a dead mimosa tree in our backyard," he began in homey fashion. "It was leaning over the house, and my mother wanted my father to cut it down so that it wouldn't damage the house or somebody. And so as a little toddler I went out and I got a stick. I beat on the trunk of that old, dead mimosa tree until I got pretty tired and went inside and took a nap, and when I woke back up and went into the backyard, the tree was down. And I remember very proudly telling my mom I did that. I caused that tree to come down. She didn't tell me that my father and the next-door neighbor had gotten a big saw and while I was asleep they felled the tree. . . . I didn't know because my mother didn't tell me that the real cause was something else altogether."

The jury—indeed, the entire audience—seemed deeply affected by this homespun story of the little Ed Stopher and the old mimosa tree. He had caught their attention and their sympathies.

Then came the payoff.

"A cause in a case like this," he went on, "cannot be determined by simply learning that something occurred first, that a man took Prozac and then subsequently did these awful things and that they're necessarily connected up. In order for anyone, including Dr. Coleman, to determine the cause of Joe Wesbecker's actions, we must know all of the facts. We need to know about the two men with the saw."

The tale was a prelude to the familiar history of Wesbecker's concealments. There were, Stopher claimed, "twenty-two important facts about himself that relate to his condition," which Wesbecker kept from his psychiatrist Lee Coleman.

The burden of the story, which Stopher recited for more than an hour, was that Coleman was the little boy with a stick and that the "big saw" was Wesbecker's scheme, which he kept hidden from everybody.

Stopher rehearsed the story well: of gun purchases, and threats, and financial dealings, and carefully laid plans, all leading to September 14, 1989, the day he stalked the Standard Gravure plant—"real calm," Stopher said.

When he had finished, he said solemnly, "I thank you for your kind and respectful treatment of me and my client. You have been exemplary.

On behalf of everybody, I thank you for the weeks, the notes, the attention, the concentration that you've given to us. Thank you very much."

When Paul Smith stood up, it was obvious that he was still sick—eyes streaming, face blotched and perspiring. He later told me that he was suffering from pneumonia and could barely stand up; during the last week of the trial, he said, he had not slept at all, and had never recuperated from a cold he had caught in mid-November.

"I'm not much for final argument in a two-and-a-half-month trial . . ." he began hoarsely. "I am not going to work on the assumption that you people can be convinced of anything that I say at this time. . . . I didn't choose . . ."

Then he stopped.

"It's the worst thing . . . personally that could happen to me," he started again, "is right here at the last of the case I would come down with laryngitis and a cold and be running a fever and not be able to communicate, not be able to concentrate like I want to. You know, it's the last thing I want, to be physically ill. It is impairing my performance, it's impairing my life. . . ."

There was a long pause while he blew his nose and composed himself.

"Certainly . . ." he began again, "the same thing was true of Joseph Wesbecker. Joseph Wesbecker did not choose his mental illness. . . ."

The parallel between himself and Wesbecker, much as the spectators felt sorry for Smith at this moment, was a bizarre introduction to his closing argument, confirming his own declaration that his performance was indeed impaired.

He began by attempting to extract some advantage from the fact that Lilly's defense strategy had been to attack the very patient whom the drug had been designed to help.

"What they're saying about Joseph Wesbecker is like . . . the defense lawyer for a rapist . . . saying that the victim of rape somehow brought this rape on herself by her particular conduct. . . ."

Thus, lamely, and in evident distress, he proceeded to argue that Wesbecker was a decent man who had managed two positive relationships, had been a responsible father and a hard worker, had struggled to lead a good life and pursue the American Dream. Whether it was his illness or lack of preparation, he appeared to be on the defensive. Much of the early part of his presentation was stated in negative terms, or posed in the form of questions. Wesbecker was not a Charles Manson or a Jeffrey Dahmer, he told the jury. "There was a lot of things said by Mr. Stopher about the early discord and problems in the family. Nothing about that was said today in his argument. If you look at Joe Wesbecker's childhood, I mean, sure, . . . his father died, his mother was young. His mother didn't give him the attention that his aunts thought she should have, but is there anything in that that's different from millions of other people?"

A little later, he appeared to be rambling: "Was Joe Wesbecker an evil man? Was he born a murderer?" he asked the jury. "When did he become a murderer? What put him on this course? Was it when he got his divorce from Sue and there started to be bitter animosity among them? Obviously that's a traumatic thing. I think probably if I had to give my psychiatric opinion, which is worthless, the . . . you know, I think that's probably where you start seeing more serious problems with respect to the disease manifesting itself. . . . But does that cause him to be a mass murderer? . . . Obviously not."

Turning to Eli Lilly and Prozac, Smith seemed to perk up, yet he continued to put questions to the jury rather than make telling arguments. At one point, in an attempt to reduce the aims of Lilly's animal trials to absurdity, he became ludicrously playful. "Lilly started giving this drug to animals," he said. "What happened? Rats became hyperirritable. Now, you say, well, okay, we couldn't ask the rat, 'Are you feeling bad today, Mr. Rat? Are you feeling less depressed today, Mr. Rat? You know, how's your family situation, Mr. Rat?' All we can do is, we can see this hyperirritablity."

Seeing that the jury were amused, he continued in this vein a little longer. "The dogs became aggressive. . . . Again, you can't say, 'Fido, are you having a bad day today? . . . The cats start growling and hissing, you stop the drug, and the cats become friendly again. Okay. Again, you can't ask Muffin the Cat how he's feeling today. . . ."

From this point, he went on to rehearse the arguments that had become familiar to us throughout the trial: Lilly's failure to report adverse events, their failure to issue appropriate package warnings in the United

States, and finally Dr. Coleman's notes on his patient from September 11, 1989: his decision to take Wesbecker off Prozac because of marked deterioration.

At last, having delivered himself of his summation in two hours, Smith looked spent.

His final words were an enfeebled recycling of Stopher's memorable story of the mimosa tree. "You know, it was like the . . . it's like the . . . somebody raked up some dry leaves and maybe consider Joe Wesbecker as, you know, in autumn people rake up the leaves and those leaves in this pile are no different before he gets Prozac, but somebody flips . . . a careless smoker flips a cigarette into that pile of leaves, which otherwise presents no danger, and that cigarette ignites these leaves. That's what happened here with Prozac. The leaves would never have burned had it not been for this cigarette. . . . These people's lives would not be ruined if not for Prozac."

Then, in the customary farewell to the jury, he said, "I thank God for you, that you're not going to be flimflammed by a bunch of psychiatrists and psychologists and corporate executives into not seeing what's as clear as the nose on your face. It's in black and white. This was a substantial factor in these people's change. Their lives will never be the same. . . . Your service will never be forgotten by me or my clients. Thank you."

Judge Potter had issued to the jurors a three-page instruction, and a three-page verdict form.

True to his reputation as "Bare Bones Potter," the instructions were brief and to the point.

Under instruction number one—"Fault of Eli Lilly & Co."—he had written:

> A drug is defective if it is improperly tested or not accompanied by suitable warnings or instructions to the prescribing physician.
>
> A drug is unreasonably dangerous if a prudent drug manufacturer being fully aware of the drug's effect and operation would not put the drug on the market or would do so with additional warnings or instructions.

You will find Eli Lilly at fault if you are satisfied from the evidence as follows:

a) That Lilly manufactured and sold the drug Prozac.

b) That Prozac as manufactured and sold was in a defective condition and unreasonably dangerous.

c) That Mr. Wesbecker ingested Prozac prior to September 14, 1989.

AND

d) That such defective condition was a substantial factor in causing Joseph Wesbecker's actions on September 14, 1989. Otherwise, you will not find Lilly at fault.

In his second instruction, Judge Potter had written as follows:

On September 14, 1989, Mr. Joseph Wesbecker had a duty not to injure or harm any plaintiff in any manner.

The Court instructs you that Mr. Wesbecker violated this duty and that you will find him at fault.

There was a third instruction, referring to Standard Gravure's duty to "exercise ordinary care to protect its employees from criminal acts of Mr. Wesbecker." The remaining forms laid out instructions for apportionment of liability.

At 3:00 P.M., the judge asked the jurors to withdraw and consult about whether they wanted to deliberate into the evening and return on Saturday, or to return the following week.

After just ten minutes, they returned to announce that they wished to be given the weekend free and to wait until Monday for further deliberation.

After the trial, the jurors would take a joint oath not to disclose any of their deliberations. They would nevertheless sketch the highlights of what happened for the lawyers. Thus Smith could tell me in May 1995 that on that Friday the jurors had taken an initial vote during the first retirement, the result of which was four in favor of the plaintiffs, three in favor of Lilly; five undecided.

39

WHEN THE JURORS met again, on Monday morning, December 12, it was with a significant alteration. Over the weekend, one of their number, an elderly woman, had suffered a minor stroke. According to Smith's later analysis of the jurors' intentions, this meant the loss of a vote for the plaintiffs. As the jurors arrived for their deliberation, they were now joined by Mrs. Ryan, whom the judge had put on standby at the end of the trial. Mrs. Ryan, according to Paul Smith, was for the defense, so, as the jurors retired, the balance of votes had been reversed: three in favor of the plaintiffs, four in favor of Lilly, and five still undecided.

Later reports, gleaned from the lawyers, indicate that there were multiple ballots: the jurors would discuss the case for forty-five minutes or so, and then take a vote.

Meanwhile, at nine o'clock, the trial lawyers convened once more in Potter's chambers. After discussing routine matters, the judge said: "I've got to plan ahead a little bit. . . ." He was referring to plans for the prospect, should Lilly lose, of a damages phase of the litigation.

"If there is a plaintiffs' verdict," he went on, "I would like to take a day's recess, and although I normally don't get involved in settlement, I would like to say something to you-all and then have you meet with a mediator to see if that portion of it could be settled, because I really do believe the dynamics there are such that it would be to both parties' benefit to settle. . . . But with that in mind, I was going to ask Lilly to have somebody present who had substantial authority to talk for the company. . . ."

The remark, recorded by the court reporter, indicates that Potter did not realize that the parties had already agreed not to proceed to a punitive-damage phase.

Joe Freeman merely confirmed that a responsible Lilly executive was in town.

Paul Smith intervened: "Had the court thought—in the event that there is a punitive-damage phase, had the court given any thought as to when that particular phase would start?"

"Within twenty-four to thirty-six hours after the verdict comes in," said Potter.

"Can I have my Christmas present sent here?" Smith asked jovially; the holiday was only two weeks off.

As the lawyers continued to banter with each other, Potter interrupted: "I asked you-all if there was anything you thought we needed to take up. Is there anything?"

"Can't think of a thing," Smith replied.

"Can't think of anything right now," added Zettler.

"No," said Stopher.

At eleven-forty-three that morning, the judge asked Stopher and Smith to come to his chambers once again. One of the jurors, a dark-haired and bespectacled young woman named Tammy Duncan, wanted to make a statement before the judge and the attorneys. "I was out in the hallway while some discussions were going on," she said, "and I overheard . . . that the Lilly lawyers were trying to settle out of court with the plaintiffs."

Potter questioned her closely to glean more details, but she could only say that she had the impression that she had overheard a conversation between two lawyers representing the different sides.

Potter told her that she had been mistaken: there was no deal. "The reason you're back there," he went on, "is because they have not settled it, and I can tell you I don't think either side has thought about that as a possibility, because each side—they're so far apart on what went on."

After the juror confirmed that her ability to reach a fair verdict had not been compromised, Potter asked her to wait outside the door.

"Does anybody have anything they want to say?" asked Potter. "Anybody have the slightest clue?"

"No," said Smith.

"I can't imagine," added Stopher. "I mean, every time I left this door, I made sure that I didn't say anything until I was over there at my table. And I certainly never talked to Nancy or to Mr. Foley about this subject at all, ever, and that is the God's truth. I can't imagine—it may well have been somebody with Court TV or a reporter or some local lawyer saying something that they didn't know anything at all about. . . . This comes as an absolute shock to me."

Potter was left to speculate whether the juror could have heard the word "settlement" in relation to another issue. "Somebody might have said, 'Can't we settle on going without an alternate,' or something, you know, used that magic word."

"It could have been that," said Smith.

"I mean, I have no idea who made the statement," Stopher said. "I'm not even sure that she knows who made the statement. But I would try to reinforce in her mind that the court has been pretty well informed about all aspects of this case, not only what's going on in the courtroom, but what's going on outside the courtroom, and that if any such statement was made, that it is not accurate."

With this the judge went out to reassure Ms. Duncan that her impression that a settlement had been in the offing was mistaken.

Meanwhile, in the jury room, the deliberations were coming to a conclusion. The number of undecideds had dropped until the defense had the nine votes needed for a verdict in its favor. "What the foreman, Mr. Holiford, did," Smith told me later, "was to take each of the jurors aside individually, saying, 'It's clear to me that the judge has instructed us to find Wesbecker at fault, so that Prozac had nothing to do with it.' "

Pro-Lilly juror Terri Morrison, whom I interviewed six months after the trial ended, confirms that she was not alone in believing that the judge had instructed the jury to find Wesbecker solely responsible for the shootings. Nor was she alone, she said, in finding Potter's criterion of unreasonable danger a "nearly impossible" standard.

At two o'clock in the afternoon, word came that the jurors had reached a verdict. The court began to fill.

At three o'clock, the jurors entered. The plaintiffs, taking the first four rows of the public gallery, stood holding hands. Foreman Holiford, the balding man who used a walking-stick, rose to his feet and announced to the hushed court that they had determined that Wesbecker, and Wesbecker alone, was responsible for the shootings on September 14, 1989.

There was a stunned silence for about seven seconds. Even the lawyers seemed amazed at the verdict. Then the plaintiffs began to wail and sob. All at once, they were hugging and hanging on to each other. Their tears were clearly spontaneous and genuine, prompted by the release of months of pent-up emotion. It was as if only now could they grieve for their loss. Nobody outside their circle knew, or could have guessed from the display of sorrow, that they had nevertheless been promised very substantial sums of money.

Karen Myatt, of Court TV, had hoped that the jurors would immediately take questions in front of the camera, but on Judge Potter's advice they returned to the jury room to receive counseling and debriefing from Roger Bell, a professor of psychiatry at the University of Louisville; the same Roger Bell had offered counseling to the employees of Standard Gravure after the shootings in 1989.

Meanwhile, the plaintiffs began to leave the court hurriedly, refusing to speak to journalists.

It was left to the lawyers on both sides and Lilly's public-relations team to make statements. Standing before the cameras in the well of the court, a jubilant Ed Stopher said: "This verdict reveals that Prozac is not unreasonably dangerous. It is not mislabeled. It was not improperly tested. And it did not constitute a substantial factor in causing Wesbecker's action—even one percent."

Paul Smith said: "This case was basically Lilly's easiest case. This was the case that they were pushing for trial. It was not a landmark case. It was the ultimate roll of the dice by all parties concerned. Because, if we win here, we would have won what they thought was one of their best cases. On the other hand, if we lose here, everybody said we were going to lose. Nobody gave us a chance anyway, since Wesbecker was obviously mentally ill."

Joe Freeman, the attorney from Atlanta, Georgia, was full of praise for the plaintiffs' counsel.

"We had very good lawyers against us," he said. "The plaintiffs' team worked very hard and really made something out of nothing. There was never anything in any of this record to really implicate Lilly. . . . So we feel like this is a complete vindication of the drug."

Lawyers on both sides explicitly denied that there had been any kind of settlement (rumors of the sort launched by Bill Bass five days before were still in the air). And Paul Smith would be quoted next day in the *Indianapolis Star*, Lilly's hometown newspaper, that he would let his clients decide whether or not to appeal (the same *Star* article reported that Lilly's lawyers were "confident" the verdict "would stand").

Ed West, head of Lilly's corporate public relations who had followed most of the trial from the public gallery, wanted to draw an immediate inference for the 160 pending lawsuits against Prozac. "I would assume," he said, "that some of these would either be dismissed or just dropped. When you peel it all back, you get into a question of money. If it becomes apparent it's very difficult to win big money in Prozac suits, this probably sends some message."

West also had a statement to read from Randy Tobias, Lilly's chairman and chief executive officer: "The verdict demonstrates," he declared on behalf of the whole company, "the futility of blaming medications for harmful and criminal acts."

Later that afternoon, on the New York Stock Exchange, Lilly stock closed at $62.63—up $1.

After two hours of "counseling," in which they had agreed on oath not to speak of their deliberations to the outside world, the jurors were released by their psychologist and attempted to slip unnoticed out of the building. Karen Myatt, with camera and lighting assistants, was ready for them. As they hurried out into the night, she ran after them and caught them in the parking lot. Not a single one was prepared to make a statement.

That evening, speaking to me on the phone, plaintiff Michael Campbell, who along with the others had been a recipient of Lilly's secret payoff, said: "It's not so much the money, although it would have been useful. It's the certainty we all have—all those of us who knew Wesbecker well—that it was this drug that made him do it . . . that more people will have to suffer until a case is proved against Eli Lilly."

———

The following morning's newspapers told a story of vindication for Eli Lilly and Prozac. *The New York Times* reported Lilly's chairman, Randall L. Tobias, as saying that the company now had "proven in a court of law, just as we have to more than 70 scientific and regulatory bodies all over the world, that Prozac is safe and effective." *USA Today* reported Joe Freeman as saying, "We feel like this is a complete vindication of the drug." The *Indianapolis News* reported that "a jury's verdict clearing Prozac of inciting a Louisville man to mass murder has lifted a cloud over the antidepressant and may even boost sales of Eli Lilly and Co."

40

ON DECEMBER 13, 1994, it seemed that the story of the Prozac liability trial had come to an end. That evening, Karen Myatt, Leslie Scanlon, and I went to an Italian restaurant on Bardstown Road, close to the church where Wesbecker's father had met his death.

That morning, Karen and Leslie had visited Judge Potter in his chambers. Leslie said: "He seemed troubled and restless. It was as if he wanted to tell us something, then changed his mind." Karen presented him with a Court TV baseball cap as a farewell present.

We agreed over dinner that it had been a fair verdict; that, even if the testimony suggested that Lilly had cut corners in adverse-event reporting and package warnings in the United States, Smith and Zettler had failed to show that Prozac had been a substantial cause of Wesbecker's actions. The decision, it seemed to us, would make it all the more difficult for future lawsuits against Prozac to succeed. This was, we agreed, a huge public-relations coup for Lilly.

As we mulled over the trial, we were united in our sympathy for the jurors. Our strongest feelings about the case centered on the absurdity of bringing so many complex and highly technical issues before a group of laypersons over a period of nearly three months.

Though we remained puzzled about the two days of consultations before closing arguments, we decided that Lilly, fearing they had antagonized the jury by overburdening them with technical detail, had made an offer to settle that had been turned down. We were each of us still unaware that the Oraflex issue had come up on the final day of the trial. We did not know that Judge Potter was ready to allow the testimony, and that Smith had decided not to bring it in.

As we made our farewells that night, we promised, without too much conviction, to meet up at Paul Smith's next Prozac trial, scheduled sometime in 1995, an action, he had told us, he was "determined not to lose."

Judge Potter might well have seemed troubled when Karen Myatt bid him goodbye on December 13, since even on the day of the verdict he had been suspicious about the failure of the plaintiffs to bring in the Oraflex evidence. His misgivings persisted throughout Christmas and New Year's until he entered the final judgment in Lilly's favor on January 25, 1995. The case was registered that day as "DISMISSED with prejudice," meaning, essentially, that the verdict could not be altered without exceptional circumstances.

His anxieties about the case continued to grow through February, fueled by local rumors of a huge and secret financial deal. Yet still he did nothing. He was waiting, as his lawyer Richard Hay now tells it, to see whether the plaintiffs would file a notice of appeal. Potter had contacted Hay after reading an account of the case in the *New Jersey Law Journal* in which Hay had expressed his amazement at what appeared to be a settlement. "It is unbelievable that the plaintiffs would reach a settlement," Hay had written, "and then want to keep it secret, particularly where the essence of their claims was that Lilly covered up information."

The deadline for filing an appeal was February 24. The date came and went without a word from Smith. At that point, Potter had jurisdiction over the case for just ten more days; he continued to fret, but still did nothing.

Eventually he asked the lawyers in the case to meet him. At this meeting in early March, he told them about the rumors; according to Richard Hay, who was now representing Potter, "They wouldn't say one way or another."

After consulting fellow judges and Hay, Potter finally acted on April 19, by publishing a motion in his court to amend the judgment of January 25.

"The court believes it more likely than not that the case was settled," he wrote, "and, therefore, the dismissal should read dismissed as settled." On the final page of his motion, Potter claimed: "On December 8, 1994, after a day's delay at the parties' mutual request and without explanation, the plaintiffs elected not to introduce the evidence they had fought so hard to get admitted. . . . The jury ultimately returned a verdict for Lilly."

In the final paragraph of the document, he ordered a "show cause" hearing, requesting the lawyers on both sides to appear before him with documentary evidence relating to any settlement, including check stubs. Potter justified his action by appealing to Kentucky Civil Rule 60.01, which declares that, even after the jurisdiction period has ended, "clerical mistakes in judgments . . . and errors therein arising from oversight or omission may be corrected by the court at any time of its own initiative."

Both sets of lawyers now combined under representation of Lively Wilson, senior partner of the Kentucky firm of Sites and Harbison, to block the motion and the subpoenas. The determination with which they responded indicated the significance Lilly attached to the judge's proposed alteration—from complete vindication to settlement. The plaintiffs' cooperation, moreover, was a token of the tough conditions underpinning the financial details: the plaintiffs, it later became apparent, would forfeit payment if they revealed the terms.

The first step of the new legal allies was to file a writ of prohibition on Judge Potter's motion in the Kentucky Court of Appeals. Potter, they argued, no longer had jurisdiction over the case; besides, the rule he cited applied only to "clerical mistakes" in judgments, not substantive changes.

Lilly and the plaintiffs contended that the liability of Lilly was the only issue tried, and that it had been decided by the jury verdict. "All of the parties at trial continue to accept that verdict and continue to accept the original judgment based on that verdict." They insisted that Judge Potter "was aware that the evidence regarding Oraflex was excluded by agreement between the parties."

By early May, a hearing for oral arguments between the two sides—Lilly and the plaintiffs versus Judge Potter—had been set for early June before three appellant judges in the Kentucky Court of Appeals in Frankfort, Kentucky.

Early in 1995, I had arranged to revisit the key figures in the trial in May in order to tie up loose ends in the story. By coincidence, a series of appointments coincided with the two weeks following Potter's motion.

First I went to Dallas to see Paul Smith in his offices on the tenth floor of a new steel-and-glass complex on the outskirts of the city. He had agreed to meet now only on provision that I did not "ask questions about any settlement."

He had cleared his calendar and he settled back on a sofa to reminisce about the case; relaxed and in good spirits, he did not have the appearance of an attorney who had just lost the $700,000 that, he said, the trial had cost him.

Waxing philosophical at one point, he said: "This is a high-risk business: you better have the money to lose. I've never gone into debt for a single cent to cover a trial. If you want to stay in contingency personal-injury cases, you've got to be willing to take that loss."

He assured me that he did not feel bitter about the case; the only episode that still rankled, he said, was Potter's decision to allow Coleman to express an opinion on Weshecker's actions after being given "tons of information by Lilly" and "being paid to read it."

I had hoped for at least some veiled clues as to what sort of deal had been struck with Lilly, but I got nothing. He ended the meeting by inviting me to an early lunch.

We went down to the lot where his car was parked—a new, bright-red Mercedes convertible SEC 600. Getting into this sumptuous $150,000 car, I said: "This smells like settlement money, Paul." He laughed and said, "My wife has got one, too."

Over lunch at the Crescent Club in downtown Dallas, I asked him about his forthcoming Prozac cases; he said simply that there had been a delay and changed the subject.

Before we parted, I asked point-blank why he had not brought in the Oraflex evidence.

"I sincerely believe it would not have made any difference," he told me. "Everybody was exhausted. In any case, it would have invited a mistrial and endless litigation. We were going to reserve it for the damages phase, when it would have been effective."

Still he was keeping up the impression that they would have proceeded to a damages phase, even though the agreement had ruled it out.

When I asked him whether he thought he might have failed in

his duty to warn the public about the dangers of Prozac, he gave me his parting shot: "My sole duty is to get money for my clients."

Back in Louisville, I had an appointment to see Ed Stopher in the boardroom of his Providian Center offices. To ensure that no ill-advised revelations took place, Ed West, head of Lilly's public relations, had driven down from Indianapolis to sit in on the session; there were also two paralegals present in the boardroom.

Like Paul Smith, Stopher warned me that he would not respond to any questions about a settlement. He was happy to talk about the case, but had nothing significant to say except when I was about to leave.

Unprompted, Stopher insisted that, in retrospect, the Wesbecker affair was crucial to understanding the workplace stress and violence sweeping America. "The real story of Joe Wesbecker," Stopher wanted to tell me, "is about stress and violence in the workplace, employer relations, and what certain people did to aggravate his problem; what certain people failed to do to help him. . . . He went everyplace to get help and never found it."

The next day, I went to see Judge Potter in his chambers in the Hall of Justice, within sight of the Old Jailhouse Building. He took me through to a conference room and invited me to sit down, but would not sit down himself. He joked a little, telling me that "doing a Wesbecker" had become a new epithet in America for going berserk at work.

Then he started pacing, his brow corrugated with anxiety.

"I wanted to call you and tell you not to come," he said eventually. "The thing is that I can't talk to you. . . . I can't tell you anything."

I got up as if to go, but he asked me to sit down again. "You learn a lot about human nature," he said, "when you do an action for liability—greed, manipulation. . . . They did a deal. The plaintiffs came off extremely well in this." Then he mouthed to me silently: "It's TRUE!"

Before I left, I asked him: "Why did you wait so long? Surely there wasn't anything you know today that you didn't know in December."

Looking bleakly out the window, he said: "I don't know. I don't know why people don't do things at the time . . . but I didn't."

———

That evening, I met two of the jurors, Carolyn Selby and Terri Morrison, for dinner at the Terrace Restaurant, in the Kadon Tower building in West Louisville. Arranging the meeting over the phone, Selby had told me that they would talk about anything but their deliberations in the jury room.

They were already seated at their table when I arrived. Selby was the bespectacled woman in early middle age I had noticed scribbling nonstop throughout the trial. She had been a secretary in an accountancy office but lost her job in the middle of the trial as a result of her long absence on jury service. She had stacks of spiral-back notebooks at her elbow. Selby had voted against Lilly.

Terri Morrison, in her mid-thirties, was a research chemist in a chemical plant. Her hair was swept back and stiff with spray; she was dressed in a matching brown top and pants. She told me that she was married with two young children. She had voted *for* Lilly.

Both jurors were now convinced that a settlement had taken place despite the lawyers' denials. Selby told me: "We're furious. I feel as if eleven weeks had been wasted as a result of the case being secretly settled."

They also felt "astonished and dismayed" in retrospect at Judge Potter's instructions. Terri Morrison said they were convinced that the judge was telling them to find Wesbecker alone guilty. They both agreed that the Oraflex evidence would have made a "huge difference" and possibly would have lost the case for Lilly.

Selby told me that she and Terri talked on the phone several times a week, always about the trial. Morrison said she continued to worry about the implications of Lilly's claim that they "massaged" figures to make lower doses of Prozac "look less good." Selby said she frequently thought about Lee Coleman's testimony. "I wrote pages and pages of questions I wanted to ask him. I stood by myself in a corridor outside that court, brimming with rage: why didn't he stretch out to help Wesbecker?"

Before leaving Louisville, I went one evening to see Michael Campbell, the only plaintiff willing to talk to me. He said—unprompted—that he would end the conversation immediately if I asked about "settlements."

He lived in a traditional clapboard house at the southern end of

Third Street, beyond the university complex. Leaning heavily on a stick, he met me on the stoop and took me into his book-lined den at the back of the house.

As the light faded, and with his wife hovering silently in a darkened adjoining room, he talked for more than two hours. He wanted to dwell on Wesbecker and an aspect of the truth he felt had been lost in the trial.

"In the twenty years I worked at Standard Gravure," he said, "we lost our pride, our manual skills, and our good wages. We went from thirty-five thousand books an hours right up to seventy thousand books an hour. The employees went from six hundred people in early 1975 down to eighty-five in 1986."

He said that after Shea came "everybody was at each other's throats." The ribbing at Standard Gravure was "unrelenting"; each person did it, and they "worked on each other's weaknesses." Wesbecker, he said, was just as bad as anybody else: "He knew how to needle people. He was kind of offbeat. But, you know, as he got more ill, his humor failed him, and he couldn't take it. Nothing was funny to him anymore. He got very rigid. He wouldn't talk anymore."

Campbell spoke about the effect of night work and overtime, how "you went home, slept a few hours, then came straight back to work, for weeks on end." He talked about the "power of the pencil," how the "guy on the bottom got drafted for the worst jobs every night. It was a tremendous strain on everyone. It was driving people against each other, and people were being laid off sick, dropping like flies."

Then he said something about Wesbecker that had not been offered throughout the entire course of the trial. "My opinion is that Wesbecker was very cunning. We knew he had stock and was obsessed with money. We used to bug him, ask him about his profits. Then, one day, he lost his temper when we were ribbing him, and it came out. He said he was planning all along to con the doctors so they would let him out on disability. He had it all figured; he was using everything to his own advantage."

"So what went wrong with the plan?" I asked.

"He lost control," said Campbell. "He really was mentally sick, and it all slipped through his fingers. And there was another thing: he could have had a physical disability, but he was proud. He wanted to keep this macho Rambo image of himself. . . . That's how he wanted to go out."

Campbell now seemed to be telling me at last that the story of Wesbecker and his rampage had nothing, after all, to do with Prozac: it had been a story of stress, derangement, and violence in the workplace.

Campbell walked with me to the door, his wife still lingering in the shadows. I asked him if he saw anything of Angela Bowman and others.

"No. We haven't been in touch since the end of the trial," he said. "We're just trying to build our lives again in peace and quiet."

It was now dark, and he watched me walk across the road until I got into my car.

Flying back to New York through Charlotte, North Carolina, the following day, I picked up the *Charlotte Observer* to find a front-page story headlined "Man kills 3, days after dismissal."

James Floyd Davis, forty-seven, of Asheville, North Carolina, had been charged with killing three former co-workers and four others in a shooting spree at an Asheville company. According to his mother, he had been taunted for his religious convictions at work, and had been fired after getting into a fight the previous week.

The lawyers representing the Lilly-plaintiffs alliance finally confronted Richard Hay (acting for Potter) in the drab and airless Court of Appeals in Frankfort, Kentucky, on June 8, 1995. Judge Potter, sporting a garish bow tie, sat with his wife and son in the audience. Presiding over the oral arguments was Judge Paul Gudgel of Lexington and two appellate judges.

In the course of the three-hour hearing, the appellate judges mulled over whether Potter had the authority to change the record in the case. They also scrutinized the testimonies of those present at off-the-record discussions in Potter's chambers on the eve of the end of the trial. The two sides had lodged affidavits that revealed striking differences.

Paul Smith declared that, after going off the record, "Judge Potter stated that he had anticipated that the plaintiffs might decide not to offer the Oraflex evidence and that he had spoken with either another judge or another lawyer with whom he consulted regularly." They had concurred, Smith went on, that there was nothing "improper or irregular concerning our decision to not introduce the evidence, even if money had changed hands." What Judge Potter did ask, Smith said, was whether or not there were still "issues to go to the jury. . . . I assured Judge Potter that there were." Smith denied that he and his fellow counsel for the plaintiffs remember the judge's asking if "money had changed hands."

The affidavits of Lilly's lawyers were essentially the same, except that they contained an additional detail. Ed Stopher asserted that Potter had said: "Whether money was paid or not—and I don't want to know—such an agreement is legal and ethical. If that's the way you-all want to try this case, it's all right with me."

To confuse matters further, the court reporter, Julia McBride, who had been present during the off-the-record discussion, said the judge was not surprised when Smith said he would not introduce the Oraflex evidence. She also confirmed that Potter said he "had discussed with another judge whether there was anything improper about the parties' agreeing to leave it out, and the other judge stated there was nothing improper about that."

But she left out a crucial aspect of both their arguments: she made no mention of anything the judge, or the lawyers, said about money.

In a document filed with the court, Potter suggested that lawyers for both sides had lied to him by denying that money changed hands before the verdict. "Lilly sought to buy not just the verdict," Potter had written, "but the court's judgment as well. This is where a 'freely negotiated settlement' ends and the court's duty to protect the integrity of the judicial system begins." Referring to motions about future damages litigation that the lawyers made to him after striking their deal, he pleaded that they "reflect an amazing lack of candor to the court."

Lively Wilson argued for the lawyers that it was commonplace for attorneys to decide during a trial not to bring up certain evidence. Richard Hay countered, "What makes this different is that there was a payment of money to withhold evidence."

"Isn't the judge's integrity at stake when he signs a judgment that doesn't accurately reflect what happened in court?" asked Judge Joseph Huddleston. The other appellate judge, Michael McDonald of Louisville, said: "The system has been tampered with by trial counsel. Isn't that why we're here?"

Later in the day, McDonald expostulated: "Haven't both sides gotten what they want? The defense can go out like Tarzan and beat their breast and say, 'We won, we won, we won,' and the opponents of Prozac can say, 'No, no, no.' "

The more cautious and troubled Huddleston disagreed. "I think the trial court has an active role to play to ensure that a just result is achieved and that the judgments or orders of the court are accurate." The agreement, he said, "was an unusual sort . . . the first I've ever heard in over thirty years of practice."

A week after the hearing, on June 15, the Court of Appeals ruled that Potter did not have authority to hold a hearing about the secret deal, because "his jurisdiction over the Prozac case had ended except for limited circumstances."

In a press interview, Ed West, public-relations director for Lilly, said: "The unseemly course of action that John Potter has been taking is outlandish behavior for a judge. Whether he's had his eye on further political office and likes to have his name in print or has some other issue in this—whatever his motivations have been, they've not been well grounded in law."

Richard Hay, on behalf of Judge Potter, commented: "I thought the Court of Appeals ruled on a technical basis, on jurisdiction only, and did not speak to the heart of what we feel is involved, and that's the integrity of the judicial system and a judge's right to see the orders of the court accurately reflect the truth."

Reporting the hearing in the September 1995 issue of *The American Lawyer*, Nicholas Varchaver asked: "But did the lawyers act wrongly in not informing Judge Potter of their agreement?"

Of six ethics experts interviewed by the journal, five asserted that an agreement, even to exchange money for evidence, is not ethically prohibited as long as all of the parties are fully informed and approve the agreement. The same experts, however, took a decidedly dim view of lawyers who mislead judges.

The magazine quoted the University of Illinois College of Law ethics professor Ronald Rotunda as saying: "The lawyer has an obligation not to lie to opposing counsel and has an obligation of candor to the judge which I think is the greater obligation. . . . When judges talk to lawyers they don't like to think they're talking to used car salesmen."

Professor H. L. Richard Uviller, who teaches legal ethics at Columbia University School of Law, commenting on Smith's part in the agreement between Lilly and the plaintiffs, was quoted as saying: "I've never heard of such a thing. He's thrown the case. You can't have it both ways. You can't have a settlement and still continue as adversaries."

Following the hearings, legal representatives of Lilly and the original plaintiffs, and the plaintiffs themselves, have refused to be interviewed about the settlement.

Attempts to deny the existence of a financial settlement were finally swept away in July, when it was revealed that plaintiff Andrew Pointer, shot in the tunnel between Standard Gravure and the *Courier-Journal* building, had been obliged to divulge his earnings in a divorce settlement. Without revealing the actual figure, his lawyer declared publicly that he was receiving a huge payment from Lilly, in three parts.

Attempts to discover the precise figure of the settlement were thwarted throughout 1995. The *Louisville Courier-Journal*, in the interests of freedom of information, filed a motion in July to unseal the divorce records. According to Cecil Blye, Andrew Pointer's attorney, the file was sealed to protect the confidentiality of the Lilly settlement. On October 25, 1995, the existence of a three-stage payment was verified, but the request to disclose the specific amount was denied.

It is likely that Smith received 50 percent of the settlement, the costs coming out of the plaintiffs' share. But his enjoyment of that reward has not been untrammeled. Following Leonard Finz's resignation in 1993, Smith had become lead counsel for federal multidistrict litigation in Prozac cases. In mid-July 1995, Smith and Zettler met in Las Vegas with lawyers in five other pending cases against Prozac to talk about future strategy. In his suite at the Mirage Hotel, Smith announced to his fellow attorneys for the plaintiffs that he had filed a motion to resign as lead counsel, pleading lack of office backup. He then intimated that he had given up on all his own Prozac cases.

"The way he put it to us," said one of the lawyers, "was that he had devoted some years of his life to Prozac, but that he was through." The same lawyer is reported as saying, "My opinion is that they've settled every Prozac case they had."

On July 27, 1995, federal judge S. Hugh Dillon approved Smith's decision to resign and declined to oblige Smith to reveal the terms of the Lilly financial settlement.

Smith has extricated himself from future Prozac cases. But his woes are far from over. In the autumn of 1995, former clients in the multi-district Prozac litigation indicated that they were considering taking legal action against him for having betrayed their interests.

After the Court of Appeals verdict Judge Potter did not give up. He took his petition to the Kentucky Supreme Court.

On May 23, 1996, as this book went to press, the Supreme Court reversed the earlier judgment and ruled that Potter could indeed conduct a hearing to determine whether Eli Lilly and the plaintiffs in the Louisville trial had misled the court about the pre-verdict agreement.

In the published statement of the Supreme Court, the judges declared that "there was a serious lack of candor with the trial court." They went on to state that "there may have been deception, bad faith conduct, abuse of judicial process or perhaps even fraud," which was "what the investigation and hearing is to determine."

Commenting on the integrity and authority of American courts of law, the judges wrote that "our system depends on the adversarial presentation of evidence . . . even the slightest accommodation of deceit or a lack of candor in any material respect quickly erodes the validity of the process."

Reacting to the Supreme Court decision, Ed West for Eli Lilly said that even if Potter's court eventually altered the jury verdict to a settlement, "it shouldn't in any way reflect negatively on the product . . . it's a question of legal procedural wrangling."

Epilogue

IN THE COURSE of the Louisville trial the litigants floated three different versions of Joe Wesbecker's life and killing spree.

Paul Smith, for the plaintiffs, portrayed Wesbecker as a depressed but basically decent man, driven berserk by a defective, mind-altering drug. Wesbecker's ability to curb his urges, which an expert witness described as "impulse control," had been destroyed by Prozac, Smith argued.

The defense, on the other hand, started by maintaining that Wesbecker's killing spree was "inevitable"—a result of inherited mental illness and an underprivileged upbringing. But when that case began to founder under the weight of contradictory testimony, the defense lawyers constructed a new argument based on Wesbecker's status as a moral agent. According to the defense, the murders were wholly "caused" by Wesbecker's unimpaired free will.

Since he was a rational individual capable of making plans and choices, argued Lilly's trial lawyer, Ed Stopher, his ability to control his actions had been affected neither by chemical intrusion nor by the influence of nature and nurture. Wesbecker had a personality disorder, defense expert witness Dr. Granacher declared, but he had "intent," he had "goals," and he was "in control." He alone bore responsibility for his actions.

It would be easy to dismiss these final and apparently contradictory diagnoses—chemical determinism versus untrammeled free will—as mere tactics in a civil dispute. After all, the goal of the plaintiffs was not so much to establish the exhaustive "truth" of a complex set of events, as to assign blame and put a dollar value on the resulting damages. It is surely significant, however, that these versions of who, or what, was responsible for Wesbecker's actions were wholly lacking in a social dimension.

The litigants' denial of Wesbecker's existence as an individual shaped by his relationships with family, neighbors, and co-workers bears the unmistakable hallmark of "reductionist" thinking—the scientific methodology by which entities are described in terms of their smallest material parts.

Reductionist explanations—explaining nature by reducing phenomena right down to the workings of atoms and molecules—have been decisively successful for Western science and technology since the second half of the nineteenth century. As an account of human identity and society they have remarkable shortcomings.

Reductionism originates with the discoveries of Galileo and Newton in the seventeenth century. They described an atomized, mechanistic world in which causal relationships could be understood and predicted in terms of the physics of falling objects, the motion of projectiles, tides, and the heavenly bodies. The idea that biological organisms too were part of a mechanistic world picture was developed by René Descartes, the seventeenth-century philosopher and mathematician, who believed that animals were machinelike automata working on hydraulic principles.

Descartes eventually extended his mechanistic model to human nature itself, thus creating one of the most troubling legacies of the Enlightenment. In our bodily functions, Descartes maintained, we are mechanistic and in all respects similar to the animal kingdom, and yet we have consciousness, rationality, and free will—faculties that reside not in the material world but in the realm of the spirit. He therefore posited the existence of two sorts of stuff—*res extensa* and *res cogitans:* material stuff, which can be observed and measured, and "thinking" stuff, the stuff of the mind, which lies beyond scientific investigation, and hence outside of nature. The frontier of body and soul, according to Descartes, was located in the brain, at the pineal gland. Thus the new sciences of physics and biology were from the outset disconnected from a theory of human freedom and responsibility.

This distinction between body and soul, widely known as "dualism," has gone through many variations since the seventeenth century. And yet dualism, of the kind expounded by Descartes, remains the inevitable consequence of a belief that would say, with Francis Crick, "You're nothing but a pack of neurons." For in order to have a human identity composed of both chemical determinacy and moral agency, it is necessary to conjure up, as did Descartes, a will that is as removed from the dynamics of a social context as it is removed from the assemblies of molecules and neurons.

The survival of Cartesian body-soul dualism into the twentieth century is a token of its extraordinary resilience, not least its potential to reduce people to exploitable mechanical objects, while nevertheless insisting that they remain wholly responsible for their actions. Hence dualism continues to create a rationale for treating people as machines while insisting that they possess an incorporeal individual freedom that transcends not only deep-seated personality disorders, but familial, workplace, and societal pressures. The social failure of such a model of human nature is its encouragement of a social climate advantageous to self-seeking individuals with a superficial humanism. It is against the background of just such a philosophy that Ronald Reagan and Margaret Thatcher could assert that there is no such thing as society, only the individual.

Ironically, for Lilly, whose fortunes are increasingly based on the premise of an exact equivalence between human behavior and brain chemistry, it was precisely the psychopharmacological notion that there could be a single chemical basis for aggression that had encouraged the plaintiffs to go to court in the first place. In other words, the application of scientific reductionism to human nature has emboldened the sort of litigation that habitually denies the dynamics of social responsibility in liability suits.

As it turned out, the defense counsel started by constructing a case built on nature-nurture determinacy, drawing on Ed Stopher's four hundred depositions. These documents should have provided ample material for a narrative of Wesbecker's social existence, portraying him in the context of the workplace, the family, and the neighborhood. But Lilly's lawyers chose to concentrate on a narrowly selective version of Wesbecker's hereditary and familial background in order to show that his murderous actions were wholly "inevitable." At the same time, in their background defense of Prozac, they reinforced a severely reductionist view of human identity summed up by Dr. Ray Fuller's reflection that "behind every crooked thought there lies a crooked molecule."

The latter line of argument was hardly surprising since the future of psychopharmacology, as revealed in the claims made for Prozac, rests on the premise that individual deviancy and unhappiness—leading to social disorder—is nothing more than specific, identifiable, and controllable chemical software programs running in the brain. Hence the role of the pharmaceutical manufacturer is to discover the links between biochemistry and behavior and then produce appropriate pharmacological "re-write" antidotes. Significantly, however, Lilly was reluctant to offer any explanation, still less apology, for the fact that Prozac had failed to help the sort of patient it had been designed for. And having failed to construct a case based on genetic and environmental determinism, they appealed to "free will," which arrived like the U.S. cavalry in the nick of time.

Yet between the lines of the lawyers' arguments and witnesses' testimony, E-mail documents, and psychiatrists' records, there was a version of Joe Wesbecker's life that was altogether different from that told in court. It was a story that had no merit for the defense and the plaintiffs since it provided no neat hypothesis of causation leading to a case for liability.

The story of Wesbecker's social disintegration and the community's part in it is complex and contains many imponderables; yet it is, I believe, closer to the truth of what happened in Louisville in September 1989 than the accounts set forth in the trial.

We were told of the breakdown of Wesbecker's relationships with his own parents, and with his wives and children. We listened to stories about his problems with neighbors and co-workers. We heard how gradually all the props and supports of his social existence fell away—family, job, church, even health care. From one point of view, Wesbecker himself seems responsible for these withdrawals. He abandoned his parish after the breakdown of his first marriage; he instigated feuds lasting years with his elder son and his mother. He withdrew from friendship with neighbors and co-workers, and finally he negotiated to take long-term disability leave from a job that had been the mainstay of his existence. In the end, apart from his fragmented relationship with Brenda Camp and his empathy for son James, there was nothing left except for Dr. Lee Coleman and his pharmaceutical products.

Wesbecker's isolation was clearly self-imposed; yet only up to a point, for it was surely compounded by indifference on the part of others. Wesbecker was not simply a man who cut himself off from his community; he was also a man who was shunned, neglected, and often denied by his community.

This is not to charge that Wesbecker's wives and relatives, his friends and neighbors, his co-workers and managers, *caused* him to shoot twenty people; it is to suggest that those who lived and worked alongside him shared a measure of responsibility for the absence of those human bonds that should have anchored him to his community, protecting him from that final murderous isolation.

In a culture increasingly shaped and driven by a reductionist view of human nature, in the guise of political and economic expedience, the prospects look dismal indeed for the reassertion of a communitarian account of human identity—as a person's ability to give to and to be for others. And yet, despite the ominous indications of the Wesbecker case, I completed this story convinced that human sociality, despite denials and repressions evident in the Louisville trial, will survive by instinct if not by education and habit; that we will continue to rediscover the need to live as members of communities, if for no other reason than that it is human to do so.

One wintry weekend in Louisville I rented a car and drove about an hour southeast of the city, to the Cistercian monastery of Gethsemani. This austere religious community, founded in the mid-nineteenth century, was home to the writer Thomas Merton from 1941 until his death in 1968. In his celebrated autobiography, *The Seven Storey Mountain*, Merton describes how, in reaction to a sense of disgust with the materialism, violence, and insanity of modern America, he had discovered a vocation for solitude and silence, which led him to this monastery among the secluded hills of southern Kentucky.

In the guest library I found his book of meditations, *Conjectures of a Guilty Bystander*. Sitting alone in the library, I came upon a passage in which he tells the story of a "vision" that changed his life. The event did not occur to him in the abbey church, nor while walking in solitary contemplation in the woods, but in downtown Louisville, at a printing plant on Fourth and Walnut, nowadays known as Muhammad Ali Boulevard.

Merton had come into Louisville on a rare visit to supervise the printing of a monastic publication. He has described the repugnance he had for the city after the peace of Gethsemani:

> Louisville leaves me with a sense of placelessness and exile . . . tired and angry people, in a complex swirl of frustration . . . the purpose of the city seems to be to guarantee that everybody has to travel about 18 to 50 miles a day through noise, stench and general anger through blocks of dilapidation, in order to get somewhere where anger and bewilderment are concentrated in a neon-lit, air-conditioned enclave.

On this occasion Merton stood outside the roaring plant watching people coming in and out of shops on the opposite side of the street, when he was suddenly overwhelmed by an unaccustomed sense of solidarity with all those strangers. "They were mine and I theirs, we could not be alien to one another even though we were total strangers . . . we were in the same world as everybody else, the world of the bomb, the world of race hatred, the world of technology, the world of mass media, big business, and all the rest."

In that moment his monkish, dualist view of human identity as an ensouled isolation had been challenged and destroyed. "It was like a waking from a dream of separateness," he wrote, "of spurious self-isolation in a special world of renunciation and supposed holiness."

It is tempting to speculate that the paths of Wesbecker and Merton may have crossed in that downtown printing plant; salutary to reflect that in their very different worlds, each had been reduced by the affliction of a sterile isolation.

For the rest of his life, while remaining true to his "interior" vocation, that vision of solidarity, based on fellowship with the unique inwardness of the other, remained with Merton, evoking a sense of shared responsibility for the world of his time.

Acknowledgments

THIS BOOK WAS MADE POSSIBLE by the cooperation of the lawyers on both sides in the Fentress-Lilly litigation in Louisville, Kentucky, in 1994.

Lilly's lawyers took some four hundred depositions on the life of Joseph Wesbecker during their discovery phase, which were made available to me in the form of indexed abstracts and chronicles.

Edward Stopher and Paul Smith supplied gaps in my court coverage by allowing me to view some sixty volumes of the transcripts of open court proceedings and chambers discussions. The court reporter, to whom I owe a considerable debt of gratitude, was Julia K. McBride. Other trial materials, including pertinent exhibits, were provided by Judge John Potter of the Jefferson County Court, who was also helpful on various legal points in the post-trial litigation.

Leslie Scanlon of the *Louisville Courier-Journal* was unstintingly generous with her time and information, as were the newspaper's librarians. Karen Myatt and Robin Levine of Court TV were helpful in supplying video material of the trial and other information. I also benefited greatly from the assistance of the librarians in Louisville's magnificent public library.

Edward A. West, director of corporate communications at Eli Lilly, and the company's team of in-house lawyers, were cooperative and courteous in answering my many questions both in person and over the telephone.

During the trial, and in May of 1995, I conducted a series of taped conversations, which are referred to in the course of my story: I would particularly wish to thank jurors Terri Morrison and Carolyn Selby; the coinventor of Prozac, Dr. Ray Fuller; and plaintiff Mike Campbell, for their time and courtesy.

In a book that draws heavily on neuroscience, I have benefited from the knowledge of experts in the field, including Dr. Michael Sofroniew,

Professor Alistair Compston, Dr. Clive Svendson, Professor Alan Cuthbert, Professor Steven Rose, and Professor Stuart Sutherland. I have also had the benefit of various legal experts, including Professor James Crawford, Dr. Barry Ryder, Peter Glazebrook, and Dr. Matthew Lohn. I must also thank Tim Jenkins and Michael O'Brien for valuable observations.

I am immensely grateful to Dorothy Wade for the original commission to cover the Wesbecker story and the trial for the London *Sunday Times Magazine*, and to Wendy Wolf of Viking for her enthusiasm and encouragement. Finally, and as ever, I wish to thank my literary agents, Bob Lescher of New York and Carol Smith of London, and my friend and publisher Peter Carson.

Sources

Chapter One

Plaintiff Mike Campbell provided an eyewitness description of conditions and industrial relations at Standard Gravure during an interview in Louisville on May 13, 1995.

Chapters Two to Five

Dr. Lee Coleman's account of his last meeting with Wesbecker, and Wesbecker's last days and hours, were described in depositions to plaintiffs' counsel and expanded in trial testimony. Individual accounts of woundings were given in trial testimony and reports in the *Louisville Courier-Journal*.

Chapter Six

The story of the Bingham media empire is told soberly in *The Patriarch: The Rise and Fall of the Bingham Dynasty*, by Susan E. Tift and Alex S. Jones (Simon and Schuster, 1990), and sensationally in *The Binghams of Louisville*, by David Leon Chandler (Crown, 1987). The most poignant and authoritative account, however, is to be found in *Passion and Prejudice*, the autobiography of Sallie Bingham (Knopf, 1989).

Gannett's takeover of the *Louisville Courier-Journal* is described in the November 1994 edition of *Louisville* magazine, "Identity Crisis at the Courier," by Maria Braden.

Of the various histories of Louisville, the most succinct and well-researched is *The New Yorker* city-in-transition profile, September 9, 1974.

Chapter Seven

A full account of the inquest into the Standard Gravure shooting deaths was reported in the *Louisville Courier-Journal*, November 23, 1989, by Jim Adams and Cary B. Willis.

Chapters Eight and Nine

I gathered crucial background on the history of Eli Lilly, Prozac, and the history of the Prozac litigation during interviews with company counselor Jim Burns and head of public affairs Ed West at Eli Lilly Center in Indianapolis on May 17, 1995. The official company history, published privately, is entitled *All in a Century: The First 100 Years of Eli Lilly and Company*, by E. J. Kahn, Jr.

Breakdown, by Professor Stuart Sutherland, was originally published by Weidenfeld and Nicolson in 1976 and reissued in 1987. A new edition is planned by the Oxford University Press in 1996.

The U.S. Justice Department's action against Eli Lilly on account of Oraflex was reported in *The Wall Street Journal* in "Eli Lilly Admits It Failed to Inform U.S. of Deaths, Illnesses Tied to Oraflex Drug," by Joe Davidson and Carolyn Phillips, August 22, 1985. I received further information from Eli Lilly's perspective during a telephone interview with Ed West on February 22, 1996.

The story of the marketing of Oraflex is reported in *Selling Science: How the Press Covers Science and Technology*, by Dorothy Nelkin (W. H. Freeman, 1987), pp. 149–50.

Chapters Ten and Thirteen

The story of Wesbecker's life and the progress of his illness was chronicled in trial testimony and in detail in Ed Stopher's depositions in preparation for the trial. I had access to portions of the deposition material; in addition, Mr. Stopher provided me with a 298-page condensed and indexed "Chronology."

Another important source of information on Wesbecker is "Little Boy Lost: The Emotional Life and Death of Joe Wesbecker," by John Filiatreau, published in *Louisville* magazine, January 1990.

Chapter Eleven

Paul Smith and Nancy Zettler told me the history of the Prozac litigation from the plaintiffs' point of view on November 13, 1994, in Louisville. I had a further interview with Mr. Smith in his offices in Dallas, Texas, on May 10, 1995.

Chapter Twelve

There is a growing and extensive literature on workplace violence. Noteworthy publications are *Violence in the Workplace*, by Raymond Flannery (Crossroad, 1995), and *Ticking Bombs*, by Michael Mantell (Irwin, 1995).

James William Gibson's excellent *Warrior Dreams: Violence and Manhood in Post-Vietnam America* was published by Hill and Wang in 1994. Juliet B. Schor's *The Overworked America: The Unexpected Decline of Leisure* was published by Basic Books in 1992.

Chapter Fourteen

The business background to Prozac in the period before the trial is to be found in a number of key newspaper and periodical articles, including: SCRIP no. 2020, April 28, 1995; SCRIP no. 1941, July 19, 1994; *The New York Times*, "A Legal Drug Culture Arises," by Sara Rimer, December 13, 1993; *The New York Times Book Review*, "On Beyond Wellness," by Daniel X. Freedman, August 8, 1993; *The Wall Street Journal*, "Eli Lilly Loses Sales," April 19, 1991; *The Wall Street Journal*, "Eli Lilly's Bid for PCS Sends Stock Down," July 12, 1994; the London *Financial Times*, "Lex Column," July 12, 1994; *The Saturday Evening Post*, "Seeking the Wizards of Prozac," by Tracy Thompson, March/April 1994.

See also the London *Sunday Times Magazine*, "Prozac Not Guilty," by John Cornwell, January 8, 1995, and *Esquire* (England), "The Wonder Drug," by John Cornwell, March 1994.

Chapters Fifteen to Twenty-eight

My account of the trial is drawn from my own notes of the proceedings, the official transcripts, and daily reports in the *Louisville Courier-Journal* by Leslie Scanlon.

Jury reaction is based on interviews with jurors Carolyn Selby and Terri Morrison in Louisville on May 16, 1995. Other background material is drawn from interviews with Paul Smith, Nancy Zettler, Judge John Potter, and Ed West, during the course of the trial.

The articles relating to Dr. Peter Breggin and based on material supplied by Lilly appeared in *The New York Times Magazine*, October 2, 1994, and *Time* magazine, "Prozac's Worst Enemy," by Christine Gorman, October 10, 1994.

Chapter Twenty-nine

The Society for Neuroscience proceedings for its twenty-fourth annual meeting are published in its two-volume *Abstracts*, and its *Press Book*.

The theories of mind-brain cited in this chapter are to be found in *The Astonishing Hypothesis*, by Francis Crick (Simon and Schuster, 1994); *Mind Children: The Future of Robot and Human Intelligence*, by Hans Moravec

(Harvard University Press, 1988); *The Emperor's New Mind*, by Roger Penrose (Oxford University Press, 1989); *Consciousness Explained*, by Daniel C. Dennett (Allen Lane, 1991); *How the Self Controls Its Brain* and *Evolution of the Brain*, by John C. Eccles (Routledge, Springer, 1994 and 1989); *Neurophilosophy*, by Patricia Smith Churchland (MIT Press, 1990); *The Computational Brain*, by Patricia S. Churchland and Terrence J. Sejnowski (MIT Press, 1992); and *Nature's Mind*, by Michael C. Gazzaniga (Basic Books, 1992).

Gerald Edelman has condensed his theory of Neuronal Group Selection into a work of popular exposition, entitled *Bright Air, Brilliant Fire*, published by Allen Lane in 1992. Oliver Sacks has written a useful critique of Edelman's work in "Making Up the Mind," *The New York Review of Books*, April 8, 1993.

Chapters Thirty-six to Thirty-nine

The moves in the settlement relating to Oraflex and Judge John Potter's subsequent attempts to make public the financial terms of the agreement are expertly chronicled by Nicholas Varchaver in *American Lawyer*, September 1995. I have also drawn on an interview with Judge Potter in his chambers in Louisville on May 16, 1995, a telephone conversation with Ed Stopher on May 12, 1995, an interview with Ed Stopher in Louisville on May 15, 1995, and an interview with Paul Smith in Dallas on May 10, 1995.

Documents relating to the post-trial litigation include Commonwealth of Kentucky Court of Appeals No. 95-CA-001215; Response by Plaintiffs and Lilly to Judge John Potter's May 31 Brief, June 7, 1995; Court's Motion Pursuant to Civil Rule 6-1 and Notice Jefferson Circuit Court No. 90C106033.

Other relevent reports appeared in *New Jersey Law Journal*, December 26, 1994; and the *Louisville Courier-Journal*, June 1, 1995, and June 16, 1995.

Index

Adler, Stephen J., 112, 113
Allen, Woody, 101
Alzheimer's disease, 217, 219
American Journal of Psychiatry, 154
American Lawyer, The, 297–98
American Psychiatric Association, 193
American Society for Neuroscience, 215–19, 222
American Trial Lawyers Association, 71
Astonishing Hypothesis: The Search for the Soul, The (Crick), 218, 219, 221

Baker, Jim, 38–39
Ball, Joseph, 25–27, 61, 128–29
Barger, Richard, 19, 29
Bass, Bill, 165, 270, 286
Bazelon, Judge D. L., 263
Beasley, Dr. (Brenda Camp's first husband), 67, 68, 69, 243–44
Beasley, Brenda, *see* Camp, Brenda (Wesbecker's second wife)
Beasley, Dr. Charles, 154, 232, 233, 234
Beasley, Melissa, 68, 69, 244, 255
"Becoming the Armed Man," 78
Bell, Roger, 285
Bingham, Barry, Jr., 32, 35, 82, 168
Bingham, Barry, Sr., 32, 34, 35, 82, 168
Bingham, Judge Robert Worth, 31–32, 82
Bingham, Sally, 32–33, 35
Bingham, Worth, 33

Biology as Ideology: The Doctrine of DNA (Lewontin), 223
Blye, Cecil, 298
Boehl Stopher Graves, 55
Bouchy, Claude, 171
Bowman, Angela, 13, 24–25, 29, 53, 107, 125, 295
Breakdown (Sutherland), 48
Breggin, Dr. Peter, 74–75, 123–24, 274–75
    testimony of, 176–87
        cross-examination, 189–96, 274–75
Bubalo, Gregory J., 39
Burke, David, 79
Burns, Jim, 55
Bush, George, 38

Camp, Brenda (Wesbecker's second wife), 5, 8, 10–12, 42–43, 60, 67–70, 83, 87, 88, 89, 94, 96, 136, 184, 186, 214, 248, 304
    testimony of, 243–46
Campbell, Mike, 20, 21–22, 28, 53, 56, 107, 164, 270, 286, 293–95
Carlson, James, 110
Center for the Study of Psychiatry, 194
Changeaux, Pierre, 221
Chemie Grünenthal, 45
Chesser, Carl, 70
Chesser, Sue (née White) (Wesbecker's first wife), 62–63, 64–65, 68, 70, 135–37, 243, 254, 255, 279
Chicago Tribune, 38–39

Chlorpromazine, 49
Churchland, Patricia, 218
Church of Scientology, 41–42, 54,
    98, 164, 165, 167–68
Citizens' Commission on Human
    Rights, 41–42, 54
Clarke, Dennis, 41–42
Coffey, Roger, 248
Cole, Jonathan, 154–55
Coleman, Dr. Lee, 54, 75, 106, 277
    coroner's inquest and, 39, 42
    deposition of, 185, 205
    described, 4
    testimony of, 6, 205–14, 293
        controversy surrounding,
        205–9, 211–13, 291
    treatment of Wesbecker and
        resulting notes, 4–8, 73, 87, 88,
        89, 95, 97, 185, 195, 205,
        210–11, 213, 259, 280, 304
Conn, Charlie, 62
Conrad, Forrest, 16, 29
Consciousness Explained (Dennett),
    220
Coroner's inquest, 39–40, 42–43, 73,
    75
Court TV, 107, 164, 270, 284, 285,
    288
Cox, Donald, 40–41, 87, 96, 247
Crick, Francis, 217–21, 222, 223, 302
Cruse, William, 91

Dalkon Shield, 109
Daniels, Mitch, 104
Dann, Laurie, 91
*Darkness Visible: A Memoir of
    Madness* (Styron), 48
Daubert decision, 181–82
Davis, James Floyd, 295
Dawes, Robyn, 111
Denmark, Prozac in, 199
Dennett, Daniel C., 220, 222
Depression, 48–52, 172–73, 217,
    219, 226, 234
    manic-, 5, 85, 96, 177, 219
    psychotic, 234–235

serotonin and, 7, 152–53, 167,
    223, 250
Wesbecker's, *see* Wesbecker,
    Joseph T., depression
Dershowitz, Alan, 110
DES (diethylstilbestrol), 46
Descartes, René, 220–21, 302, 303
Desyrel, 6, 95
Dillon, Judge S. Hugh, 299
Distillers, 45–46
Dobbs, Dr. Dorothy, 146–48
Dualism, body-soul, 219–24, 263,
    302–3
Duncan, Tammy, 283, 284
Dunner, Dr. David, 170
Durham decision, 110–11, 263

Eccles, Sir John, 220, 222
Edelman, Gerald, 221, 222
Elavil, 6
Eli Lilly and Company, *see* Lilly and
    Company, Eli
Emperor's New Mind, The (Penrose),
    220
Eveready Battery Company, 80

Farley, Richard, 91
Fawcett and Haynes Printing, 11, 62,
    63, 65, 136, 137
FDA, *see* Food and Drug
    Administration (FDA)
Fentress, Joyce, 54, 56
Fentress, Kenny, 20, 21, 29
Fentress suit, *see* Wesbecker
    plaintiffs' liability suit against
    Eli Lilly
Fialuridine (FIAU), 104
Finz, Leonard, 54, 56, 71, 72, 298
Fluoxetine hydrochloride, *see* Prozac
Food and Drug Administration (FDA),
    47, 104, 121, 154, 155–56, 174,
    197, 242, 267–68
    Prozac approval process, *see*
        Prozac, FDA approval
        process
Ford Motor Company, 109

Frazier, Don, 86, 87, 90, 94,
    247–50
Freedman, Daniel X., 100
Freeman, Joe, 156, 159, 172–75,
    181, 183, 199, 200, 202–4, 205,
    228, 229, 285–86, 287, 290
    Breggin cross-examination,
        189–96, 274–75
    opening statement, 120–22
    punitive damages and, 240–41,
        283
    secret settlement and, 271
Fuller, Dr. Ray Ward, 51, 102–3,
    182, 215, 275, 303
    deposition of, 138–43
    testimony of, 225–29

Gannett Corporation, 34–35, 81, 82,
    168
Ganote, Bill, 3, 20, 29
Ganote, Charlie, 3, 20, 87, 89
Ganote, Linda, 54, 56
Gazzaniga, Michael, 221
Geigy, 49
Gerard, Ralph, 102, 139
Germany:
    Prozac in, 171, 199, 212, 230–31,
        232, 235, 241
        package inserts, 117, 156–57,
            232
    psychiatry in, under Hitler,
        192–93
Gibson, James William, 77–78
Glaxo, 104
Gnadinger, Paul, 20, 21, 22
Gorman, Christine, 124
Gorman, Chuck, 21, 22
Gosling, Tommy, 3, 66, 92
Granacher, Dr. Robert, Jr., 257–67,
    276, 301
Greathouse, Dr. Richard, 39–40, 42,
    43
Greist, Dr. John, 158, 159
    testimony of, 237–39
Griffin, Gerald, 95
Gudgel, Judge Paul, 295

Halcion, 6, 93
Hall Security Service Inc., 41, 54, 75,
    106, 249, 250–51
Hatfield, Stanley, 16–18, 29
Hay, Richard, 289, 295, 296, 297
Hays, Ruben and Foley, 133, 166
Henry, Dr. Steve, 27–28
Hinckley, John, 91
Hoffman, Bill, 20, 21, 22–23, 29,
    270
Holiford, Mr. (jury foreman),
    284–85
How the Self Controls Its Brain
    (Eccles), 220
Huberty, James Oliver, 77
Huddleston, Judge Joseph, 296, 297
Human Relations Commission,
    Louisville, 85–86, 90, 253
Huntington's disease, 219
Husband, James, 16, 29

Imipramine, 49
Impulse control, ix, 180, 223, 262,
    263, 301
Indianapolis News, 287
Indianapolis Star, 286
Indocin, 6
Iproniazid, 49

Johnson & Johnson, 104
Journal of Analytical Toxicology,
    183
Jury, The (Adler), 113

Kandel, Eric, 216
Kapit, Dr. Richard, 183
Kelly, Archbishop Thomas, 37
Kline, Dr. Nathan S., 49
Kramer, Peter, 6, 98–100, 101, 124
Kuhn, Dr. Roland, 49

Laing, R. D., 176
Lampton, Patrick, 69, 70, 85
Lancet, 183
Lattray, Tim, 61–62, 63
Leber, Dr. Paul, 154, 155, 171

Leitch, Bonnie, 55
Leventhal, Dr. Morton, 6, 70, 257
Lewontin, R. C., 222–23
Lilly and Company, Eli, 43, 44–47,
    103–4
  Oraflex and, *see* Oraflex
  Prozac and, *see* Prozac
  the verdict and, 286–87
Listening to Prozac (Kramer), 6,
    98–100, 101, 124
Lithium, 11, 39, 49, 83, 85, 181
Lithobid, 6
London *Financial Times,* 101
London *Sunday Times Magazine,* ix
Lord, Dr. Nancy, 196–204, 262
Los Angeles Department of
    Children's Services, 80
Louisville, 57–58
Louisville Courier-Journal, 31–34,
    35, 37–38, 39, 40, 43, 63, 91,
    106, 107, 168, 298
  trial coverage, 115, 122
  see also Scanlon, Leslie
Louisville Times, 31, 34, 35
Lucas, James, 40–41, 42, 87, 89–90,
    91, 93, 95–96

McBride, Julia, 296
McCall, Don, 40, 43, 88, 94, 96, 97
McDonald, Judge Michael, 296–97
McDonald's, 109
  massacre at San Diego, 77
McGoldrick, John, 225, 229–30, 273,
    274–75
McStoots suit, 55
Mantell, Michael, 81
Mattingly, Dan, 85–87, 253
Menendez brothers, 110
Merck, 103–4
Merton, Thomas, 305–6
Metten, Charles, 87–88
Milk, Harvey, 110
Miller, Dr. Frank, 28
Miller, Jackie, 3, 14–16, 29, 56, 79
Mind-brain relationship, debate over,
    219–24, 263, 302–3

Minnesota Multiphasic Personality
    Inventory (MMPI), 237–39
Minsky, Marvin, 222
Mitchell, Jim, 3
M'Naughten ruling, 111
Molloy, Dr. Brian, 51
Montgomery, John (Wesbecker's
    uncle), 60, 61, 83, 91, 94,
    131–32
Montgomery, John T. (Wesbecker's
    grandfather), 59
Montgomery, Nancy (Wesbecker's
    grandmother), 12, 59, 60, 61,
    62, 63, 94
Moody, Dr., 102
Moore, Dr. David, 85
Moravec, Hans, 220, 222
Morris, B. Hume, II, 54, 56
Morrison, Terri, 284, 293
Moscone, George, 110
Multiple sclerosis, 219
Myatt, Karen, 107, 164, 270, 285,
    286, 288

National Rifle Association, 38–39
Navane, 6
Needy, Sharon, 13–14, 25, 29, 125
Neuharth, Allen, 34
Neuronal Group Selection, 221, 222
Neurophilosophy, 218–19
Neuroscience, 215–23, 224, 225
Neurotransmitters, 50, 51, 139, 152,
    178, 225
  serotonin, *see* Serotonin
New Jersey Law Journal, 289
New Republic, The, 100
Newsweek, 38, 55, 87
New Yorker, The, 101
New York Review of Books, The,
    100
New York Times, The, 98, 287
New York Times Book Review, The,
    100
New York Times Magazine, The, 123
Norepinephrine, 152
Norpramin, 6

Oklahoma City bombing, 78
Oraflex, 104–5, 155
  evidence at Wesbecker trial
    concerning, 156, 240, 267–69
    withholding of, xi, 271–72,
      288, 289, 290, 291, 293, 295,
      296
  Lilly's misdemeanor in handling,
    x, xi, 46–47, 117, 145, 156, 241,
    242
Osby, Damian, 110
Overworked in America (Schor), 82

Pamelor, 6
Parkinson's disease, 219
PCS Inc., 103
Penrose, Roger, 220, 222
Penthouse, 192
Percodan, 6
Pharmaceutical Association, 50
Philosophical reductionism, 218–19,
  221, 222, 260, 263, 302, 303
Pointer, Andrew, 18, 19–20, 29, 107,
  265, 298
Popham, James, 41, 87, 96
Potter, Judge John, 73, 75, 112, 122,
  123, 124, 133, 150, 156, 159,
  161, 163–64, 174, 181, 184,
  187 88, 192, 193, 194, 196,
  199, 201–2, 229, 242, 250, 256,
  260–61, 265, 273
  Dr. Coleman's testimony and,
    205–9
  described, 107–8
  jury instructions, 276, 280–81,
    284, 293
  Oraflex evidence, ruling on,
    267–69, 288
  secret settlement of Wesbecker
    case and, x–xi, 270–71, 272,
    283–84, 288, 289–90, 292,
    295–97, 299
Principles of Neural Science, 216
Prozac, 98–105, 165–66, 173–75,
  180–83, 225–36, 304

clinical trials, ix, 51, 121, 144–46,
  149, 182–83, 197–201, 212,
  223, 227, 229, 230, 234–35,
  239, 240, 266, 279
  concomitant drugs in, 147–48,
    197, 199–201, 203–4, 227, 241
discovery of, 51, 140, 226
dosage, 52, 145, 159–62, 173–74,
  235, 236
FDA approval process, 6, 51–52,
  116, 146–48, 170–72, 183, 197,
  203–4, 230–32, 235, 241, 266–67
impulse control and, 180, 186,
  223, 262, 263
liability suits against Lilly, 54–56,
  286
  multidistrict legislation,
    54–55, 72, 298–99
  of Wesbecker plaintiffs, *see*
    Wesbecker plaintiffs' liability
    suit against Eli Lilly
marketing of, 52, 98, 101–3, 223,
  239, 240
new drug application (NDA),
  51–52, 197, 203
overseas, 104–5, 154–55, 199
  Germany, 117, 156–57,
    171–72, 199, 212, 230–31,
    232, 235, 241
package warnings, ix, 122,
  156 57, 185, 223, 232, 235,
  241, 279–80, 288
  in Germany, 117, 156–57,
    232
serotonin levels and, 7, 51, 102,
  141, 152–53, 167, 179, 180,
  219, 223, 228–29
significance to Lilly's success, x,
  55–56, 101, 103, 105, 154, 156,
  272
suicidal ideation and, 54, 145–46,
  154, 155, 157, 170–71, 174–75,
  183, 199, 212, 231, 241
violent behavior and, 54, 117, 154,
  155, 158, 170, 174–75, 199,
  201, 219, 227, 263–64

Prozac (*cont.*)
  Wesbecker on, ix, 6, 7, 39, 41–42,
    88, 95, 96, 181, 182, 185–87,
    210–11, 213–14, 255–56
Psychology of Freedom, The
    (Breggin), 190
Psychopharmacological view of
    human behavior, 57, 218–19,
    223, 260, 263, 303, 304
Public Citizen Health Research, 47
Purdy, Patrick, 38, 77

Reagan, Ronald, 91, 303
Reductionist view of human nature,
    218–19, 221, 222, 260, 263,
    302, 303, 305
Restoril, 6, 93
Reuters, 122
Rich, Ivan, 88, 90
Ring, Leonard, 71, 72
Ritalin, 99
Rose, Stephen, 219
Rothenburger, Vernon, 40
Rothman, David, 100
Rotunda, Ronald, 297–98

Sacks, Dr. Oliver, 222
Sallee, Paul, 17, 18, 29
Sampson, Charles, 160
Saturday Evening Post, 102, 139
Scanlon, Leslie, 107, 115, 122, 164,
    270, 288
Scherer, Gordon, 20–21, 265
Schizoaffective disorder, 5–6, 89,
    234, 235, 241
Schizophrenia, 176, 177, 219, 234
Schor, Juliet B., 82
Schulman, Bob, 35
"Seeking the Wizards of Prozac,"
    102–3
Segal, Herbert L., 40, 88, 90
Seidenfaden, David, 16–18, 29
Selby, Carolyn, 106–7, 293
Selective serotonin reuptake
    inhibitors (SSRIs), 51, 104,
    120–21, 140, 223

Senler, Dr. Vikdam, 6, 85
Serotonin, 102, 114–15, 120, 178,
    225, 226–27
  aggression and, 7, 219, 226
  depression and, 7, 152–53, 167,
    223, 250
  Prozac and levels of, *see* Prozac,
    serotonin levels and
Seven Story Mountain, The (Merton),
    305
Shea, Michael, 35–36, 37, 40, 41, 42,
    53, 81, 82, 84–85, 86, 96, 97,
    247, 251, 294
  deposition of, 253–54
Shedden, Dr. William, 47, 144–45
Sherrill, Patrick, 79
Slater, Dr. Irwin, 144–46, 151
Smith, Cora, 60
Smith, Paul, 71–76, 123–38 *passim,*
    144–62 *passim,* 166–68, 174,
    176–88, 191, 193, 194, 196,
    223, 224, 226, 259–60, 261,
    265, 288–92, 298–99
  closing arguments, 278–80
  Dr. Coleman's testimony and,
    205–13
  cross-examination of defense
    witnesses, 226–29, 230–36,
    238–39, 249–50, 251–52, 255,
    266–67
  described, 71–72
  opening statement, 114–18
  Oraflex evidence and, 267, 268,
    271, 288, 291, 295, 296
  punitive damages and, 241–42,
    273, 283
  secret settlement and, 270, 271,
    272, 283, 295–96, 298
  the verdict and, 285, 286
SmithKline Beecham, 103–4
Soma, 93
Standard Gravure, 54, 63, 75, 90–91,
    106, 253, 281
  chemicals used at, 2, 81, 83–84,
    248

ownership changes, 32–36, 82, 84–85, 168–69, 247
security at, 40, 42, 96, 249, 250–52, 254
Wesbecker's job stress, *see* Wesbecker, Joseph T., job stress and
Wesbecker's shooting spree at, *see* Wesbecker, Joseph T., shooting spree and suicide
working conditions at, 1–3, 33, 35, 66–67, 75–76, 81–82, 83–84, 247–50, 294
Stein, John, 16, 26, 29, 53, 87–88, 107, 128, 264
Stizler, Sam, 41
Stockton, California, massacre, 38, 77, 78, 91
Stoke, Sheila, 95
Stopher, Edward H., 55, 57, 58, 71, 74, 75, 124–32 *passim,* 135, 137, 149–50, 159, 204, 223–24, 239, 243–51, 253–65, 273, 285, 290, 292, 301, 303
closing argument, 275–78
Dr. Coleman's testimony and, 205, 206, 208–9, 213–14
opening statement, 118–20, 239
Oraflex evidence and, 267–69
secret settlement and, 283–84, 296
Strong, Tom, 26
Styron, William, 48
Sutherland, Stuart, 48
Szasz, Thomas, 176, 191

Talking Back to Prozac (Breggin), 124, 176
Tallarigo, Lorenzo, 161–62
Taylor, Cecil, 88, 90
Teicher, Dr. Martin, 54, 154–55, 167, 174, 183
Thalidomide, 45–46, 109
Thatcher, Margaret, 303
Thompson, Dr. Leigh, testimony of, 235, 236, 269

defense attorney, questioning by, 172–75
plaintiffs' attorneys, questioning by, 149–62, 170–72
Thompson, Tracy, 102–3, 139
Throneberry, Grady, 42, 86, 87, 90, 96, 250–52
Ticking Bombs: Defusing Violence in the Workplace (Mantell), 81
Tilford, Jack, 38
Time, 38, 78, 91, 123–24
Tingle, John, 18–19, 65–66
Tobias, Randall, x, 286, 287
Tofranil, 6, 85, 88
Toxic Psychiatry (Breggin), 74, 176
Trazodone, 93
Tricyclics, 157

United Kingdom, Committee on the Safety of Medicines, 154, 155, 199
USAir, 79
USA Today, 287
Uviller, H. L. Richard, 298

Valium, 6, 49
Varchaver, Nicholas, 297
Vogel, Steve, 168–69

Wall Street Journal, The, 47, 54, 101, 112
Warman, Paula, 15–16, 29, 41, 86, 92, 94, 96, 125–26, 253
Warrior Dreams (Gibson), 77, 78
Wernicke, Dr. Joachim, 160–61
testimony of, 229–36
Wesbecker, James (son), 5, 9–10, 12, 41, 64, 67, 94, 135, 137, 196, 214, 243, 259, 304
problem with exposing himself sexually, 5, 9, 64–65, 68–69, 88, 93, 130, 254
testimony of, 254–56
Wesbecker, Joseph Kevin (son), 5, 63, 64, 65, 67–68, 130, 196, 243, 255

Wesbecker, Joseph Kevin (son)
(*cont.*)
testimony of, 133–35
Wesbecker, Joseph T., xiv
Dr. Coleman's treatment of, *see*
Coleman, Dr. Lee, treatment of
Wesbecker and resulting notes
delusions, 7–8, 185, 186, 210–11
depression, ix, 5
manic-, 5, 85, 96
disability benefits, 92, 93, 94, 121,
125–26, 137
guns and, 3, 38, 56, 62, 67, 77, 87,
89, 90, 91–92, 93, 96, 97,
185–86, 213, 245, 248, 277
history of mental illness, 3, 6, 70,
85–87, 93, 137, 235, 243–45,
249, 254, 257
MMPI, 237–38
"impulse control," ix, 186, 223,
262, 263, 301
intent versus chemical
determinism, question of,
260–64, 276–77, 301, 304
job stress and, 3, 5, 40, 41, 43, 64,
66, 69, 70, 75, 85–91, 168–69,
245, 248, 249, 253
personal history, 5, 57–70, 71,
83–97, 129–31, 184, 195–96,
224, 279, 301, 304–5
on Prozac, *see* Prozac, Wesbecker
on
schizoaffective disorder, 5–6, 89
shooting spree and suicide, ix,
13–23, 26, 89, 168, 233, 304
threats prior to, 40–41, 42,
56, 87, 88–89, 94, 95–96,
185–86, 196, 248, 251–52
suicide attempt, 6, 70, 87, 137, 245
Wesbecker, Martha (née
Montgomery) (mother), 59–62,
65, 71, 129–31, 184, 196
Wesbecker, Murrel (grandmother),
59, 60, 130–31, 195
Wesbecker, Thomas (father), 59,
129, 184

Wesbecker plaintiffs' liability suit
against Eli Lilly, ix, 56–58,
71–76, 106–8, 114–299
the defense:
case presented by, 224–78
closing arguments, 274–78
opening statements, 118–22,
239
strategy of, ix, 55, 57, 71, 75,
165–66, 223–24, 263, 264,
276, 301, 303–4
see also Freeman, Joe;
McGoldrick, John; Stopher,
Edward H.
discovery, 57, 58, 71, 74, 75–76
final judgment, 289
motion to amend, 289–90,
295–96, 299
the jury, 106–7, 108, 165, 184,
187–88, 283–84, 288, 293
deliberations, 281–82, 284
instructions to, 276, 280–81,
284, 293
jury verdict, x, 284–87, 288
Oraflex evidence, *see* Oraflex,
evidence at Wesbecker trial
concerning
the plaintiffs, 71–76, 223, 301
case presented by, 124–62,
170–214, 301
closing arguments, 278–80
expert witnesses, 74–75,
123–24, 176–204, 205–13
opening statement, 114–18
see also Smith, Paul; Zettler,
Nancy
punitive damages and, 240–42,
273, 282–83, 296
secret settlement, x–xi, 270–73,
282, 283, 285, 286, 288–93,
295–98
West, Danny Lee, 248
West, Ed, 56–57, 108, 150, 165–66,
167, 274, 286, 292, 297
White, Dan, 110
White, Lloyd, 20, 29

Wible, James, 20, 29
Wible, Sarah, 54, 56
Wilson, Lively, 290, 296
Wolfe, Dr. Sidney, 47
Wong, Dr. David, 51, 102, 140
Wood, Richard, 47, 161
Workplace violence, 78–81, 295

Zerbe, Dr., 160
Zettler, Nancy, 72–73, 74, 114, 133,
    138–43, 149, 161, 166, 167–68,
    205, 229, 239, 242, 255, 283,
    284, 288, 290, 298
  Dr. Lord's testimony and, 197–202
  Oraflex evidence and, 267–68

About the author

JOHN CORNWELL is an award-winning investigative journalist who writes regularly for the London *Sunday Times Magazine* and occasionally for *Esquire* (England) and *Vanity Fair*. He was formerly editor of the London *Observer*'s Foreign News Service. His true-crime study, *Earth to Earth*, won the Gold Dagger Award for nonfiction in Britain and was nominated for an Edgar Allan Poe Award in the United States. His other books include *A Thief in the Night, The Hiding Places of God,* and *Nature's Imagination.*

John Cornwell is also senior research fellow at Cambridge University, where he directs the Science and Human Dimension Project. He has been a visiting fellow at the Neurosciences Institute at Rockefeller University in New York, and has traveled the world researching the social impact of neuroscience.

He lives in England.